Burma: Food, Family & Conflict

Art direction and graphic design: Yukari Taki

ISBN: 978-84-949480-0-8
Legal deposit: V2885-2018

Printed and bound by Gutenberg Press Ltd.,
Tarxien, GXQ 2901, Malta, www.gutenberg.com.mt

REFERENCES:

Who Really Killed Aung San? Lemkin, R. BBC2 documentary, 19 July 1997

Halliday, R. (1917). *The Talaings.* Rangoon Government Press, Rangoon.
Available online: https://archive.org/stream/talaings00hallrich/talaings00hallrich_djvu.txt

Furnivall, J. S. (1939). The fashioning of Leviathan. *Journal of the Burma Research Society*, Volume 29, pp. 1-138

Furnivall, J. S. (1948). *Colonial Policy and Practice: A Comparative Study of Burma and Netherlands India.* Cambridge: Cambridge University Press; and New York: New York University Press

Herbert, P. (1982). 'The Hsaya San Rebellion (1930-1932) Reappraised'.
Melbourne: Monash University, Centre of Southeast Asian Studies.
Working Papers, No. 27, pp. 1-16.

Collis, M. (1938). *Trials in Burma.* Faber and Faber

Warren, C. V. (1937) *Burmese Interlude* London: Skeffington

Final Report of the Riot Inquiry Committee. (1939). Government of Burma. Rangoon. Available online: https://ia801609.us.archive.org/22/items/in.ernet.dli.2015.206317/2015.206317.Final-Report.pdf

Tinker, H. (1975). 'A Forgotten Long March: The Indian Exodus from Burma, 1942'. *Journal of South East Asian Studies.* Available online: https://www.jstor.org/stable/20070108?seq=1#page_scan_tab_contents

Thein Pe Myint's *Wartime Traveler.* Translated and Edited by Robert H. Taylor. Athens: Ohio University Press, 1984

BURMA:

FOOD FAMILY & CONFLICT

BRIDGET ANDERSON *and* STEPHEN ANDERSON

South-East Asia early 1900s

FAMILY TREE

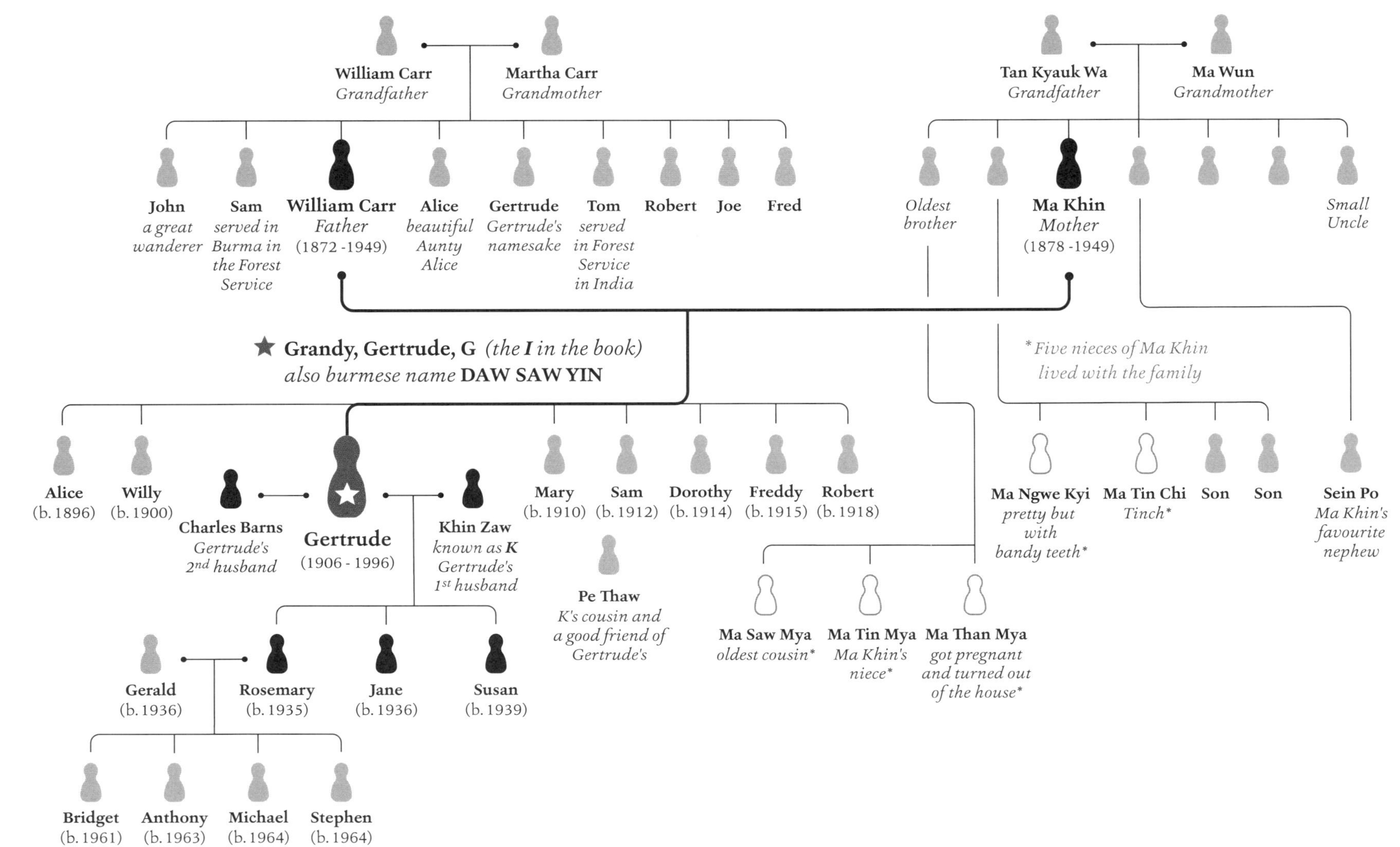
William Carr
Grandfather
Martha Carr
Grandmother
Tan Kyauk Wa
Grandfather
Ma Wun
Grandmother
John
a great wanderer
Sam
served in Burma in the Forest Service
William Carr
Father
(1872 -1949)
Alice
beautiful Aunty Alice
Gertrude
Gertrude's namesake
Tom
served in Forest Service in India
Robert
Joe
Fred
Oldest brother
Ma Khin
Mother
(1878 -1949)
Small Uncle
★ Grandy, Gertrude, G (the I in the book)
also burmese name DAW SAW YIN
* Five nieces of Ma Khin lived with the family
Alice
(b. 1896)
Willy
(b. 1900)
Charles Barns
Gertrude's 2nd husband
Gertrude
(1906 - 1996)
Khin Zaw
known as K
Gertrude's 1st husband
Mary
(b. 1910)
Sam
(b. 1912)
Dorothy
(b. 1914)
Freddy
(b. 1915)
Robert
(b. 1918)
Ma Ngwe Kyi
pretty but with bandy teeth*
Ma Tin Chi
Tinch*
Son
Son
Sein Po
Ma Khin's favourite nephew
Pe Thaw
K's cousin and a good friend of Gertrude's
Ma Saw Mya
oldest cousin*
Ma Tin Mya
Ma Khin's niece*
Ma Than Mya
got pregnant and turned out of the house*
Gerald
(b. 1936)
Rosemary
(b. 1935)
Jane
(b. 1936)
Susan
(b. 1939)
Bridget
(b. 1961)
Anthony
(b. 1963)
Michael
(b. 1964)
Stephen
(b. 1964)

To Dad for the cheese on toast,
Ant and Mike for the laughs,
and above all to three inspirational women,
Mum, Grandy and of course Ma Khin.

CONTENTS

RECIPE CONTENTS

RECIPE CONTENTS

MAKING DIFFERENCES: BETWEEN TWO WORLDS

TENSIONS IN BURMA

WAR

ENDINGS

INTRODUCTION

Our grandmother, Grandy, had an acerbic wit and a sharp eye. She loved her grandchildren deeply but was by no means blind to our faults. Our mother was a successful hospital doctor with four small children, so inevitably Grandy was called upon to help look after us. She devotedly moved to Newport in South Wales when our parents settled there to bring us up. There were many migrants there and our Catholic school catered for Irish, Polish and Italian families, but it was overwhelmingly European, in the colonial sense of the word. Strangers were forever asking us 'Where are you from?', and Grandy would answer, in her expensive English accent, that she was an eskimo. One question she didn't mind answering though was her age. The correct response was surprise (and quite right because she never looked her age, her skin was unwrinkled and her hair, though grey, was cut short and spiky), whereupon she would like you for knowing how to flatter her, though mind you, if she didn't like you, you would probably never know, so polite and gracious was she - until you'd left!

All my life she told me stories. 'The problem with us is too much talky talky,' she would comment from time to time. As a child, what fascinated me were not the happy-ever-afters, but the tales of fear and horror and the feel of touching an emotion that was too big for me yet to experience. My memories of walking home with her from school are not memories of streets or the park or of houses, but of William Golding*, Piggy's shiny pink conch shell, the squelch of sea anemones and the dark, hot buzzing of flies. I can still feel the disappointment I

* Explanations of selected words appear in the glossary (page 248)

experienced when I took *Pincher Martin* from her shelves at the age of six and found it utterly incomprehensible, the words bearing no relation to the exciting world she had opened to me apart from that last magically recognisable phrase, 'he didn't even have time to kick his sea-boots off'. But the very best stories were her own, about her father, the grand English judge, and her mother, beautiful and passionate, and their lives in a big house in Rangoon with lots of servants and carriages. They were tales of dashing romance and drama, a secret wedding to a Burman, a long trek to India to escape the Japanese. Even the names were exciting: Sir Oscar and Lady de Glanville, Khin Myo Chit - which, Grandy explained, means 'lover of my country'.

I loved her stories. It seemed that half of her lived in a completely different world from me. For her 'monsoon' was more than an empty word. She could use words like 'Thakhin' and 'boxwallah', which to me related, not to the real world but to TV serials and old-fashioned books. I particularly loved to hear her talk about her grandmother, Ma Wun. She too was a story teller, and Grandy described how she would listen, spell bound, to her fairy tales about Me Htwe or the Unlucky King, or the Golden Crow. 'Tell me one', I would beg, and when Grandy began, 'There was once a King of Burma...', I would screw my eyes up tight and imagine that I was in the house in Bassein listening to the old voice of Ma Wun - and soon I would be transported into the world of mythical kings, turtles and magical transformations.

The stories continued to fascinate me and as I grew older I began to demand detail and personality. I put the different incidents together and illustrated them with old photographs laid out on the living room carpet. There was Lady Carr in her best silk longyi and Sir William in his judge's wig, Grandy as a young woman holding a cigarette holder 1920s style. I also became more sensitive to quite how hard Grandy was on herself. She was critical of others but most of all, harsh on herself, for being lazy and unattractive and unintelligent. I saw none of this. She had a mind like a razor and was always so well turned out. Her middle name was 'Saw Yin' which someone once told me meant 'clean and tidy', but I later learned that it means 'deliberately charming'. She always lived up to both.

After I left university, I wanted to understand our family history in a more comprehensive way, a life unfolding rather than a series of vignettes. I recorded a series of interviews with Grandy and researched in the India Office Library. It was really exciting to find the documentation on the institutional upset that followed her father's marriage, and to realise that the bundle of papers on the shelf in Grandy's spare room were the early literary attempts of a former Prime Minister of Burma. But I also realised how we differed. I was (and am) convinced of the profoundly negative effects of colonialism on people historically and into today. Grandy was more ambivalent, acutely aware of its racism, but sensitive to the good intentions of men like her father and often very harsh on her mother. I wanted to record what she said, but was so conscious of the silences, not only of her mother, but of the people in the Burmese countryside, whose opposition to colonialism was and is so often dismissed as backward and foolish, and whose names and sacrifices are forgotten in an English language historiography that continues to be shaped by colonial assumptions. I don't claim that this book escapes those assumptions, but I hope that at least they are visible.

This book has been put together through tape recordings of Grandy, and historical research [1]. We have used the colonial place names: *Rangoon* for Yangon, *Burma* for Myanmar, and *Moulmein* for Mawlamyine. This is how Grandy referred to them, and she would have refused to call them anything else. However, Steve and I use the contemporary nomenclature. Sometimes, for ease of reading, we have made specific connections between historical context and Grandy's life that fit the story, but only in the most minor ways. She really did sit next to Nehru and had trouble with Aung San. She was also very, very funny, and I miss her deeply.

Bridget Anderson, Bristol, 2018

Professor of migration, mobility and citizenship, working for a borderless world.

[1] This research also informed the BBC documentary, aired on 19 July 1997, *Who Really Killed Aung San?* Before she died Grandy strongly counselled against making this, but for one of the few times in my life, I didn't take her advice.

Mum was born in Burma but came to Britain shortly after the war. She trained as a doctor in London which is where our Welsh Dad met and fell in love with her, allegedly over a shared cadaver in an anatomy class. Initially his parents weren't too keen on the match - unsuitable partners being a recurring theme in our family, but love conquered all, and they had four children in rapid succession. I was the last.

Mum was always busy. She was appointed consultant at a provincial hospital in South Wales, but despite her demanding job, she always cooked for her family. Her meatball curry was to die for and she'd serve it up with dahl and pungent fiery balachaung that Dad would heap on to his plate while telling us that he'd never eaten garlic, let alone spicy food before he'd met Mum.

On our birthdays, she would let us choose our favourite dish and prepare it lovingly - mine was snails with garlic butter, something I'd once tried on holiday with my parents in Lyon. Poor Mum, shopping for snails in Newport! Occasionally Dad would guiltily relieve Mum of her responsibility as the family caterer and take us all out for dinner at Casa Antonio, where we'd tuck into paella and suck the heads of garlic sodden prawns. We enjoyed foreign holidays when travelling abroad was a luxury, and still not teenagers we had our first taste of authentic Mediterranean food. It was hardly pushing back the frontiers of gastronomy, but it set a standard. Food was an important part of life and something to be shared and enjoyed.

Mum's job meant she couldn't always be at home when we got back from school, so our grandmother was called upon to help. Grandy would be there to make our tea: shortbread, flapjacks, cheesecake and her wonderful toffee. She had learnt to cook when she got married, confessing that before then she'd never so much as fried an egg as there were always servants to do the household chores in Burma where she had been brought up. I was her favourite and loved to be in the kitchen with her. She would stir a heavy cast iron pot of bubbling condensed milk and sugar, and as it slowly darkened and caramelised she'd tell me 'going slowly, coming nicely', entertaining me with stories about her life in Burma that were so vivid I could almost feel the cloying tropical heat and hear the sounds of the jungle.

It was Grandy, who first told me about Ma Khin. Grandy's father, an English judge in Burma had met this beautiful native girl and they had married. But this was no fairy tale, and I understood immediately how difficult life must have been for them and for their children, Grandy included. After all, weren't my siblings and I the offspring of a similar mixed marriage? Newport is on the border between Wales and England, but none of us felt able to participate in the assertions of Welshness of the children of the many white immigrants to our Catholic school. It was all about race. We knew we didn't look like 'British' should even though we felt it (Grandy used to say exactly the same thing): half-and-half's who didn't really know what to answer when quizzed about where we were from. All that weird foreign food that we ate at home only proved that we didn't really belong anywhere. We had a loving and happy family life but trying to fit in at school wasn't easy. A sense of belonging that eluded us seemed to be deeply rooted in our family history.

As I became older I grew more interested in food. As an undergraduate student, I'd cook for myself and my housemates, often calling Mum or Grandy to ask for recipes that they gladly shared over the phone reminding me '... and don't forget the going slowly, coming nicely'. I graduated and taught physics in South London for a few years, but I was becoming increasingly passionate about cooking. In 1991, I took up a teaching job in Valencia, a city I fell in love with the moment I set foot in its central market.

During the long summer holiday, I went to work at a cookery school in Italy and met Alastair Little, then one of London's most talked about chefs. Cooking was getting the better of me and I took the decision to throw in my teaching career and take up a job offer from Alastair at his Soho restaurant as a trainee chef. I returned to Valencia a few years later and opened my first restaurant, Seu Xerea in 1996.

Seu Xerea was a little bit of Soho in the heart of a Spanish provincial city, a fusion of Asian and Mediterranean food that was completely new to the locals. But what seemed to really arouse their curiosity was me. And back we went to that tiresome question '¿De dónde eres?', 'Where are you from?'. 'London' was just not the right answer! I started to put up pictures of my family on the walls of the restaurant. Ma Khin in her silk longyi, next to Sir William Carr in his judge's wig, Grandy sitting on the steps with her children at the house in Safrajaing Road where she lived during the war, K, my Burmese grandfather reading the news broadcast on Indian radio. And these became my prompts to talk to my customers about where I was from.

In 2014, I opened Ma Khin Café. I wanted to give a voice to Ma Khin who had struggled so hard to bring up her children in a hostile colonial environment, and to Grandy who had lived through the Second World War and been politically active during the end of colonialism. Proud and confident today of where I'm from, Ma Khin Café, like this book, celebrates the cultural traditions and encounters that have marked the history of our family and extends the same welcome to everyone without having to ask 'Where are you from?'

***Stephen Anderson**, Valencia, 2018*
Chef and restaurateur

UK MILK
Sweetened
Beverage Creamer

FOOD INTRODUCTION

Stephen Anderson

Influences on the recipes

This book started life more than thirty years ago. As Grandy got older we became increasingly concerned that the treasure trove that was her prodigious memory and her skillful story telling would one day be lost for good. 'Nearer now than yesterday,' she'd joke, but it saddened us to be reminded of the approach of what she wryly referred to as the big sleep. So Bridget recorded Grandy as she told her stories, transcribing the tapes, structuring the text and conducting detailed research in the India Office Library to provide a historical background. The result was a fascinating personal account of the decolonisation of Burma seen through the eyes of our grandmother. But as Bridget's academic career and family took priority, this singular historical document remained unpublished.

When I opened my second restaurant, Ma Khin Café in 2014 in Valencia, Spain, it was inspired by the smells, tastes and stories that Grandy had shared with me from an early age. Those stories encouraged me to travel to Burma and India, to find inspiration for the menu at Ma Khin Café, and I visited the places that form a part of this story. I found myself climbing the steps of the Shwedagon Pagoda where Ma Khin had stopped to chat with stall holders. I poked through baskets of tiny oranges and mountain strawberries at the bazaar in Kalaw just as Alice and Ma Khin had done. I even ate shan noodle soup in the dining room at The Grey House, now a boutique hotel, seventy years after Sir William Carr and Ma Khin had abandoned it for the last time. And my wanderlust has taken me further afield, to Thailand, Vietnam, Laos, Malaysia and Singapore, countries that Grandy never visited but whose food forms a part of the menu at Ma Khin Café.

Bridget and I decided to bring together the story and recipes in a single book and this is the result. The recipes you will find cover not just Burma but a wide area of Southern and South Eastern Asia. This is a geographical area with enormous gastronomic diversity. There are of course plenty of Burmese dishes here. (If you are looking for a more comprehensive collection of traditional Burmese recipes I would strongly recommend Naomi Duguid's excellent *'Burma: Rivers of Flavor'*). Indian and Chinese dishes feature heavily too, partly due to the historical and contemporary presence of these communities in Burma, but also because of the family links to China through Ma Khin's father, and to India where Grandy spent the war years. And then there are the recipes from other South East Asian countries which are more my story than Grandy's.

The importance attached to eating is common throughout Southern and South-East Asia. The heavily polluted air in Delhi is not just due to car exhausts and the burning of crop stubble. Every morning across the city thousands of charcoal braziers are lit to prepare chapatis for breakfast. Street food is often the traveller's first point of contact with the region's food, but food carts are not there for the backpackers. In a region where the working day is long and people live in distant suburbs, this is an affordable alternative to a restaurant lunch and an essential service for millions of office workers and labourers. Street food is a great leveller, because the quality of the food attracts people from a wide range of economic backgrounds. Local people have their favourite places for each speciality and at the best pavement eateries long queues are a common sight.

At the end of the working day, most people in the region eat at home, restaurants being an option for only the wealthiest. Food is shared among the family, the elders being served first. In Burma if they are absent, a small portion of rice is set aside as a mark of respect. Food in Asia is important no matter what the time of day, and it is no surprise that when two Burmese meet a commonly exchanged greeting is 'Sa pyi pila' literally, 'Have you eaten yet?'

Migration has mixed and melded the gastronomic traditions of this part of the world. The Chinese theory of heating and cooling foods has extended across the subcontinent. Depending on our constitution we are classified as having a hot or cold nature, and our diet should compensate our natural imbalance to achieve a healthy equilibrium. The seasons also affect what constitutes a suitable diet, so spicy, bitter, or calorific foods (all considered heating) are eaten more in winter and green vegetables, duck, and dairy products (cooling) are more commonly consumed in the summer. Food is a vital part of good health and 'heating' ingredients are used to treat cold symptoms such as chills and tiredness, whereas cooling foods are said to cure rashes and sore throats.

Apart from the Chinese theory of heating and cooling foods, there are a whole range of unwritten rules across South Eastern and Southern Asia when it comes to ensuring a healthy and balanced diet. In Vietnam, the five senses are connected to five organs and these should be stimulated when eating by five nutrients, a curious mix defined as powder, liquid, mineral, protein, and fat. There are also five tastes: sweet, sour, salty, bitter, and hot, and a meal should also include five colours. It's all quite a challenge for a home chef! In neighbouring Thailand, a strong emphasis is placed on the aromatic qualities of the finished dish, with citrus and spicy ingredients giving the food its characteristically fresh flavours. The absence of animal protein for the majority of the population of India is compensated by the consumption of wheat, pulses and vegetables. Spices are used to raise these humble ingredients to a whole new gastronomic level. Despite being near neighbours, Burmese cuisine makes limited use of spices, preferring the pungent flavours of ginger, shallots, chilli, ngapi (fermented fish paste) and fermented soya bean paste. Rice is the staple ingredient and is served alongside fish, meat, soup, vegetables, salads and relishes. At a time when our diets are under constant scrutiny and we are bombarded daily with often contradictory information about which foods are good for us, it's salutary to remember that variety, balance, and a limited intake of animal fats and protein coupled with the consumption of local, seasonal produce are features of healthy traditional diets the world over.

I never tire of telling the staff at my restaurant that eating well is not just about food, it's about eating joyfully. On a recent visit to Burma we had arranged to spend a day trekking in the hills of the Shan states. Our route home took us through fields where the residents of a local village had just finished collecting the rice harvest. They were celebrating with a meal, and bottles of Burmese rum and they called us over to join them. Banana leaves were laid out in front of us and a spicy chickpea curry with chicken was served up with rice and relishes. Though we didn't share a common language, the food brought us together, and we laughed and communicated and in no time we had learnt each other's names, the family relationships, who was lazy, who ate the most, who was the boss, and who the joker. It was humbling to be so warmly welcomed by people who had so little but gave us so much with a simple meal.

Using the recipes

The angular forms of the Roman and Greek alphabets evolved as symbols to be carved in stone. Babylonian cuneiform script was etched into clay tablets that dried into permanent records. The circular forms like strings of pearls, so characteristic of the Burmese alphabet, evolved from the early traditions of Burmese scribes who wrote with ink on dried leaves. My approach to cooking is in the spirit of Burmese scribes and the spirit of Ma Khin, nothing is written in stone.

During her visits to England, my great grandmother, Ma Khin would adapt the dishes of her childhood to the ingredients she could find, delighted to discover that rhubarb brought a refreshing tang to her vegetable curry, that sorrel could replace Burmese sourleaf and that she could rustle up a passable version of balachaung using anchovy paste instead of ngapi. Today, at least in larger cities around the world, the presence of well stocked Chinese supermarkets means that most of the ingredients in this book can be found fairly easily. But just in case you have difficulty tracking down some of the more unusual ingredients, I've included

Ginger
Star Anise
Crispy garlic
Fried shallots
Peanuts
Turmeric
Ngapi
Dried shrimp
Chillies
Cassia bark
Lemon grass

alternatives in a number of recipes. I'm sure you will have your own ideas, so feel confident to explore. Try the food as you go along, and don't be afraid to change quantities. I have tried to make the quantities suitable for four people in most recipes, but I don't quote exact weights in grams for spices, herbs and other flavourings. I have measured ginger in centimetres, garlic in cloves, spices and herbs in teaspoons and tablespoons, but these are all pretty arbitrary, because at the end of the day it's the taste that matters and you must be the final judge of that. If you have not cooked this kind of food before you might want to start with the recipes I've labelled 'easy'. You can get used to processes like spice roasting and grinding, as well as how to adapt for your personal tastes, and then move on to the more challenging recipes.

I have endeavoured to fit the recipes into the text, and the connection is sometimes a little distant, so I have included an introduction at the beginning of each recipe. My selection criteria comes down to choosing the dishes that our guests at Ma Khin Café enjoy, recipes that represent our family story from my great-great-grandmother Ma Wun to me. Enjoy cooking these dishes and sharing the results ... and don't forget the 'going slowly, coming nicely'.

Common ingredients in the recipes

Rice

Rice is the staple ingredient of South East Asian and Burmese cuisine and Burma was once the world's largest exporter of rice. But disastrous economic policies in the second half of the 20th century and a lack of investment have made Burma dependent on rice imports. The poor price paid by international markets for relatively low-quality Burmese rice means you are unlikely to find a packet on your supermarket shelves. For the recipes in this book you can use long grain Thai fragrant rice for the South East Asian dishes, or basmati rice for the Indian dishes. If a recipe requires a certain kind of rice, this is specified.

There are no hard and fast rules about cooking long grain rice. If you have a rice cooker, rinse the rice once and cook it with an equal quantity of water plus a couple of tablespoons per person extra and a little salt. Alternatively, rinse the rice and cover with about 2cm of cold water. (You can measure this by placing your index finger so that the tip just touches the rice. The water should come up to the first joint). Add salt, bring to the boil then cover and cook for ten minutes. Turn off the heat and leave the rice to rest covered for ten more minutes. My mother swears by her own method of cooking rice. She brings a pot of salted water to the boil and drops in the rice. It's a foolproof method because you just taste the rice and when it's sufficiently cooked, drain it and return it to the hot pan for a few more minutes so that any residual moisture is absorbed.

Glutinous or sticky rice is a staple of Northern Thailand and Laos. In spite of its name, it contains no gluten and is perfectly suitable for coeliacs. It must be soaked before cooking for at least four hours and is then steamed in a bamboo basket set over a pot of boiling water. Glutinous rice is used in many Burmese and Thai desserts, including sticky rice with mango (page 79).

Ground toasted rice adds an interesting savoury crunch to Laotian dishes. Though usually made with glutinous rice, it works just as well with other varieties. Warm a dry frying pan and toss the uncooked rice over a medium flame until it begins to brown. Grind the toasted rice in a food processor until it has the texture of coarse sand. It keeps well in a screw top jar.

Spices

What would South East Asian food be without spices? The wonderfully warming citrus astringent taste of cardamom, the earthy taste of cumin, the pungent intense aroma of cloves. When I cook at home, my neighbours often ask 'What were you cooking that smelt so delicious last night?'. And that's just what spices do for food, they create anticipation and they don't defraud! Try to buy small quantities of whole spices or share out larger packets with friends. Freshness is important and that way you are constantly renewing your stock. Invest in a coffee grinder and toast whole spices in a dry frying pan before grinding them. You'll be amazed just how intense the aromas are compared to packets of ground spices that may have been sitting on a supermarket shelf for months. With turmeric, cumin, coriander, garam masala, chilli powder, black pepper, green cardamoms, cloves, cassia bark or cinnamon, nutmeg or mace, mustard seeds, fennel seeds, fenugreek, and saffron you can cook pretty much everything in this book.

Chillies

In Burma, pregnant women are advised not to eat chillies as they are said to cause baldness in babies! It is hard to imagine that prior to Columbus' voyage to the Americas in 1492, chillies were unknown in Asia. How different the region's food must have been before the arrival of these addictive little devils! Green and red chillies are used fresh, in salads and stir fries. In Burma, dried red chillies are soaked and pounded with other ingredients to make curry pastes, and chilli flakes are usually present on the table to add a sprinkling to a bowl of Shan noodles or mohinga. In Thai cooking, curry pastes are also made with dried chillies except for green curry, for which long fresh green chillies are pounded to a particularly fiery paste.

Ngapi

The use of fermented fish products is ubiquitous in Asia and interestingly was once equally common in the Mediterranean. The Romans were great consumers of garum, salted mackerel and tuna guts, fermented and dried in the sun before being pickled in brine. In Burma, ngapi is a generic term for 'pressed fish', which may be made with shrimps or fish. You can buy fermented fish paste in Chinese supermarkets. Keep it in the fridge tightly sealed (it smells dreadful), and before using, wrap it in tin foil and dry roast it in a heavy frying pan. Ngapi is an essential ingredient in balachaung (page 185) and many Burmese dishes from the coastal areas. In the Northern Shan States of Burma, fermented soy beans are often used instead of ngapi. These dry discs that look suspiciously like cow pats are difficult to find outside Asia, but vegetarian readers can substitute ngapi with yellow bean paste, which can be found in Chinese supermarkets in Europe.

Fish sauce

In a similar process to the production of ngapi, fish sauce collects the liquid result of the process of fermenting fish. Small fish and shellfish are heaped into concrete tanks and the liquid produced as it all ferments, flows off to be filtered, boiled and bottled.

Dried shrimp

Another essential to our store cupboard is dried shrimp. You'll find these in the cold section of your Chinese supermarket. They should be pink and not a tired brown, though beware of anything that looks excessively and artificially rosy! In Asian markets shrimp are graded by size, the bigger being the more expensive of course.

Fruit and vegetables

Maha Bandoola Street in Yangon's Chinatown is one of the city's biggest food markets and a feast for the senses. Enormous crayfish as big as your forearm, prawns the size of a dinner plate and piles of fried crickets vie for your attention alongside stacks of recently plucked chickens whose living companions cluck miserably under wicker baskets. And for the fainter hearted, piled high on carts, a vast selection of tropical fruit and vegetables. Stinking durian sit alongside the more palatable jack fruit and mangosteens, with their thick fibrous skin concealing tender white segments that are wonderfully sweet, acidic and fragrant. Mangoes are harvested ripe as they should be, and then there are custard apples, Grandy's favourite (she would spoon out the vanilla flavoured fruit and keep the pips to play jack stones with her siblings). Tiger nuts are used to make a refreshing milky drink which strangely enough is widely consumed in Valencia, where it is called orxata. And keep an eye out for Burmese grapes, more like a fibrous lychee than a grape, which can be peeled and eaten directly or fermented into wine.

The vegetable stands in the market are no less interesting, with aubergines, from the tiny pea variety to the white bulbous and aptly named eggplant, bitter gourd, wing beans, okra, green tomatoes, and all kinds of leaves: sour, bitter, and fragrant.

At Ma Khin Café we try as far as possible to use locally produced fruit and vegetables, fortunate as we are to enjoy enormous variety in what is known as the garden of the Mediterranean Coast. Why bring vegetables from the other side of the world when recipes can be adapted to use local ingredients? Many Chinese vegetables are now grown locally, and at my allotment in Valencia I have had great success with lemongrass, long purple Chinese eggplant, and bitter gourd. But if you can't get more unusual vegetables, think about the flavour and texture you want to achieve in the finished dish. Turnips and pumpkin are interchangeable in a curry, courgettes can replace okra in a stir fry and cucumber can even substitute green papaya in a salad. I've not tried it, but I'm sure brussel sprouts would be great in a Thai red curry, and slices of water chestnut could substitute for banana root in mohinga.

Ginger, shallots, and garlic

These deserve a special mention as they crop up repeatedly in many Burmese recipes. The Burmese use crispy shallots and garlic to sprinkle on salads and soups. You can make them by half filling a suitable pan with neutral oil. Drop a cupful of thinly sliced shallots into the oil and heat over a high flame until the shallots begin to bubble. Now lower the heat as you need to maintain this temperature (about 160ºC) in order for the shallots to lose their water. If you go too fast they will caramelise on the outside while still soft inside. Stir frequently so that the shallots brown evenly. After about ten minutes when they have turned

a dark golden brown, strain through a metal sieve placed over a clean pan. Shake the shallots out of the sieve onto several layers of kitchen paper to drain them of any excess oil. You can store crispy shallots in an airtight plastic container.
The same process can be applied to make crispy garlic. The oil left after frying crispy shallots and garlic can be used for dressing salads.

Herbs

Herbs are the perfect fresh foil to the more earthy and intense contribution that spices make to the taste of Asian food. Thai holy basil with its unique aniseed/ liquorice taste is a true blessing. I couldn't imagine eating a vegetable korma without coriander (though tarragon is a great alternative) or a lamb biryani without mint. Dill sets off a Vietnamese cha ca and elevates it to something exquisite. Don't be dainty with herbs in these recipes, as flavours should be hearty and stand up to the stronger presence of spices and chilli. You may be lucky enough to find fresh kaffir lime leaves, lemon grass or curry leaves in an Asian food store. Even if you don't need them that day, snap them up. These more robust leaves freeze well (unlike the other previously mentioned herbs) and even when frozen are so much better than the dried alternative.

Nuts and oil

Peanuts and peanut oil are commonly used throughout Asia. Sunflower or rapeseed oil are suitable alternatives as both have a neutral flavour. Olive oil is not suitable for Asian cooking as the wonderful fruity flavour simply doesn't fit in. Sesame oil with its characteristic nutty taste is for specific dishes only and is not suitable as a general-purpose oil.

Roasted peanuts are used in several recipes in this book and may be substituted for cashews or almonds. To roast the nuts, place them on a tray in an oven preheated to 180ºC. After 5 minutes stir the nuts so that they cook evenly and return them to the oven for another 5 minutes or until golden brown. If you are allergic to nuts, try substituting with deep fried cooked chickpeas.

Fish

The Burmese are huge fans of fresh water fish, not surprising in a country criss-crossed by great rivers. But the availability of wonderful Mediterranean fish in Valencia has led me to adapt recipes to what I find easily available here. I hope my grandfather K will forgive my use of sea bream instead of catfish in mohinga – an abomination in his eyes! - but having eaten both the authentic Yangon version and my own, I'm inclined to stand by my preference. The sustainability of the oceans is something that should concern us all, and in the Burmese way, I'd strongly recommend making fish dishes a part of a meal rather than the centrepiece. Eating well is about eating fairly too.

Meat

In contrast to Europe and North America, meat is a less important part of the daily diet for many people in Southern and South East Asia. When meat is consumed, flavour is hugely important. I'd recommend investing in a small charcoal grill, which is probably the fastest way to get a really authentic smoky Asian taste to your meat. If a barbecue is too much trouble, try seasoning the meat with smoked salt, which is available in many supermarkets. Make sure to buy the best quality organic meat you can afford. Given that in Western Europe we throw away half of the food that we buy, it makes sense to buy good quality and sustainable ingredients and make the effort not to waste anything.

Chicken stock

Chicken stock is used throughout this book, so to avoid repetition I'll include a recipe here. Given the dubious content of chicken stock cubes, I would strongly recommend making your own. It's easy, satisfying and can be frozen in 500ml plastic containers.

INGREDIENTS

Two free range chicken carcasses (approximately 1kg)
6 free range chicken wings
½ tsp black pepper corns
2 bay leaves
1 large carrot
1 medium white onion
2 stalks celery
1 small bunch parsley
4 cloves garlic

Put the chicken carcasses and wings in a stock pot and cover with 4 litres of water. Bring to the boil, lowering the heat as a thick scum begins to form. Use a small ladle to skim these impurities from the surface before they have a chance to cloud the stock. Add the bay leaves and pepper corns and allow the stock to simmer gently for at least 1 hour. Meanwhile chop the vegetables and parsley coarsely and crush the garlic cloves. Add these ingredients to the stock and continue to simmer for 20 minutes more. Drain the stock and return it to the pan, boiling vigorously to reduce to a volume of about 2 litres.

This makes a light chicken stock, suitable for wonton soup (page 241) or as a base for khao swe (page 104). If you want to freeze the stock you can reduce it still further to just 1 litre so that it occupies less space. Just dilute it again when you come to use it. To avoid over-salting, do not be tempted to season the stock until you have reduced it to the desired concentration.

Eggs

The Burmese love boiled eggs and they crop up again and again in salads, soups, and rice dishes. Bring a pot of water to the boil with a tablespoon of vinegar and a teaspoon of salt. The eggs are less likely to crack if they are at room temperature so take them out of the fridge a few hours before cooking. Lower them carefully into the water and simmer very gently for 7 minutes (for a runny yolk) or 9 minutes (for hard boiled). Lift out the eggs with a slotted spoon and plunge them into ice cold water until cool. Peel the eggs starting at the wide end and rinse off any fragments of shell.

Noodles

I wish we were able to buy fresh noodles in Europe in the same way that we can buy fresh pasta. On a recent trip to Vietnam, I really appreciated the texture of fresh rice noodles in bun cha and cha ca. Likewise the delicate spring roll wrappers for poh piah rolls that we ate in downtown Yangon. But cooking is often about making do with what you have, so make appropriate use of the dried noodles which you can find in Chinese supermarkets.

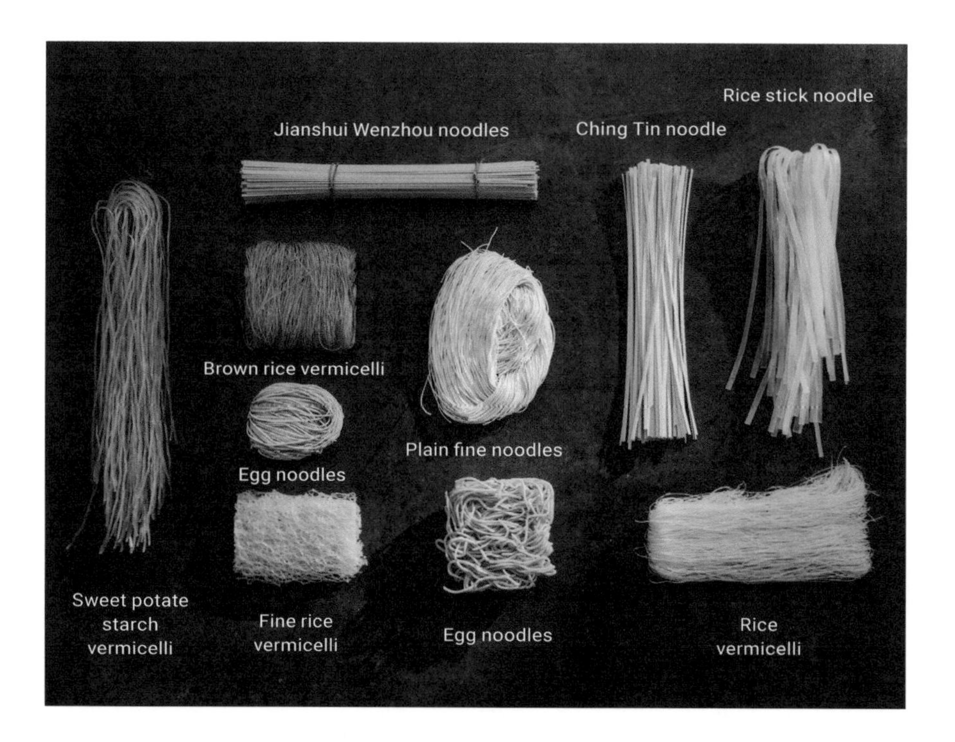

Batterie de cuisine

You don't really need any special equipment for the recipes in this book. A good small paring knife and a cook's knife are the only things I take with me if I have to cook in someone else's kitchen and I just make do with what else is available. But there are some tools that make life easier.

For making curry pastes, you'll need a food processor if you don't want to spend hours pounding the paste with a pestle in a granite mortar. Larger food processors are fine for making curry paste on an industrial scale, but for the smaller quantities described in this book you'll probably find the ingredients tend to stick stubbornly to the sides of the bowl hopelessly beyond the reach of the spinning blades. I use a small food processor of the kind that comes as an attachment to a hand-held blender. I'd also recommend investing in an electric coffee bean grinder for grinding spices.

A 'spider' is a Chinese slotted spoon usually made from copper or stainless-steel wire. It's great for lifting food from boiling water as it drains the food very efficiently. Equally, a wire basket is handy for cooking noodles. Both can be bought in Chinese supermarkets.

A good pestle and mortar is useful when crushing is more important than mincing. I use it to grind coarse salt with saffron, which really brings the colour out.

A small rolling pin will help when making samosas. Twenty centimetres is a good length. Try to buy a simple wooden cylinder without any handles, as samosas are rolled by turning the pastry with the left hand while the right rolls the edges of the circle with the rolling pin and handles get in the way.

Oil temperatures are important when frying food, so a reliable thermometer that reads up to 200°C is a useful tool. Infra-red point-and-shoot thermometers are easy to use and relatively cheap.

BEGINNINGS
(- 1912)

The Mon Talaing

It began with chaos, the seasons, wind and water. Then came the earth, minerals, plants, and the animals having no bones. There was no knowledge of time. Then animals having bones came into being, and finally a woman appeared. She was called Itthangeyasangasi and she fed on the perfumes of flowers. Through her came people and from the two sons of a prince and a dragon mother were born the Mon people. One of the sons founded the city of Thaton, and the other died young to be reborn as a famous disciple of the Buddha. Their religion was pure and their rulers wise, until the Burmese King Alompra invaded Thaton. He carried away the scriptures, the monks, the wise, those with spiritual insight and the Mon court, and brought them to his capital of Pagan. And so Pagan flourished but Thaton was laid waste[2].

Me!

I remember nothing of Prome, the town where I was born in 1906. I was called Gertrude after one of Father's sisters. I didn't like her much and have always hated the name. It doesn't shorten well either and I was relieved in later life to be given the nickname 'G'. A great improvement on 'Gertie'. Father was a judge with the Indian Civil Service, and when he was stationed there he brought with him my mother, Ma Khin, a Mon Talaing woman, and my two oldest siblings, Alice and Willy. ☞ | P 46 **MON PRAWN CURRY** |

I have only scraps of family lore about those early days. I've been told that I was the first and only child in the family to have had a Madrassi ayah to look after me and that she was not at all a good nurse, for she used to have tiny pills of opium knotted into a corner of her sari which she used to keep me quiet when I cried. A large louse had once been found on my baby head that must have fallen from hers and that was considered an omen of great good fortune and prosperity that, alas, never materialised.

---

[2] Halliday, R. (1917) *The Talaings*. Rangoon Government Press, Rangoon. Available online: https://archive.org/stream/talaings00hallrich/talaings00hallrich_djvu.txt

Portrait of G

My grandmother and grandfather

My grandmother, Ma Wun, told of how her mother remembered watching the arrival of the first Europeans in Moulmein, and how she thought they were an ugly, coarse people with very red faces. This must have been some time after 1825. The first Commissioner, Mr Maingy had originally set up his headquarters at Amherst but it became apparent that Moulmein had greater strategic advantages, and so British garrisons and officials were transferred there. At the time, it was little more than a fishing village and from the sea to the border was jungle and forest, cut only by rivers and watercourses which offered the main means of transport between one village and the next. The British wanted to build roads for trade, but it was difficult and Mr Maingy imposed compulsory labour on local families for some months of the first two years. He found however that this had detrimental effects on the rice harvest so in the end sent for convicts from Bengal. I know that Moulmein is famed for its large prison, and I suppose this is one reason why it so dominates the place.

I have always been fascinated by the town. Everybody says how attractive a place it was, standing at the mouth of the Salween River with a ridge of hills behind, dotted with golden stupas. By the time Granny Ma Wun was born in the late 1850s, it had developed into Britain's first military and administrative capital in Burma, strung out along a single street which extended along the river about two and a half miles. Its glory days were over by then and it was well into its decline. By 1852, when the British annexed the Delta region which is where Rangoon is - attention had turned to rice growing and Moulmein began to fade into obscurity [3].

One of the drivers of Moulmein's prosperity had been the Hokkien Chinese who traded along the Tenasserim coast even before the British had landed there. Granny Ma Wun told me that my grandfather was born in 'The Big Country' and had come from a poor family. A friend had told him that there was money to be made abroad and he had taken a boat to Penang in Malaya. Apparently, it was a very difficult journey, the passage was stormy and the boat was overcrowded. He had arrived as a 'sinkeh' or a new recruit and had to work off his passage for a year for a master, but after that was able to trade on his own account. He set up a small business in Moulmein and ended up staying and joining what was probably by then a sizeable Chinese community. Granny said he liked to spend time in the Chinese tea house in the bazaar, drinking tea and eating gyozas. It was said to be decorated with large inscriptions, paper lanterns and banners. ☞ | P 49 **GYOZAS** |

The Chinese were considered 'pauk paw': like family. Marriage to a local woman was quite common and certainly much more acceptable than marriage to Indians who were dubbed 'kalar' or foreigners. He and Granny had seven children,

---

[3] The early days of British rule in Burma, including the efforts of Commissioner Maingy, were described and analysed by JS Furnivall (1939) in 'The fashioning of Leviathan', *Journal of the Burma Research Society* (29) 1-138

and my mother, Ma Khin Hnyaw, born in 1878, was the third. She and all her brothers and sisters had rather unusual names that I've never come across again. 'Khin' means loving and 'Hnyaw' is the smell of oil cooking. In later life, my Burmese friends would tease me that she was called 'loving fried fish'. Usually in these kinds of marriages the daughters were brought up as Burmese and the sons as Chinese, but my grandfather died of a lingering illness when they were all still young, and Granny Ma Wun had brought them all up in her ways and they spoke no Chinese.

Mother

His early death meant that the older children had to set to and earn a living. My mother rolled cheroots - not Kipling's 'whackin' white' ones, but the ordinary brown stumpy ones about the size of a cigar. Unusually she herself did not smoke cigars nor chew betel. She sold them in Daingwunkin bazaar, where she had her own stall and she used to keep her accounts in her head. People today think that feminism is a twentieth century invention, but in Burma women always worked. It is true that according to Buddhist precepts a woman is of a lower spiritual level than a man and a wife must always respect her husband's 'hpon', his male holiness, but on the other hand this means that he does not know how to deal with earthly matters like handling the family finances.

The British were always very admiring of the independence of Burmese women, but I think they were also rather afraid of them. The most famous of all Burmese women - before Aung San Suu Kyi of course - was Queen Supayalat, the wife of the last king of Upper Burma, King Thibaw. She is always portrayed as arrogant, ambitious and insanely jealous, and many atrocities happened during their reign. She supposedly colluded with her mother, Hsinbyumashin, in poisoning all rivals for her weak and simple-minded husband's affections and urged him to massacre his relatives. All this would have been happening when Mother was a girl, as the Kingdom of Ava, or Upper Burma, was invaded by the British in 1885 when she was about twelve.

I'm sure if you go there now you'll find the Daingwunkin bazaar run down, but it must have been the heart of the town at that time and it was there she met my father. He had taken up his first appointment as Assistant Commissioner at Moulmein in November 1893 and was one of her customers. Lower Burma has a very wet climate and Mother often used to tell us romantic stories about how she used to dry his tobacco leaves by putting them under her mattress.

Mother, Ma Khin Hnyaw

Father

My father, William Carr, worked for the Indian Civil Service. In the parlance of the day he was an 'ICS man'. In the 1870s and 1880s when Father was growing up, to be British was to be great, to share in the most noble history, heritage and culture in the world. He used to tell me how he liked to read boys' magazines, and they were packed with exciting stories about life in the British Empire. There was a poem from one of them he used to recite, I think rather tongue in cheek:

> 'Boys of spirit, boys of will,
> Boys of muscle, brain and power,
> Fit to cope with anything,
> These are wanted every hour.'

That summed up Father to me, and I've always thought that he was the ideal ICS man. They had a certain mythology about them and Philip Mason wrote a famous book about the ICS in the 1950s called '*The Guardians*', which likened them to the ruling caste of Plato's Republic. This was their ethos, wise and dutiful with a moral commitment to govern, not merely as rulers, but to guide by example.

Father, William Carr, 1895

Father was very bright. He was the third of seven sons and two daughters of a Lancashire cotton manufacturer. It is hardly surprising that an educated boy from an evangelical family should want to try for the ICS open competition. He told me that there were two other sons of manufacturers among the candidates of 1891 and at the exam he met the son of an upholsterer (who was not successful even though he'd gone to a crammer for a year to prepare for the exam). Candidates could sit as many papers as they wanted, from Greek to Mechanical Philosophy, and the thirty-two who had the highest total marks became probationers, permitted to join the service after two years, subject to exams and a certificate of moral suitability.

Probationers chose the province where they wanted to serve in the order in which they came in the open competition. At that time Burma was ruled as a Non-Regulation Province of India, meaning it was considered a backward area in need of stronger, more personalised government. ICS men there were given a freer hand by their superiors and as well as governing they heard criminal cases, but nevertheless it tended to be a place left for the lower ranking candidates. Indeed, the year after Father joined, the ICS changed the arrangement because they were concerned about the quality of the people serving there. Father had ranked sixth and had a wide choice so it was a surprise to everyone that he chose Burma. I asked him once, 'Why Burma?' but he answered only that it seemed a good sort of place. I think the fact that his older brother, Sam, was already in Burma working for the Indian Forest Service must have influenced his choice, for the two of them were very close. But, as he later explained in a letter to the Government of India complaining about the slowness of his promotion, the most important consideration was his career. His exam mark meant that he would rank first in Burma among the officers who entered in his year, and since Upper Burma had only recently been occupied, promotion opportunities would be good. So, he started in Burma as an Assistant Commissioner, in charge of revenue, education, health, roads, jails, local taxation, and government in an area about half the size of an English county. Quite a challenge for a young man in his early twenties.

Family disapproval

Mother said, quite openly, that living with Father meant she was able to help her family more substantially than she had when earning the meagre profits from selling cheroots in the Daingwunkin bazaar. When Father's butler came and invited her to live with him, Granny Ma Wun was very distressed that that her daughter was becoming the mistress of an Englishman. Apparently, there was a tremendous scene and she threw all her daughter's bedding out of the window. There was no formal wedding ceremony in Burmese village life and under the rule of the Burmese kings any foreign immigrant could be required to live with a Burmese woman, so there was a tradition of relationships between

Burmese women and foreign men. But when the man was English the young woman's family knew very well that he felt quite free to abandon her and all their children if they were not bound by a formal contract. I think it must have been because of such worries that Mother's family were so hostile.

It wasn't only Mother's family who were outraged. Father's family also strongly disapproved of the arrangement. It was Mother herself who told me how she'd feared Father's older brother, Uncle Sam, who used to visit when he was on leave. He did his best to stop the relationship and turned her out of the house whenever he came visiting. He was solicitous for his favourite and promising brother's career. It was sad for everyone. I pitied her in those early days of their relationship. She had to be very nice to the butler because he was in charge of the household, and unless she was nice to him he wouldn't put in a good word with his master. Assistant Commissioners were moved from station to station rarely staying for more than two or three years in the same town. She followed Father from posting to posting, fifteen years old and far from home. She lost her first baby because, she said, she loved to play hopscotch on the sand in the moonlight and one energetic game brought on a miscarriage.

Having a Burmese mistress was also strongly discouraged by the British authorities. It was considered to lower the prestige of the English who were supposed to keep a certain distance from the local population. There were all sorts of rules drafted to try and prevent such marriages. The suggestion was to require reports of the woman's antecedents, her social standing and her property, as well as those of her family including parents, uncles, aunts, brothers, sisters, brothers-in-law, sisters-in-law and first cousins. Furthermore, if she had previously been the man's mistress, the government would prohibit the marriage. In the end, these suggestions were rejected on the grounds that penalising men who married rather than those who kept mistresses might only encourage illicit connections and it would undoubtedly cause problems with the church. However, every young officer was warned of the danger he would incur should he enter either a marriage or an irregular connection with a Burmese woman and was made very aware of the damage it could cause to his career prospects.

Early married life

But Father was not like most of the British men who took Burmese mistresses. I later learned that in 1901 he had informed the ICS that he wished to marry her and was only dissuaded with great difficulty. He was a man brought up to do the right thing, and that included making a decent woman of the mother of your children. They were married in 1906 shortly after I was born, having been together for ten years. Mother used to claim their irregular union had lasted so long by then, that when they finally did get married she'd lost all interest in the idea. She said that she could not understand why Father had chosen to marry her after she had me, an ugly, black child, when he had stubbornly refused to do so despite Alice and Willy, her two eldest fair-haired children who were such a credit to their English father.

Father was transferred back to Moulmein in 1908. By this time he'd married Mother and had been a judge for two years. An ICS man would usually make the choice between the judiciary and the executive side of the service early in his career, but because Burma was a Non-Regulation Province, the executive and judiciary were not separated until 1905. Then a superior judicial service was created in Lower Burma and some of the judicial work was taken from the ICS executive officers. For some reason, the judiciary seemed to be the preferred option among those ICS men who were married to Burmese women. Father elected to join this service, partly because he was more temperamentally suited to the work, but partly I suspect for ease of promotion.

Unusually for a Burmese house the Session Judge's official residence in Moulmein had three storeys, and the third storey was left unfurnished and used by my mother for storing durians. They had to be kept out of reach of my father's nose because they smelt more and more strongly as they ripened, and how the English loathed that smell! I seem to remember that storey as a dusty, spooky place. It is very likely that my image of it has been built up entirely from hearsay and I don't really remember it at all, but it has always haunted me, and when I have dreamt in later life about a house where I'm trying to find my way about or find something, it's always a house with a third spooky storey. In those early years I seemed, I was told, always stricken with fear, never speaking above a whisper: 'Say Papa', my mother would teach me, and I'd whisper, 'Pa-pa'. 'Louder!' Still only a whisper. And again. And again! Truly a hopeless creature.

Funnily enough, much as I loved and depended on him in those early years, I never felt entirely easy with Father. Perhaps Mother had something to do with this. She had enormous respect for him and never tired of telling us what a great and GOOD man he was, so that we saw him as a being exalted above us. And she had the Burmese Buddhist's sense of a man's greater holiness. At the pagoda, it is the man who enters the inner sanctum to approach the image of the Buddha with offerings, and at home on washing day the woman's longyi must always be hung below his. We must have absorbed some of Mother's attitudes, but what distanced Father from us much more in those early years was the language barrier. Although I had been speaking, reading and writing English at school for years, until I was about nine years old I spoke nothing but Burmese at home and Father's spoken Burmese was rather halting, although of course he wrote the language very correctly.

Our English family

Father, although great and dominant in our lives, was not real as Mother was. He had a family, but they were far away in improbable England, and we'd never met them. We had heard tell of them and seen their photographs - I remember big head-and-shoulders portraits of his mother and father that used to hang in a prominent place in every house we lived in.

Father with siblings, 1897

There was a rather striking group of Father with his siblings: six brothers sitting one above the other on a flight of front door steps of their mother's house in Southport, Father second from the top and with his two sisters one on each side of him. Inset, on the top right-hand corner, was his eldest brother who was away at the time the picture was taken. That was John, we were told, who was a great wanderer, now in one country, now in another. I remember he sent Father a sjambok and we were told it was a cattle whip from Africa. But where was Africa? Another faraway place. Above Father was his brother Sam, the one who had served in Burma in the Forest Service. By the time I had been born he'd been promoted to a senior job in India. And that was our Aunty Alice, Father's elder sister - wasn't she beautiful. How different from his younger sister, Gertrude, on the left, whom I had the misfortune to be named after and who was very plain. No wonder, said Mother, that she'd never married, while Alice was married to a very rich man. And those four below Father were his younger brothers, Tom, Robert, Joe and Fred, our English uncles. But they were not real these people. We didn't know them in the flesh, as we knew Mother's people. She told us lots of stories about her childhood, how naughty her brothers had been at school, but we knew nothing of Father's schooldays because, simply, we were not on chatting terms.

Our Burmese family

Our relationship with Mother on the other hand, was entirely easy. We spoke her language and she was with us all day. And we grew up with her people. As well as us children there were five Burmese cousins aged between eighteen

Mother and family, Pagoda Hill, Kalaw

and nine who lived with us. Two of them were the children of Mother's eldest sister, who had been abandoned by her wealthy Chinese husband. They were called Ma Ngwe Kyi, pretty but with bandy teeth, and Ma Tin Chi, and the three of us were more or less of an age and went to school together. The other three were the daughters of her oldest brother. He had married a local girl, and both parents had died when we were very young. They were called Ma Saw Mya , Ma Tin Mya, and Ma Than Mya. Ma Saw Mya was the oldest and she was rather handsome, she was the sort of head nanny to us. Ma Tin Mya was vivacious and plain and she did the Burmese cooking, and Ma Than Mya was a bit older than me, not as tall or handsome as her oldest sister and still young so she was sent to school.

That meant there were five orphan daughters of Mother's siblings entirely dependent on her. Wealthy Burmese women often took in poorer girl relatives who did the light housework and looked after the children. They were not paid anything but the woman of the household was expected to send them to school and arrange suitable marriages for them when the time came. Our cousins used to organise our games, make the beds, cook, wash, sweep, that kind of thing. Mother was particularly fond of Ma Ngwe Kyi and used to take her round visiting friends and dress her up nicely, I think because she was her favourite sister's eldest child. ☛ | P 51 NAN GYI THOKE |

Our lovely Granny, Ma Wun, came to stay quite often. She had made up with Mother over her association with Father when it became obvious that he was not going to abandon her and that he was able to look after her and the family. Granny was a lovely, gentle woman, who always had a cheroot between her teeth and a betel box by her side. She had a special affection for me because like her, I was 'Inga thami', Tuesday's daughter, born on a Tuesday. I loved her dearly, because she told the most marvellous stories. Stories about Owl who didn't pay his debts and can only come out at night, or Me Htwe, a beautiful heroine. After many misadventures, Me Htwe came home to roost in a large bael fruit in the garden of an old couple, who picked it and put it in their rice bin to ripen. Every morning when they went out to sell their small wares in the bazaar Me Htwe emerged from the bael fruit and did their housework.

Mother - rage and grace

Mother was totally unlike gentle Granny. She was a tempestuous creature, never morose, but given to great rages. As a child I feared these rages, especially when she turned on me with cries of 'Mi Htoo! Mi Htoo!' which means 'Stupid! Stupid!', and I couldn't understand why. She had a habit of launching into a long tirade of steadily increasing recrimination out of all proportion it seemed to the small misdeed or mistake that had sparked it off, rebuking not only the present wrongdoing, but also all other crimes the poor miscreant might ever have been guilty of in the past and would be guilty of in the future - and she would extend her rage further to include everybody else who had ever taken part in such crimes. At those times, the whole household would fall silent speaking only in whispers.

Very often it was poor relatives who came begging from Moulmein that started her off. Mother could not forget that when her father was lying bedridden in his last illness these same people had kept their distance and offered her mother no help. She'd make no bones about reminding them of this: 'When we were poor, what help did we get from you? I swore then that one day I would earn a bag of gold and hit you on the head with it'. And she'd send them away with a flea in their ear. She was no soft touch with her siblings either. Ma Wun's favourite son was her young brother, who we called Small Uncle. He was a no good and he spent what little he had on gambling. Small Uncle came to Granny Ma Wun and he was telling her all his troubles and crying, and Granny sent me to go and ask mother for some money. My Mother said: 'Crying is he? Well tell him to make some powder out of a playing card and rub it into his eyes and they won't be so sore.'

She knew the value - and the power - of money, but she wasn't miserly. She was a good businesswoman. She made small savings out of housekeeping and stashed away among clothes and linen many a long roll of silver rupees, which turned out a godsend in the early twenties when the Alliance Bank of Simla failed and ready cash was hard to come by for a time. She appreciated a good head for business and not every relative was sent away empty-handed. Her favourite nephew, Sein Po, was a handsome charmer and a very smart operator who had set himself up in business and prospered but sometimes needed a loan. He never came empty handed himself. He always brought her a length of best Bangkok silk and he never failed to repay the loan punctually, offering due interest, which she would generously waive. He was a great friend of mine, Sein Po. He always insisted to us that Mother's long tirades were nothing to get panicky about: 'They're just talk. She likes to talk, you know, so all you have to do is listen humbly and you'll have no more trouble.'

I have told you dreadful stories about Mother and her rages and dramas, but I have been grossly unfair. She was simply the prisoner of her time and place, of her upbringing and her later circumstances, and aren't we all? She lived in an English world but spoke no English. She knew only too well both where she had come from and that the world was changing and she wanted the best for her children. Quite often I feared her, but I admired her greatly. She'd had little schooling but she had energy and character enough to rise above her many disadvantages. She was a lady as to the manner born, my mother.

MON PRAWN CURRY

Serves 4 | prepare 30 mins | cook 30 mins | easy

There is a saying in Burma: Mandalay for talking, Rangoon for boasting, Moulmein for eating. On a recent visit to Ma Khin's home town a monsoon storm threatened, and we took shelter at a food stall under rickety poles holding up plastic sheets. In no time bowls of rice and steaming prawn curry appeared and as we sat under the blackened sky and the thundering rain threatened to burst the banks of the Salween river, there was no talking, no boasting, just eating.

INGREDIENTS

For the curry paste:
6 dried long red chillies
2 fresh bird's eye chillies
2cm ginger
2 cloves garlic
6 shallots
1 tsp fermented fish paste
1 tsp ground cumin
½ tsp ground coriander
½ tsp turmeric
¼ tsp ground cinnamon
½ tsp salt

For the prawn curry:
2 tbsp sunflower oil
750g large king prawns with shell and head on
1 litre light chicken stock (page 29)
1-2 tbsp tamarind paste
½-1 tbsp palm sugar
1 small aubergine
250g okra
2 medium green tomatoes
2 tbsp chopped coriander

Break off and discard the stem of the dried chillies and shake out the seeds. Put them in a bowl, cover with cold water and leave to soak for 1 hour. Slice the tops from the fresh chillies and discard. Cut open the chillies and remove the seeds. Peel and coarsely chop the ginger and garlic. Peel the shallots and cut them into quarters. Put all the ingredients for the curry paste in a food processor and grind until smooth. You will have about four large tablespoons of curry paste, enough to make two curries, so freeze half.

Peel the prawns and separate the head from the body. With a small paring knife, tug the black intestine from the body of the prawn and discard. Keep the shells and heads. Cut the aubergine into 2cm cubes. Slice each okra into pieces about 2cm long. Cut the tomatoes into similarly sized pieces.

Fry the shells and heads of the prawns in 1 tablespoon of sunflower oil and when coloured pink, add the chicken stock. Boil until the stock has reduced by half then strain and set aside.

Heat the remaining oil in a heavy casserole dish and fry 2 generous tablespoons of curry paste for a few minutes over a medium heat, stirring as the paste becomes aromatic. Add the reduced stock and season the soup with the tamarind paste and palm sugar. It should be tart with just a hint of sweetness. Add the aubergine and okra. Cook for 5 minutes then add the prawns and tomato and cook for 3 more minutes. Serve immediately sprinkled with chopped coriander.

GYOZAS

Makes 24-30 pieces | prepare 45 mins | cook 15 mins | medium difficulty

Though often associated with Japanese restaurants, gyozas are really a Chinese dish, brought back to Japan by troops returning home at the end of the Second World War. My image of Ma Khin's father is of him sitting at a steamed-up window in the Chinese tea house, sipping tea and dipping gyozas in vinegary soy sauce looking down at his fellow traders in the streets below.

INGREDIENTS

For the gyozas:

1 packet of gyoza wrappers (available from Chinese supermarkets)
200g minced pork
75g frozen peeled prawns defrosted
4 leaves of Chinese cabbage
4 spring onions
1 tsp chopped garlic
1 tsp grated ginger
½ tbsp sesame oil
2 tbsp light soy sauce
½ tsp sugar
1 tsp ground white pepper
1 tsp corn flour
¼ tsp salt

For cooking and serving the gyozas:

4 tbsp light soy sauce
1 tbsp rice vinegar
2 tbsp sunflower oil
2 tbsp sesame oil
Water
1 tbsp chopped chives
1 tsp toasted sesame seeds

Slice the cabbage leaves and spring onion thinly and chop the prawns. In a mixing bowl combine all of the ingredients for the filling, squeezing the mixture with a clenched fist until it oozes out between your fingers. Allow the filling to rest for 20 minutes in the fridge. Mix together the soy sauce and rice vinegar.

Lay a round gyoza wrapper on a dry surface and place a spoonful of the filling in the centre. With a wet finger, moisten the edges of the pastry, and fold it over to enclose the filling. Skilled gyoza makers can form pleats, a fiddly business for the amateur, so don't be afraid to just pinch the edges closed with your fingers.

Choose a good non-stick frying pan with a lid. Cook the gyozas in batches. Put half the sesame and sunflower oil in the pan with 50ml of water. Bring to the boil and add sufficient gyozas to comfortably fit in the pan. Cover and steam the gyozas for 5 or 6 minutes. Remove the lid and allow any remaining water to evaporate. The gyozas will begin to fry and crisp in the remaining oil. Turn once and when crispy on both sides remove from the pan and place on a serving dish. Repeat with the rest of the gyozas. Sprinkle with chives and sesame seeds and serve with the soy and vinegar sauce.

NAN GYI THOKE

Serves 4 | prepare 20 mins + 2 hours to marinate | cook 60 mins | easy

This unusual salad of cold noodles and warm chicken curry is often served for breakfast or as a mid-morning snack. Thoke means salad, and nan gyi refers to the type of noodle. The noodles used in Burma are made with rice flour, but sadly it's difficult to find these fresh noodles in Spain, so we settle for Japanese udon noodles. I am sure Burmese cooks would thoroughly disapprove of using wheat in place of rice noodles, but the texture and size of udon suits the dish. You could also try making the salad with cellophane rice noodles. Just follow the cooking instructions on the packet.

INGREDIENTS

For the chicken curry:

400g boned and skinned chicken thighs
1 tsp Madras curry powder
1 tsp garam masala
2 tbsp sunflower oil
1 medium onion chopped
1 tsp finely chopped garlic
1 cm grated ginger
1 stalk lemon grass
¼ tsp chilli powder
1 tsp paprika
200g chopped tinned tomatoes
½ tsp salt

For the salad:

1 packet udon noodles
A handful of fresh bean sprouts
¼ white cabbage shredded
4 spring onions chopped
2 tbsp shallot oil
2 tsp fish sauce
Juice and zest of 1 lime
2 soft boiled eggs (page 30)
1 tbsp chopped coriander
2 tbsp ground toasted rice (page 24)

Cut the chicken into bite size strips and season with the curry powder, garam masala and salt. Mix well and leave to marinate for 2 hours. Remove the older leaves from the lemon grass and finely chop the white part.

Heat the oil in a heavy pan and fry the onion over a medium heat until it begins to brown. Add the garlic, lemon grass and ginger and continue to fry until aromatic. Add the chilli powder and paprika and stir everything well before adding the marinated chicken. When the chicken begins to colour, add the tomatoes followed by 400ml water. Bring to the boil then lower the heat and simmer gently for 30-40 minutes until the chicken is tender and most of the liquid has evaporated.

While the chicken curry is cooking, bring a large pan of salted water to the boil and cook the noodles according to the instructions on the packet. Drain and refresh them in iced water. Put the cold noodles in a mixing bowl and add the shredded cabbage, spring onions and bean sprouts. Dress cautiously with shallot oil, fish sauce and the zest and juice of the lime - fish sauce can be overpowering so be careful not to add too much. Arrange the noodle salad on a serving dish. Spoon over the warm curry and top with slices of boiled egg. Sprinkle with chopped coriander and ground toasted rice.

BASSEIN: PADDY BIRDS AND SIMNEL CAKE[4] (1913-1917)

Arriving in Bassein

We left Moulmein in 1912, when Father was stationed at Bassein in the Irrawaddy Delta. I imagine we must have gone there by boat, but I don't remember the journey at all. What I do remember, and most vividly, is arriving at the house we were to live in. It was built of wood on solid pillars of teak, with a large garden and as our carriage turned into the drive, a great mass of yellow cosmos in full bloom flashed on the eye. It was a steamy, end-of-the-monsoons kind of day and the damp air was filled with the smell of that cosmos. I absolutely rushed at it, but someone cried, 'Snakes! Snakes!', so I wasn't allowed to go among them. Even now, every time I smell a cosmos I see that sheet of gold. They were right about the snakes and I distinctly remember a great snake coiled around one of those teak pillars that was chased away and killed.

There were nasty smells in that garden too. In the corner, diagonally opposite the cosmos behind the house, were a number of tall trees where lots of paddy birds nested. They were beautiful creatures individually, but in hundreds, living messily over our heads, calling harshly to each other and their eggs sometimes dropping from their nests to rot on the ground, they were a great nuisance. But they were beautiful and an easy target for the Indian servants, who shot them down with catapults to eat their flesh and sell their lovely tail feathers for trimming English ladies' hats. All this against my mother's strict orders and so always done when she was out. When darkness fell the paddy birds would disappear and the flying foxes swoop in to roost, hanging upside down on the branches of the trees. They smelt bad and they made strange, squeaky noises. Fearsome looking creatures - blood-sucking vampire bats we were told, and we children were terrified of them.

In spite of the bats we had some wonderful times in that garden. There were tamarind, mango and banana trees and clumps of bamboo, and we used the stems and seeds for our games. We wrapped little bundles of tender tamarind in banana leaves for a mysterious, positively magical game I loved to play.

[4] 'Paddy Birds and Simnel Cake' was the title of a Radio 4 programme from the 1980s that interviewed Grandy about her early life. She was very pleased that an extract also featured in Radio 4's Pick of the Week.

Securely fastened with a stick for a pin, each little bundle was carefully buried in a hole in the ground and the earth firmly patted down over it. Then we'd take it in turns to jump on the covered hole, reciting an incantation calling on the spirits for salt and oil for our salad. And when we dug up our bundle again the tamarind leaves would be moist and delicious! The spirits had granted our prayer! ☞ | P65 MANGO CHUTNEY |

Alice and Willy were in England. As with most ICS families they had been sent back to England to study in boarding schools when they were about eight or nine years old as the education in Burma was not considered of a high enough standard. This meant that when we arrived there were three children, myself just six, my little sister Mary two and a half and Sam the baby and of course the five cousins. My nights were very interrupted in those days, for Mary was a real little terror when she was a child. I remember when we were first in Bassein she'd wake up every night in the small hours and scream for the gramophone that Father had brought back from England with him. It was one of those old wind-up ones with an enormous brass horn, rather beautiful, scallop-edged and looking like a great lily. Most of the records were of Harry Lauder singing, and night after night our sleep would be broken by the loud strains of *Roaming in the Gloaming* and *Annie Laurie.*

Our imperial household

Like all imperial households we had a large staff of servants whose living quarters were away from the house, a row of one room huts well back in the compound with a separate lavatory and wash house. As with all servants in households like ours, they were Indians. The British had ruled India for much longer than Burma and Indians were felt to be better acquainted with European households, and besides no Burmese would lower himself to do that kind of work. There was a driver, a gardener, a cook to make Father's English food, and a boy (who in India they called a 'bearer' which is a kind of butler). A paniwallah boiled water for the baths and did the washing up and all the jobs to do with water, except the latrines which was the work of the sweeper and washing clothes, which was done by the dhobi. The rest of the jobs, the Burmese cooking, the bed making, the dusting, and, of course, looking after us, was the work of our Burmese cousins.

The dhobi was not resident but he came once a week on Dhobi Day. The family clothes would be put into piles depending on what kind of garments they were. One of the Burmese cousins or in later years, Alice, would sit on a stool with a little book. The dhobi counted out in Hindustani the number of items of each type of clothing and she noted it down. When they had finished, he would put it all in one of the sheets and go off with a white bundle on his shoulders.

The next week he'd come back with the bundle rather smaller because all the clothes had been washed and ironed, and the process would begin again.

There was no electricity in the districts, so no fans, and instead we had a punkahwallah. He had to sit on the floor and pull at a cord, and from time to time, poor fellow, he would fall asleep, and the punkah would stop turning, and you would shout, 'Hey! Pull that punkah!'. Outside our house there was a chaprassi who was paid by the government to stand at our front door. He wore a uniform with a red sash across his chest and in the middle of it was a big brass disc with DIVISIONAL AND SESSIONS JUDGE engraved around the rim. The chaprassi in Bassein was severely pockmarked not just on his face but also on the soles of his feet, and he used to show us how they were pitted with scars. He must have liked to frighten us because when on one occasion a frog hopped by and we all shrank away from it, he said, 'Look, it's nothing to be afraid of,' and he picked it up in one fist and squeezed it. Squeezed it to death! I was absolutely horrified.

Bassein routines

There were two kinds of meals in our house, English food for Father cooked by the Indian cook and Burmese food for us and Mother cooked by one of the cousins under Mother's supervision. Mother would send them out to the bazaar and examine the ingredients they brought back, giving them instructions on how to make the most of them and overseeing the cooking process. The final result would be sent upstairs to us at five o'clock. ☞ | P 67 **FRIED RICE WITH SPICY CHICKEN WINGS** |

In the early years, we used to eat with our hands in the Burmese way, but later we had to use a spoon and fork so that our hands didn't smell. Father's English dinner would be ceremonially served up to him at eight o'clock in the dining room downstairs, and Mother would sit with him and have a small helping of every dish. It started with soup, then there was a fish course, then meat and finally pudding. When he had finished, the pudding would be sent up to us. It was often custard, or bread and butter pudding. When she came to stay with us, this was Granny's favourite treat. She particularly loved the crust on the top, and she and Mary would always have fearful rows about this crust. Granny was served first and she would take all the crust there was, and Mary would let out a loud howl and say: 'Granny's taken all the jo'. 'Jo' meaning 'crust', you see. ☞ | P 68 **BREAD AND BUTTER PUDDING** |

After dinner Father would come upstairs to settle down for a read before bedtime in his easy chair, with a whisky and soda beside him. We children were organised to go to him for a goodnight kiss and a chocolate - never more than one each.

I can see him now, sitting in that chair, holding a big oval tin labelled 'Cadbury's King George Chocolates', doling them out, each one wrapped in silver foil.

Bassein beyond our door

Looking back at those early days in Bassein I see them as a kind of Golden Age, when we were all happy and had lots of family fun, but in fact Bassein was not a pleasant place to live. It was not so bad for us as the residences of principal officials, the American Baptist Mission, the Post Office, etc. were comparatively healthy, but the town had no uncontaminated water supply. Cholera, dysentery and typhoid periodically swept through the place, particularly the unsanitary poorer areas built on the swamp and marshy land that lay on the other side of the river from us.

J.S. Furnivall, who was to become my great friend when I was at Rangoon University wrote a marvellous book that looked at the British development of the Irrawaddy Delta into a 'factory without chimneys' for the production of rice [5]. Burmese peasants came in their thousands and they brought millions of acres of jungle and swamp under rice cultivation. They cleared the land by burning undergrowth, chopping trees and, in kanazo areas, flooding the roots for two years. Having 'opened' the area, they were attacked by displaced wild animals, including tigers and elephants and plagued by insects. By the time we arrived the frontier areas were in a state of semi-anarchy as rich landowners paid retainers to fight battles over boundary rights and terrorised small cultivators into giving over land to large estates. More and more cultivators were unable to repay debts and farms were handed over to money lenders or landowners, often Indian or Chinese. The tenants continued to work on the land, trapped in ever greater debt. It was a tinderbox. Father would not have dreamed of telling us about it at the time, but years later he said that his Division together with Pegu, also in the Delta, then accounted for over half the violent crime of Burma, and Burma was considered one of the most lawless provinces in India.

We were not immune, though, from a sense of insecurity. My unhappiest memories of Bassein are of the times when Father was away on tour. Everyone went to bed earlier, and a police constable came to stand guard outside the house. We had a trapdoor made of solid teak in hinged sections that was folded over the stairwell. It was additional protection that was deployed when Father was away, because the stairs came up from an open verandah downstairs. I was really scared then: what were the dangers that so formidably threatened us? But the good thing was that when the trapdoor went down we had coffee made with jaggery, and that was a big, big treat. Jaggery is a brown sugar, like fudge. I have happy memories of Father's tours from Bassein too, and those were of the times when some of us went with him to Henzada, on a train that ran on

[5] Furnivall, J.S. (1948). *Colonial Policy and Practice: A Comparative Study of Burma and Netherlands India.* Cambridge: Cambridge University Press; and New York: New York University Press

Portrait of Father

rails bedded on beautiful white pebbles. We stayed in the Circuit House, above Father's courtroom. An hour or two before the court sat, the exhibits in the case would be laid out on Father's desk - sometimes a blood-stained dagger! And from upstairs we'd watch the criminals being marched in to wait in the backyard. We knew they were coming when we heard the tramp, tramp, tramp of policemen's boots and the clank, clank, clank, of prisoner's chains. Then we would lie on the floor and use a hairpin to scrape away between the boards so we could peer through the chinks at Father. It would almost inevitably end in us having fearful giggly fits, and Father would storm out of the courtroom and upstairs in a great towering rage - he who was always so kind and gentle!

I didn't know that barely a week before we had moved into our lovely house, the district of Henzada had seen an attempt at a bloody uprising. Rebels had been organised from Bassein to Mandalay, and the revolt was to be the sign to attack the British, seize arms and sweep down to Rangoon to drive the foreigners into the sea. The plot was inspired by the 'Galone Saya San', a herbal doctor, renowned for the efficacy of his cures and his devotion to Buddhism.

He seems to have been a very inspiring man. Hundreds of recruits were tattooed and initiated in ceremonies to make them invulnerable to English bullets. Of course, the magic charms didn't work, and they were set upon by armed police, and four of them were killed, including their leader, Kyauk Lone.

There was never any talk about this kind of incident in our household and I learned about this much later from Thein Pe, a nationalist student of mine. I do remember though at the time I was frightened by the piece of paper that I once saw on Father's desk. It said JUDGEMENT. It haunted me because I knew Christians were enjoined to 'Judge not, that ye be not judged'. Was Father going to be judged too? I did know that he was absolutely anti-capital punishment. He talked a lot about it because even in those days there was an anti-capital punishment movement. He said he certainly didn't approve of capital punishment in Burma because most of the crimes were crimes of passion. I don't know how far his feelings were affected by the fact that they had to watch a criminal execution in the course of their training and I think it must have made a terrible impression on him.

Getting closer to Father - books!

It was in Bassein that I began to get closer to Father, and as language separated us early on, later it was language that drew us into an easier relationship. When we lived in Bassein a boxwallah called on us from time to time. Boxwallahs were door-to-door salesmen employed by big shops in Rangoon to peddle their goods in smaller towns in the districts. Our boxwallah (an Indian of course) carried on his head a small but deep black tin trunk with 'Mrs Wood' printed on it in white letters. Mrs Wood's shop in Rangoon sold millinery and haberdashery, and ladies' and children's clothes. We children crowded round the boxwallah when he squatted on the verandah to open his box and display his goods to Mother. He sold all sorts of odds and ends: ribbons and laces, trinkets and soft toys, and small garments, but best of all, for me, books! Very thin little paperbacks, no more than pamphlets, printed on shoddy paper between hideous lime green covers. They were children's books all about a character called Mabel who had various adventures.

One day Father saw me reading *Mabel in Christmas Toyland.* 'What's that you're reading? Here, let me have a look at it', he said, and he made me read it to him, correcting my mispronunciations. Soon afterwards a box of books arrived from a shop in India - now was it Hall and Anderson in Calcutta? or Thacker Spink & Co in Bombay? I can't remember. But I do remember the books that came: *Robinson Crusoe, Gulliver's Travels, Pilgrim's Progress* and *Little Women* all in the Everyman edition. I devoured them all, and a whole new world opened before me. Father kept an eye on my reading: 'You don't want to read that', he'd say, 'it's very badly written. Read this, it's very well written'. How do you tell a book that is well written from one that isn't? That was a question that puzzled me for years.

Father liked to teach me things. When he had time, he would take me for long walks in the heat, pointing out things of interest, explaining why that dog is hanging its tongue out, and answering my questions. 'Why is corrugated iron wavy?', I remember asking. And he devised a little experiment with paper, coins and a bowl to show me how the waves made it stronger. He was a very meticulous man and he passionately liked people to get things right. I remember many years later, when I was grown up with children of my own, a book called *Siamese White* by Maurice Collis was published and at once became the talk of the town. I asked him what he thought of it. He shrugged his shoulders: 'Oh a best seller, of course, not surprisingly - but he doesn't get his detail right', and he turned up chapter and verse to show me where Collis had made the moon rise in the wrong part of the sky at the wrong time of the night in the wrong month of the year! He had a fixation about the movements of the moon and got very cross when people made mistakes about them. Apparently, a similar error appears in Kenneth Grahame's, *The Wind in the Willows* in Chapter 7, and he wrote an article on it for the Rangoon Gazette. It was not published - the paper probably judged that few of its readers were likely to be as dedicated students of the movements of the moon as Father was. He had better luck on more newsworthy subjects. When the journalist, C.P. Scott died he contributed an article in which, after due obeisance to C.P. Scott, he was away on one of his hobby horses: the loose use of language in contemporary prose, illustrated with a collection of grammatical atrocities perpetrated by eminent columnists in reputable papers.

His social life was similar to that of most ICS men, or so it seemed to me in those far off Bassein days. He played tennis and bridge at the Club and at weekends he'd be in his dark room developing photographs; he'd been a keen photographer for many years and had a Butcher's half-plate camera with a tripod and a black cloth to put over his head when he was focussing his shots. Sometimes he would go snipe shooting. They looked pathetic - small birds with long-beaked heads. They would be roasted for Father's dinner, and Ma Than Mya would rescue any leftovers, shredding the meat and serving it up in a delicious salad. ☛ | P 71 **FRIED PORK RIBS WITH CRISPY HERBS AND NUOC CHAM SAUCE** |

Looking back at those early years in Bassein I see it as a very happy time. But now I wonder what was it like for Father? He was happy with us often, I know, but how happy was he otherwise – in his work? in his relationships with others? I remember he had one great friend, Mr. Arnold, indeed he was the only close friend I ever knew him to have. That is probably another reason why I look back at that time with such pleasure. In later life, I looked up Arnold in the Indian Office Library and found he was a great intellectual. He had written a book about psychoanalysis at a time when Freud really wasn't that well known. When I discovered that, I understood it was their intellectualism that brought Father and him together.

Starting school

I went to school at St Joseph's Convent on our side of the river. It was run by nuns of a French order. Reverend Mother wore spectacles and had a funny little knobbly nose, and Sister Edmond was small and lively and very clever. She liked me a lot because I read books. I remember when Mary was sent to school she howled her head off and kicked the nuns. It was a long time before she agreed to go to school at all. The nuns also ran an orphanage and I sometimes saw young Burmese and Karen boys carrying great steaming buckets of delicious smelling Burmese soup from their kitchen across the yard.
☞ | P 72 **CAULIFLOWER AND CHICKPEA CURRY** |

The orphans were not pupils at the school though. The intake was largely Eurasian, many of them with Portuguese names, and most of them Roman Catholics (hence 'Judge not, that ye be not judged'). If both our parents had been English we'd never have been sent to such a school, to pick up 'that dreadful chi-chi accent', though I wasn't aware of this at the time of course.

I really enjoyed school. The only thing that made me uneasy was tiffin time, when everybody ate packed lunches out of tiffin boxes, little round metal lunch boxes in two or three tiers with rice packed into the bottom tier. We did not have tiffin boxes but had our meal brought from home by the Indian butler, who laid out a white napkin for us to eat off and waited on us. ☞ | P 75 **CURRY PUFFS** | I was the odd one out, and I didn't like it. I suspect that was why a horrible little boy called Eric liked to cut me down to size. He used to mock us because we called our parents Mama and Papa instead of Mummy and Daddy like they all did. One day he stared long and hard at me, (and he wasn't so good-looking himself), and said, 'You don't look English. None of you look English except Mary'. When I got home I rushed to the mirror, and blow me, I saw he was right! One day, after Eric had been particularly horrid, Father comforted me by telling me that Lord Liverpool, who was once Prime Minister of England, had a Eurasian mother.

All the same I went on believing myself English - Father was English, so of course I was too. We definitely were not properly Eurasian because Eurasian also meant that you inhabited a particular social position – in the same way that Armenians, Jews or Parsees had a particular kind of status. From time to time I did feel an uneasy sense of separation. I remember once at a big garden fete I was selling buttonholes from a small tray slung around my neck. Mother had grown some miniature chrysanthemums, bright yellow, that were exactly the right size for buttonholes, so those were on my tray. I was quite proud of them, until I saw a pretty little English girl, with golden hair and blue eyes also selling buttonholes, but hers were tiny little pink rosebuds! Outclassed, as usual!

Simnel cake and Buddhist festivals

At home we were not Burmese and preserved certain distinctions between our cousins and ourselves: they wore Burmese clothes while we never did; indoors, in strict compliance with Burmese custom, we all went barefoot, but outdoors they wore Burmese slippers and we wore shoes and socks; they spoke to their elders in strict Burmese and did not neglect the due obeisances, while we just spoke colloquially to everybody; they were Buddhists and we were Christians, so they shared Mother's devotions but we went to Sunday School.

I knew exactly how England would smell because every year my English grandmother sent us an enormous Christmas parcel. Inside were presents for everybody: dolls, Hornby trains, big fairy tale books and little pieces of costume jewellery, and always a Lancashire simnel cake with thick toasted almond icing and marzipan on top. When we opened it, there was a smell of simnel cake and English new books (which was quite different from the smell of Indian new books) which we called 'the England smell'. I imagined that in England everything would smell like that. Though I have to admit that sometimes I used to think, 'But does England really exist? Maybe they have made it all up!'.
☞ | P76 **SIMNEL CAKE** |

Our half-and-half life at home in Bassein meant that we had the best of both worlds and we had fun, not only at Christmas but also at Buddhist festivals. We loved Thingyan, the Burmese New Year in April, the most riotous of occasions. A spirit from the highest heaven visits the earth and brings the rain. The old year's dirtiness must be washed away and the New Year welcomed in with a tremendous throwing of water at everyone and everything. We didn't go out on the streets of course, but we had a water festival inside the house, upstairs, where the floors were scrubbed wood and the furniture light cane, so that getting wet didn't matter. The whole family took part, Mother and the older cousins less rowdily, more sedately than us younger ones. We rushed about in terrific excitement, squirting water from brightly painted tin syringes that we had bought in the bazaar. I can still see Father wearing his baggy Shan trousers, his cheeks all round in a jolly smile, chasing us with a great dripping bath sponge in his hand and roaring with laughter when he caught and drenched us and we screamed with delight. We always ate a special kind of rice with jaggery balls on those occasions. ☞ | P 79 **STICKY RICE WITH MANGO** |

The shadow of war

World War 1 broke out during the second year we were in Bassein. It meant an end to home leave and officials stayed in their posts, so no transfer out was possible and this was the reason we were stuck for five years in Bassein. The outbreak of war marked the end of what I think of as the Golden Days in Bassein. A number of things happened that changed the tenor of our lives. Father joined the local volunteer force - all the men did - and he'd go off once a week or so in a khaki shirt and shorts and Sam Browne, khaki puttees on his legs, to do his military training. I was supposed to go to England to school that year. I had been really looking forward to following my big brother, Willy, and sister, Alice, and becoming properly English, but my English granny advised Father not to send me claiming it was because life in England was too hard. This worried Mother, and she badgered Father to bring Willy and Alice back to Burma. He wouldn't hear of Willy being brought back, but Alice was a girl and getting on for eighteen, so she was brought back early in 1915.

Alice and Mother, 1927

Father went to Colombo to meet her. That was the last port of call for passenger liners sailing from England to Burma, a journey lasting a whole calendar month, the last five or six days being from Colombo to Rangoon. Liners were not safe for that last part of the journey as the German cruiser *Emden* had been active in the Indian Ocean, and there was fear that ships were still vulnerable. Father promised to send Mother a telegram, letting her know that Alice was safe, which I, as the only person in the house able to read English would have to translate into Burmese. He gave me a lesson in telegraphese: his telegram would say 'Derbyshire arrived Colombo', and this meant Alice was now safely with him and would soon be home again. I was eight and a half, and proud to be entrusted with this job. But pride, as always, goes before a fall. It happened that our Uncle Tom, Father's brother in the Forest Service in India had shot himself in a lonely outpost in central India. While Father was away in Colombo, Uncle Sam wrote giving details of Uncle Tom's suicide. I had to translate it for Mother, and when I got to a passage that said, 'Tom had been drinking', she interrupted with, 'What had he been drinking?'. In all innocence I said, 'Water, I expect', whereupon Mother blew up: 'Mi Htoo!' she shouted angrily, 'Mi Htoo!'. I didn't know what had hit me. Why was she so angry? How had I been so stupid? It was not until many years later that I understood. Mother had expected the answer WHISKY, for her the root of all evil.

The shadow of England

At last Father came home, bringing Alice with him, a very grown-up Alice, who spoke English all the time in a funny voice. We all stood round as she unpacked her trunks - the England smell again! No marzipan, but still, that special smell. What was it? I don't smell it now I live here. Her clothes were things of wonder: great thick navy serge coats and skirts, which were put away quickly with moth balls; gloves, new to me and rather sinister like dead men's hands, disembodied, black and smelling strangely; beautiful evening gowns such as we had never seen. Auntie Alice had helped her to buy them, Alice said. 'How much did they cost?'. 'About three sovereigns each.' Three golden sovereigns for one dress! What wicked extravagance! Sovereigns were treasured stores of gold for Burmese ladies, to be put safely away and hoarded against a rainy day, and not to be squandered on clothes. The older cousins, who had been Alice's playmates as children and were used to treating her familiarly, watched her undress and roared with laughter when they saw her corsets. They had never seen such a thing, and found it excruciatingly funny, 'Amele, amele, oh dear, oh dear, how can you bear to wear such a thing? Aren't you hot?'. They prodded her with their fingers, collapsing into heaps of giggles. But Alice had grown up and away from her old playmates. She ordered them out of her room, and thereafter kept her distance.

In fact, Alice's homecoming brought a new formality to the household. She had learned all kinds of British ways, and she was shocked to find that we spoke Burmese to Father. There wasn't much talking because Father was a man of few words, and not being much of a linguist he didn't prattle in Burmese, it was just one word, and another word in answer. She told us we must speak to Father in English, so a new regime was started and I felt rather shy at first. But the changes upset the cousins most of all. At that stage Ma Tin Mya, who had originally done the cooking, had run off. She had been discovered meeting a young man secretly in the garden and was devastatingly reprimanded. She had met lots of nannies who were getting money for doing the work she was doing for nothing, and she obviously felt this was a pretty poor kind of life, so she had left and we were never allowed to see her again. Mother's 'second in command' as it were, was the oldest cousin, Ma Saw Mya. She took her responsibilities very seriously and she had charge of the keys of the storeroom, doling out groceries to Father's cook and the butler, checking their bazaar accounts, and so on. Alice took over all these duties and there was a terrible row when Ma Saw Mya had to hand over the keys. The cousins all had boxes where they kept their precious things, and after Ma Tin Mya did a bunk, Mother kept the keys to those boxes so they wouldn't run away. So she came and demanded her box key from Mother and left our house to join her sister working as a nanny. Alice also replaced Ma Ngwe Kyi as Mother's visiting companion. Ma Ngwe Kyi became the cook and from then on Mother and Alice were almost inseparable.

Alice proved a more useful companion than poor Ma Ngwe Kyi could be. She was a great help when Mother entertained as the Judge's wife. She knew how to organise dinner parties for the people who 'dropped cards' on us, and she could translate for Mother when guests couldn't speak Burmese. She extended Mother's social contacts with the European ladies of the station and together they went regularly to the wartime work parties arranged by Mrs Gillespie, wife of the local Steel Brother's boss, on the commercial west bank of the river. They were both busy for days before the biggest war effort in Bassein, a grand fete called 'OUR DAY' made memorable for me by a wonder that I saw: a camera obscura, my first introduction to moving pictures and pure magic!

It was the first of several introductions to modern life, because shortly after that I passed the 4th standard exam, the top of the school at St Joseph's convent, and had to go to boarding school in Rangoon. Father took me to the Diocesan Girls' High School, on what seemed a long and complicated journey, by train and boat. Did we arrive late in the evening, or very early in the morning? I can't remember, but I do remember having buttered eggs for chota hazri at the Railway Hotel in Rangoon, wondering what they might be - and what a delicious discovery they were! I suppose your generation would call them 'scrambled eggs'.
☞ | P 80 **THAI CRAB OMELETTE WITH SRIRACHA SAUCE** |
Another new thing I saw at that hotel was a telephone, a great enough wonder when I saw Father using it, but an even greater wonder when I saw a little English girl, much smaller than me, talking into it as though it were the most ordinary thing in the world.

MANGO CHUTNEY

Makes about 1kg | prepare 30 mins | cook 120 mins | easy

I envy Grandy being surrounded by tropical fruit trees, able as a child to pluck ripe mangoes, custard apples and mangosteens straight from the tree. In more temperate European climates, having too many mangoes is like having too much money - you fantasize about what you would do with it all! This is a great recipe should you suffer the terrible misfortune to find yourself with a glut of mangoes.

INGREDIENTS

4 firm mangoes
1 white onion
2 fresh long red chillies
2cm piece ginger
1 tsp cumin seeds
1 tsp fennel seeds
1 tsp mustard seeds
1 tsp green cardamom
300ml cider vinegar
500g brown sugar
1 tsp salt

Peel the mangoes and cut into irregular chunks about the size of the top of your thumb. Chop the onion and slice the chillies into fine rings. Peel the ginger and slice finely. Put the spices into a dry frying pan and toast over a medium flame until they become aromatic.

Put all of the ingredients into a preserving pan and bring to the boil. Lower the heat and simmer gently for 2 hours until most of the liquid has evaporated and the chutney is quite thick. Allow to cool for 10 minutes then spoon the mixture into sterilised jars* and seal. Leave for at least 2 months to mature before using.

*To sterilise the jars, place them in an oven heated to 140°C for 5 minutes. Fill the jars while they are still warm.

FRIED RICE WITH SPICY CHICKEN WINGS

Serves 4 | prepare 30 mins + 2-4 hours standing time | cook 30 mins | easy

Fried rice is the perfect mid-week dinner, and a great way to use up leftover boiled rice. In fact, it works much better when the rice has been sitting in the fridge for a day. You can use all sorts of vegetables in the stir fry, frozen peas, runner beans, chopped peppers, water chestnuts... Chicken wings are ubiquitous in Asia, and cooked this way they are incredibly moreish and messy, so change into an old t-shirt before tucking in.

INGREDIENTS

For the spicy chicken wings:

12 chicken wings
75g light brown sugar
1 tsp chilli flakes
25g light soy sauce
150ml rice wine or dry sherry
1 tsp finely chopped garlic
1 tsp grated ginger
½ tsp coarse sea salt

For the fried rice:

50g frozen peas
50g peeled carrot cut into 5mm dice
50g fine French beans cut into 1cm lengths
1 egg
2 tbsp sunflower oil
25g whole dried shrimp
½ tsp chilli flakes
1 tsp finely chopped garlic
1 tsp grated ginger
500g cooked long grain rice prepared the previous day (page 24)
2 tbsp chopped roasted peanuts (page 28)
2 tbsp crispy fried shallots (page 27)
1 tbsp fish sauce

To serve:

1 tsp chopped chives
1 tsp toasted sesame seeds

Cut the tip off the chicken wings and cut the wing in two at the joint. Sprinkle salt on the wings and leave to rest in the fridge for 2-4 hours.

Put the sugar, chilli flakes, soy sauce, rice wine or dry sherry, chopped garlic and ginger in a saucepan and bring to the boil. Simmer gently until the sauce thickens (about 30 minutes). Remove from the heat.

Dry the wings with kitchen paper and fry at 120°C for 15 minutes until cooked through. Lift the wings out of the oil and drain them in a sieve placed over a metal bowl.

Prepare the ingredients for the fried rice. Fill a mixing bowl with ice cubes and 2 litres of water. Bring a large pan of salted water to the boil. Blanche the frozen peas for 2 minutes. Lift the peas out of the water with a 'spider' (page 31) or slotted spoon and refresh them in the iced water. When cold, recover the peas and set aside. Repeat this process with the carrot and French beans (these will need slightly longer cooking). You want the vegetables to be cooked but still crunchy.

Beat the egg in a bowl. Heat 1 tablespoon of oil in the wok and cook the egg as you would a French omelette. Remove the omelette from the wok and cool on a plate, then cut into pieces.

To make the rice, heat the remaining oil in the wok and fry the chilli flakes, dried shrimp, garlic and ginger for 1 minute. Add the peas, carrot and chopped French beans and stir fry, tossing or stirring continuously. Add the cooked rice and stir and toss so that the any clumps of rice break up and the grains begin to crisp on the hot surface of the wok. Add the pieces of omelette, peanuts, crispy shallots, and fish sauce. Keep warm.

When you are ready to serve, heat the oil to 180°C. Carefully return the wings to the oil and fry again for 5 minutes until crispy. Drain as previously and place on kitchen paper to absorb any excess oil. Paint the wings with the sauce and sprinkle with sesame seeds. Serve the wings on a bed of fried rice sprinkled with chopped chives and sesame seeds.

BREAD AND BUTTER PUDDING

Serves 4 | prepare 20 mins | cook 30 mins | easy

My first sortie into a professional kitchen was under the auspices of Alastair Little at his eponymous Soho restaurant so admired by the 1990s glitterati. Alastair showed me how to make this dish and when I next visited Grandy, I proudly showed off my newly acquired skills by preparing the pudding for her. She loved it, and said it reminded her of the puddings that she enjoyed as a child, sent up to the nursery from her father's table. 'Of course, we didn't have brioche and cream then, just stale bread and milk. You young people don't know how lucky you are!'

INGREDIENTS

1 vanilla pod
600ml cream
600ml milk
4 eggs
120g butter at room temperature
170g sugar
1 brioche
50g raisins soaked in rum

Heat the oven to 150°C. Now make the custard: carefully slice through one side of the vanilla pod and scrape out the seeds with a teaspoon. Add both seeds and pod to the milk and cream in a saucepan. Bring this mixture to the boil then set aside. Beat the eggs in a bowl with the sugar and add the hot milk and cream mixture, stirring to dissolve the sugar. Strain to remove the vanilla pod and set aside.

Butter a deep 30cm x 20cm oven proof dish. Cut the brioche into thick slices and butter generously. Arrange the slices in the prepared dish like roof tiles with the buttered side down. Pour the custard on top. Now place the ovenproof dish into a slightly larger roasting pan and pop the whole thing into the oven. Pour hot water from a kettle into the roasting pan so that it comes half way up the sides of the baking dish. Bake the pudding for 20 minutes in this improvised bain-marie then sprinkle the raisins on top. Continue to bake for 10 minutes more, or until the custard is just set. Remove from the oven taking care not to splash yourself with the hot water. Lift the baking dish out of the hot water in the roasting pan. Allow to cool before serving.

FRIED PORK RIBS WITH CRISPY HERBS AND NUOC CHAM SAUCE

Serves 6-8 as a shared starter | prepare 30 mins | cook 120 mins | medium difficulty

I fell in love with this dish at a cheap eatery in Vientiane. At Ma Khin Café we often use lime leaves and lemongrass in salad dressings, chopping them extremely finely because they are so fibrous. In this dish, the lime leaves and lemon grass are fried so they become wonderfully crisp and can be happily munched and swallowed with the rest of the ingredients. This is a real finger-licking good dish. You may like to experiment with quails or even snipe, but pork ribs work just fine.

INGREDIENTS

For the ribs:

1kg pork ribs cut into 4cm pieces
1 tsp chilli flakes
1 tsp five-spice powder
Salt
2 tsp finely chopped garlic
2 tsp grated ginger
3 tbsp light soy sauce
3 tbsp dry sherry
2 tbsp ketchup manis (Indonesian sweet soy sauce), or thick soy sauce
1 litre sunflower oil for deep frying

For the nuoc cham sauce:

Juice of 1 lime
2 tbsp palm sugar or white sugar
4 tbsp water
1 tbsp fish sauce
1 bird's eye chilli

To serve:

24 kaffir lime leaves
4 stalks lemongrass
8 whole dried Sichuan chillies
12 small whole garlic cloves
1 tbsp cornflour
1 cucumber peeled and sliced
4 spring onions
1 tsp toasted sesame seeds
2 tbsp sweet chilli sauce (available from Chinese supermarkets)
1 tbsp chopped fresh coriander

Put the ribs in a large mixing bowl and sprinkle with the salt, chilli flakes and five-spice powder. Add the ginger, garlic, soy sauce, sherry and ketchup manis and mix well. Spread out in a roasting tray, cover with aluminium foil and bake at 120° for 1.5 hours. The ribs should be tender but they must not brown, so lower the heat if necessary and cook for slightly longer. Remove the ribs from the oven and leave to cool then refrigerate until you are ready to serve.

To make the nuoc cham sauce, slice open the chilli remove the seeds and chop finely. Warm the water in a small pan with the palm sugar until dissolved. Allow to cool then add the other ingredients.

Prepare and julienne the spring onions. Place them in a small bowl of water with some ice cubes so that they become crispy. Tear the central vein from the lime leaves. Cut each stalk of lemon grass into 6cm lengths then cut each of these pieces into fine strips lengthwise. Crush the garlic cloves.

Heat the oil to 170°C. Fry the lime leaves for about 30 seconds (be careful, they will spit as they crisp) then drain on kitchen paper. Now fry the strips of lemon grass, followed by the whole garlic cloves and the dried chillies. Dust the ribs with corn flour and fry until crisp. Be careful when frying not to allow any of the ingredients to burn as this will impart a nasty bitter taste to the finished dish. Assemble the dish on a large flat serving plate with layers of cucumber, spring onion, fried ribs, crispy herbs, chilli and garlic. Dress with nuoc cham sauce and sweet chilli sauce and finish with toasted sesame seed and chopped coriander. Serve with jasmine rice.

CAULIFLOWER AND CHICKPEA CURRY

Serves 4 | prepare 20 mins | cook 40 mins | easy

I eat out a lot, and love cooking simple food at home. It's a chance to redress the balance, as restaurant food invariably has an excess of animal protein and fats. So my store cupboard is stuffed with lentils, chickpeas and other pulses, which are transformed into something delicious with the judicious use of spices and the addition of some seasonal vegetables. Asafoetida is often added to chickpeas and pulses in Indian recipes to aid with digestion. It is not essential but may save your guests from the more embarrassing consequences of eating chickpeas and cauliflower!

INGREDIENTS

2 tbsp vegetable oil
5 fresh or dried curry leaves
1 piece mace
8 cloves
1 whole dried red chilli
1 medium white onion chopped
1 tsp garlic finely chopped
2 tsp grated ginger
1 tsp coriander powder
2 tsp cumin powder
1 tsp ground turmeric
½ tsp asafoetida
1 tsp garam masala
200g chopped tinned tomatoes
500g cooked chickpeas
1 small cauliflower
250ml natural yoghurt
50g roasted cashew nuts, chopped (page 28)
2 tbsp chopped coriander

In a heavy casserole, heat the vegetable oil and fry the curry leaves, mace, cloves and whole dried chilli for a few minutes until fragrant, then add the chopped onion. When the onion begins to brown add the garlic and ginger and fry for a few more minutes. Add the coriander powder, cumin, turmeric and asafoetida and stir well. Now add the tinned tomatoes and the chickpeas followed by about 500ml water. Bring to the boil and allow everything to simmer gently for about 20 minutes. Meanwhile, grind the cashews to a coarse powder in a food processor.

Cut the cauliflower into florets. Bring a large pan of salted water to the boil and blanche the florets for 5 minutes. Scoop the cauliflower from the boiling water and add it to the chickpeas. Allow everything to cook together for 5 more minutes. The curry should be quite thick. If it is still very liquid, turn up the heat and reduce while stirring constantly to avoid burning. Stir in the yoghurt, garam masala and chopped cashew nuts. Serve immediately sprinkled with the chopped coriander and accompanied by basmati rice.

CURRY PUFFS

Serves 4 | prepare 60 mins | cook 20 mins | medium difficulty

'My dear Mary: I did beat you in eating curry puffs. I had 6 at tea on Wednesday – making a martyr of myself in order to finish them- but as I didn't have any sandwiches I suppose we may call it a draw.'

Sir William Carr in a letter to his daughter Mary, 5 March 1938

INGREDIENTS

For the pastry:

500g plain flour

1 tsp salt

250g butter at room temperature in 1cm dice

120ml cold water

For the filling:

2 tbsp sunflower oil

8 fresh curry leaves

1 medium onion chopped

250g finely chopped chicken breast

1 tsp Madras curry powder

¼ tsp chilli powder

½ tsp turmeric

½ tsp ground black pepper

1 medium sweet potato in 5mm dice

1 medium potato in 5mm dice

½ tsp salt

5 tbsp water

In a mixing bowl combine the flour and salt. Gradually rub the butter into the flour with your fingertips until the mixture is crumbly. Add the water, gathering the mixture together until it forms a ball. Try not to knead the mixture too much. Allow to rest for 10 minutes then roll out to a thickness of 3mm. Cut out circles with a 10cm pastry cutter, place these on greaseproof paper and refrigerate until ready to use.

To make the filling, heat the oil in a large frying pan and fry the curry leaves with the onion until translucent. Add the chicken and brown slightly, breaking up any clumps of meat. Add the spices and then the potato and sweet potato. Fry for a few minutes until the spices are aromatic then add the water and continue cooking until the potato is tender. Allow to cool.

Take three or four circles of pastry out of the fridge. Lay the circles on a dry surface and paint the edges with a finger dipped in cold water. Place a spoonful of the filling in the middle. Fold the pastry over the filling and press to seal the edges.

Once you have prepared all of the curry puffs, heat a deep fryer to 170°C. Fry the curry puffs until golden. Serve with mango chutney (page 65).

SIMNEL CAKE

Serves 8-12 | prepare 45 mins | cook 2.5 hours | medium difficulty

It's easy for me to imagine Grandy enjoying 'the smell of England' as she opened the parcel from her English family. As a child, long before I had set foot in Spain, Dad would take us all out for dinner at Casa Antonio, owned by Antonio of course, who had come to South Wales to escape the poverty of 1950s Spain. The restaurant was decorated with bulls' heads, fishing nets and mantillas, and Julio Iglesias provided the background music. It all seemed so exotic to us, but it was the food, dripping with olive oil and aromatic with rosemary and garlic that I remembered years later when I arrived in Valencia. The smell of Spain!

INGREDIENTS

For the marzipan:

200g ground almonds
200g icing sugar
1 egg separated
½ tsp vanilla essence

For the cake:

200g currants
200g sultanas
100g candied peel
2 tbsp rum
¼ tsp saffron threads
50ml milk
175g strong plain white flour
1 tsp baking powder
50g ground almonds
175g butter
175g soft brown sugar
3 large eggs
¼ tsp allspice

Prepare the marzipan. Mix the almond and icing sugar in a bowl. Separate the egg. Mix the yolk and vanilla essence with the icing sugar and almonds. Beat the white and gradually incorporate it into the marzipan. Wrap in film and chill.

Prepare the cake mix. Soak the dried fruits in the rum. Warm the milk and add the saffron. Leave to infuse. Mix the flour, baking powder and ground almonds in a bowl. In an electric mixer, cream the butter and sugar until fluffy. Add the eggs one by one followed by the flour, all spice and ground almonds. Finally add the fruit together with the saffron and milk.

Spoon half of the mixture into a 22cm lined, loose-bottomed tin. Separate a third of the marzipan from the prepared ball and roll it out, cutting a circle to fit over the cake mix. Cover with the rest of the cake mix and cover this with a piece of buttered greaseproof paper with a 5cm hole cut in the top to allow it to rise. Bake for 2.5 hours at 130°C until a skewer poked into the top layer comes out clean. Allow to cool.

Roll out the rest of the marzipan on a surface sprinkled with icing sugar to form a circle that overlaps the cake by about an inch. Roll any trimmings into 11 balls. Place the marzipan circle on top of the cake and the 11 balls around the perimeter and toast with a blow torch, or place under the grill for a few minutes.

STICKY RICE WITH MANGO

Serves 4 | prepare 15 mins + 3-4 hours soaking | cook 50 mins | easy

The Burmese have a traditional dessert served during the water festival consisting of balls of sticky rice flour stuffed with palm sugar and served in syrup. I confess I find these and many Asian desserts excessively sweet, and when I visit South East Asia I tend to eat fruit rather than sugary desserts. An exception is Thailand's national dessert of sticky rice and mango. I love the salty/sweet glutinous rice, combined with juicy mango ripened on the tree.

In Thailand, sticky rice is cooked in a woven bamboo basket with a lid that sits on top of an aluminium pot. You can improvise a steamer by wrapping the soaked rice in muslin and placing it in a metal sieve. Rest the sieve over a pot of boiling water and cover the pan with a tight fitting lid. If the pot and sieve have the same diameter, the basket of the sieve will be suspended over the water. Make sure the water does not touch the rice in the sieve.

INGREDIENTS

150g Thai glutinous rice
300ml coconut milk
2 tbsp sugar
1 tsp salt
½ tsp corn flour
1 ripe mango, peeled and sliced
1 tsp toasted sesame seeds

Cover the rice with water and leave to soak overnight. You can shorten this time to 3 or 4 hours but do not skip this step as the rice will never cook if it hasn't been previously soaked. Strain the rice and wrap it in a piece of muslin then place it in the top half of a double boiler. Cover and cook for 30 minutes.

Meanwhile warm the coconut milk in a saucepan with the sugar and salt, stirring until the sugar has dissolved. When the rice is cooked, place it in a bowl and pour three quarters of the coconut milk on top. Stir and set aside for 20 minutes during which time the rice will absorb the coconut milk.

Beat the remaining quarter of coconut milk with the corn flour, warming gently until it thickens. Place a spoonful of rice in a bowl, cover with mango slices and spoon the coconut sauce on top. Sprinkle with sesame seeds and serve.

THAI CRAB OMELETTE WITH SRIRACHA SAUCE

Serves 2 to share | prepare 10 mins | cook 10 mins | challenging

I first tried this dish at Krua Apsorn, one of Bangkok's most popular restaurants. Despite being deep fried, it is not at all oily and the crispy outside reveals a wonderful fluffy interior. The same dish works really well with oysters. Sriracha sauce (a hot chilli sauce) is one of those guilty commercial pleasures. I always have a bottle in the fridge.

This dish involves deep frying in very hot oil. Keep small children at a distance and be extremely careful.

INGREDIENTS

4 eggs
100g white crab meat, or 4 fresh oysters coarsely chopped
1 tbsp fish sauce
2 tbsp chopped spring onion
50g bean sprouts
½ tsp ground black pepper
Sufficient sunflower oil for deep-frying
Sriracha sauce
Coriander leaves to garnish

Beat the eggs with a balloon whisk until light and airy. Add the crab or oysters with the fish sauce, spring onion and bean sprouts. Season with a little black pepper.

Put a 10cm diameter, 8cm high ring mould in the centre of a pan suitable for deep frying. Pour in the oil until it reaches 1cm from the top of the ring mould. Depending on the size of your pan, you may need more or less oil, but do make sure you use a pan that is wide enough to be able to turn over the omelette comfortably and deep enough so that you don't splash yourself as you turn it. Heat the oil to 190°C and pour in the egg mixture. Be very careful as it will splutter and expand rapidly. Allow the egg to crisp and brown for 1 minute. Slide a metal spatula under the mould and grip the side of the ring with tongs then deftly turn over the whole thing to cook the other side for 30 seconds more. Remove the omelette and drain thoroughly on kitchen paper.

Decorate with streaks of sriracha sauce and coriander leaves. Serve with steamed rice.

RANGOON LIVES
(1917-1922)

Education in Rangoon: Rule Britannia and the Highland Fling

I didn't like boarding school at all, especially in the evenings. The Diocesan Girls' High School was at the edge of a residential area on Signal Pagoda Road, which runs into Sule Pagoda Road in the heart of the town. From six to seven in the evenings all the boarders from the middle school upwards had to do homework for the next day in a classroom supervised by a teacher. It was always dark by six o'clock and sitting in silence, my eyes bent on homework, I listened to the trams running on Sule Pagoda Road, grinding noisily to a halt, and then trundling off again with a pinging of bells - alien sounds, that made me feel very far from home.

We were taught by European teachers and we had European exams. Everything was in English. After homework, there was a short service in the boarding school chapel, always with an evening hymn. How they harped on death and what mournful tunes they had! I felt more homesick than ever and dreaded what was yet to come: going to bed. At home, we slept with a dim light burning, but here we were left in the dark, left in the dark all night. My dormitory was a long room with a row of beds on either side. Matron's room was at one end and sometimes, lying awake at night, I'd prickle with fear to see her walk down the room between the rows of beds, in a long white nightgown, her hair hanging down her back and a candle in her hand.

There were no 'proper Whites' in our school. Proper Whites were people who had come out from England and who were middle class and English with the kind of status that Father had. Most of the girls were Eurasians and a fair number were Armenians and Domiciled Europeans. Domiciled Europeans could have two white parents, but the family would have been settled in Burma with no intention of returning. Such people did not send their children to England to be educated – often they just didn't have the money. They were associated with the Eurasians and were not considered White even though they were whiter than me. Race was much more complicated than skin colour. There were very few Burmese, and the few that were there, were known by Anglicised names and wore European clothes for school although there was no school uniform. It was a much bigger and better school of course, and it made me aware of a much wider world than I'd known at Bassein. It was a very competitive system with marks and weekly medals made of thin silver and shaped like shields for the top girl. The many teachers, the four big buildings, and the highly organised, well ordered school day greatly impressed me, and at first, I worried that I wouldn't be able to do the work. Teaching throughout the school was in English, and Burmese was neither spoken nor taught, not even as a second language, though French was compulsory. We got to know something of English literature and at the top of the school they read Shakespeare. There was no science taught except mathematics and arithmetic. A curious thing, though it didn't strike me so at the time, was that although in Geography our lessons dealt in greater detail with Burma and India than with Great Britain and other parts of the world, in History we were taught no Burmese or Indian history at all. We learned only English history - in a very '1066-and-all-that' kind of way. Similarly, in dancing lessons we learned how to do the Highland Fling, the Irish Jig, and the Hornpipe, but we knew no more of Burmese dancing than we knew of Burmese history. In our singing lessons, we had to learn *Rule Britannia* and *Land of Hope and Glory*, and the national anthems of all the allied countries of World War 1 in English translation. Every year on the 24th of May, Empire Day, we were marched in single file to the Maidan, to join columns of uniformed soldiers and policemen, Boy Scouts and Girl Guides, etc. to sing *Land of Hope and Glory* and *Rule Britannia*. For some reason, my Mother would never let me join the Girl Guides. I never really understood why this was except that it seemed to be part of a general prohibition against our going out anywhere on our own initiative.

When it was time for me to go back to Rangoon for my second term, Father was on tour in Henzada, and Mother, Mary and I were with him at the Circuit House. The journey from here was shorter and Father was busy, so Mother took me back to school. We didn't stop at the Railway Hotel but stayed instead with one of Mother's Sino-Burmese cousins, Kyee Ma Lok, who lived with her Chinese husband in Rangoon's Chinatown area, a jangle of sights and sounds and food smells such as I'd never known before. Everything in their house had a strange look and feel and smell. The first thing I saw as I went through the door was a sort of altar with terrifying-looking images on it and joss sticks burning. That evening I had my bath under the skies. I had to pour icy cold water over myself with a tin dipper from tall Pegu jars on top of an open roof. I was positively glad to get back to school where, although I had to bathe in cold water, at least it was under a tap in a bathroom behind closed doors.

☞ | P 102 **HOKKIEN PORK WITH GINGER** |

Dear Granny dies

I settled down better at school that term all unaware of disaster at home, where Mother's favourite niece Ma Ngwe Kyi, (the one with the bandy teeth) had died of bubonic plague. Father had also lost his best friend in Bassein, Mr Arnold, the Deputy Commissioner, who died suddenly of cholera. I think these two deaths made my parents both feel they'd had enough of Bassein. Father had had five gruelling years there and needed a rest. Home leave in England was out of the question because of the war, so he took a year's local leave and brought everyone to Rangoon.

I could live with my parents again, but not at first in our own home. Father had bought a house in Rangoon some years before, but it was let and until the tenants moved out we lived in rented accommodation in 6 Camp Road, which was near a railway station. There were a lot of pariah dogs swarming about, and I was very frightened of them. I remember there were dog poisoners who used to put down poison to get rid of them, and there were problems with water supply and the servants had to get water from wells. Still we were well away from the river which was very unhealthy. That land was occupied by mills and factories, and the barracks and rooms of the Indian coolies who worked there. I noticed a lot more Indians in Rangoon, where they provided most of the industrial and port labour. Most of the Burmese in contrast were dependent upon agriculture for their living.

The diseases in Rangoon were different from Bassein, largely influenza and tuberculosis, but when dear Granny, Ma Wun, died in 6 Camp Road, it was from plague. She had nursed Ma Ngwe Kyi devotedly and she too became ill with the disease. Just before she died she asked for 'Inga thami', Tuesday's daughter, to give her a plain gold ring. Mother went out and bought one and that evening I was sent in to her. It was very eerie: I slipped the ring on her finger while she murmured something - I have no idea what, and then I fled. I have never fathomed the significance of this, and Mother, if she ever knew, never told me. The next morning Mother had very swollen eyes and she told me, 'Don't go into Granny's room'. Of course, that sent me straight to Granny's room because I knew then that she was dead. She was lying with her face covered and I peeled back the cloth to see her, and there was her dead face. I was horrified and fascinated too, but I just had to cover her up again and go to school, and by the time I came home she had been buried. I missed her dreadfully.

Behave with decorum

I suspect another reason for Father taking leave was that he had been passed over for Chief Justice of Lower Burma in favour of Mr Rigg, who ranked several positions below him. The British Imperial hierarchy just did not like officers

Portrait of Mother and Father

having Burmese wives. They thought that their judgement might be unconsciously perverted by their spouse even if they were people of ability. I caught disturbing snatches of talk between Father and Mother - Mother indignant because Father had been passed over for promotion and Father just shrugging his shoulders and looking out of the window. I was unsettled by a vague sense that all was not well, that some misfortune was pending.

Whether it was because I was older or because we were in Rangoon I don't know, but I felt our ambivalent status much more keenly than I had in Bassein. A man called Spense was our family doctor. He was an awful old charlatan who wore an orchid in his buttonhole and had a wonderful bedside manner but not much else. He had come to our house and seen two very beautiful Burmese-made stone water filters. He liked them so much that Mother said she would give one to him. I was sent round in the car to make sure it was handed to Dr Spense or his wife *in person* so it was not stolen by one of the servants. Their chaprassi took it in and came back and said, 'Memsahib gives her salaams', meaning 'OK go home'. And I said, 'No, I want to see the Memsahib' and this went on for some time. In the end, the Memsahib did appear looking cross and said, 'Yes dear, did you want some sweets?' I was furious. I said: 'My Mother said I was to give it to you personally, that's all', and marched off. I didn't want any sweets. I felt awful. I knew if I'd been an English child she would have invited me in and made much of me. 'Yes dear, did you want some sweets?' The Burmese would call me 'Bomagalay', little white girl, but I knew the English didn't think that.

I remember asking Father around that time, 'Do you sometimes feel ashamed of us because we none of us look English?' 'You don't notice things like that about your own children', he replied. But I went on putting two and two together along those lines. I accepted we were his dearly loved children regardless, but why didn't he join the Pegu Club, or the Gymkhana Club? I once asked him. 'Don't like it', he said, 'A lot of snobs'. In Rangoon, he'd practically stopped playing bridge and all his social contacts were official. He had no personal friends he went golfing with, no best friend like Mr Arnold of Bassein.

Maybe this made Mother even more determined that we should act in a suitably English way, and that her daughters in particular should conduct themselves with decorum. When I was ten, the little boy next door wrote me a letter. I never saw the wretched thing, but it caused me a deal of trouble I can tell you. Alice intercepted it and read it to Mother who blew up. She was so angry with me for receiving a 'love letter': 'Mother's milk still wet on your lips and you are having love affairs!' At the age of ten, I ask you. From then on, she kept an eye on me. 'She,' pointing at me, 'she likes men'. Nothing could have been further from my mind!

In Rangoon, our daily routine was no longer what it had been in those Golden Days of Bassein. No more ceremonial distribution of chocolate after Father's dinner, no more bedtime stories, but for me it was a compensation that I was old enough now to be allowed to stay up with Father after the younger children had gone to bed. I particularly loved those evenings when the English mail was delivered, once a week, more or less regularly, and the newspaper would tell us when the boat was due to dock. Often it was as late as ten at night that the postman, (always an Indian), would call out from downstairs: 'Sahib, Sahib, English mail', and Father would go down to unlock the heavy front door with many clankings of bolts. I loved those evenings, when I was allowed to unwrap the packet of newspapers and magazines while Father read letters from his English family. Once a month came the literary magazines; *The Strand*, *Blackwood's*, *John O'London's Weekly* and *Cornhill*. *The Strand* was my favourite, with its picture of a red London bus and other traffic on the street and St Mary le Strand in the middle distance. Then there was a *Times Weekly Edition*, and a children's newspaper for us, and for Alice an extraordinary magazine called *Home Chat*, full of recipes and romance. Alice liked love stories. I remember when we went to the small subscription library together she would always look in the catalogue under R for Romance while I would search M for Murder and Mystery, and C for Crime.

Kalaw - a place of enchantments

Early in 1918, Father took us all on a lovely holiday to Kalaw in the Southern Shan States, a small town over 4000 feet above sea level, set in beautiful pinewoods. It was an absolute revelation to us children because it was cold. So cold that we had to have a fire in the house to keep us warm. The town was still undeveloped then and very different from the bustling, popular hill station it became in later years. There were only two European style houses, both owned by a Colonel Green who lived in one of them and let the other to occasional visitors, and that was where we stayed.

Colonel Green was an eccentric old gent, long retired from the Burma Commission into which he had been drafted from the Army in the years following the annexation of Upper Burma. His Burmese wife of many years was a picturesque old lady who wore the most bizarre Burmese clothes, the jacket heavily trimmed with lace and frills and tucks as Burmese ladies' jackets never usually were. She rarely went out but liked having visitors and telling them stories of how her husband had taught her to ride a horse in England when he'd taken her there on his leaves, and how she'd gone hunting with him. Colonel Green, pink-cheeked, blue-eyed and white-haired, was a great talker too. He talked about so many different things that I couldn't always follow him, but most of all he loved to sing, and tell us of the importance of voice production. I didn't project my voice correctly at all, so he taught me breathing exercises and urged me to practise them so that I too would be able to sing. It was Colonel Green who showed Father and me our favourite walk, up Pagoda Hill, on top of which lived a hermit, a Buddhist monk, with his acolyte. We would set out early in the morning, when the leaves and pine needles were so wet with dew that I kept slipping on them, until I overcame my fear of spiders crawling over my feet and learnt to take off my shoes and socks. I felt triumphant when I reached the top and I always enjoyed our call on the hermit, who liked chatting to visitors.

The market at Kalaw, 1937

More often, Father went alone on long walks exploring the countryside while we children revelled in a new delight: freedom of movement, such as we had never been allowed before, rambling about in the woods around our house. We used to love to go and pick wild raspberries. They were bright orange! I have only ever seen them in Kalaw and only on that occasion. By the time we went again there were no more, but that first visit we ate enormous quantities and made ourselves sick. They were delicious! We went on excursions with Mother too, and particularly exciting was going into the town with Mother to shop on 'bazaar day'. On every fifth day the hill tribes, the Palaung, Kayan and Pa-o [6] came down into our valley from their mountain villages with all kinds of goods to sell at the Kalaw bazaar, produce from their small farms like fresh vegetables, oranges, chickens, and pork. The hill tribes also brought hand-woven cottons and silks, sold by the yard or by the longyi-length, delicate silver ornaments, daggers big and small with carved handles and Shan bags and baskets of all shapes and sizes. The Pa-os dressed soberly in black but the Palaung and Kayan women wore loose smocks of thick, hand-woven cotton in brilliant reds and blues. The Kayan women had necks like giraffes extended by many heavy brass rings, but the Palaungs preferred cane - cane rings round their hips and a tangle of fine cane for turbans. Mother loved bazaar days, and so did we. We had all fallen in love

---

[6] 'Grandy actually used the term 'Paduang' for the Kayan people and 'Taungthu' for the Pa-o people, terms which these groups now consider offensive so we have chosen to use the correct term.'

with Kalaw and its many enchantments, above all, the heady aromatic smell of pines that filled the air. We loved it so much that some years later Mother and Father decided to build a house there, just down the road from Colonel Green's. It was modelled on a kind of English home counties mock tudor design but with Burmese touches and a verandah on red bricks rather than teak pillars. They called it The Grey House. We used to stay there regularly to escape the heat of Rangoon and my parents planned to retire there.
☞ | P 104 **KHAO SWE** |

The Grey House, Kalaw, 1937

From left: Mary, Freddy, G, Sam, Robert and Dorothy, 1922

Back in Rangoon after that holiday we were able to move into our own house, 8 Sandwith Road, in an inner suburb where our neighbours were mostly Eurasians and Armenians. The house itself was smaller than the one in Bassein, but it had modern amenities: electric lights and piped water. No more oil lamps and no more horses and carriages; instead, Father bought his first motor car, a red Ford tourer, and hired a tall handsome Muslim driver who wore a red fez. He used to drive us to school, myself, Mary, Sam, Dorothy and Freddy. Robert was about two and a half and the driver took a great liking to him and let him play with the car. Very soon Robert was speaking fluent Hindustani with the driver, though with the family, of course, he spoke in Burmese, but rather less fluently. The garden, though it had some interesting trees in it, was not big enough to play in, so on fine afternoons we'd walk with our cousins to the grounds of the nearby Jubilee Hall, built to commemorate Queen Victoria's Golden Jubilee. More interesting, but frightening, was the Freemasons' Hall. Standing at one end of Sandwith Road, within sight of our house, it was an ominous presence and many stories were whispered among the children of the neighbourhood of the scary things that went on there at night: people drank blood out of human skulls, we were told, and did all kinds of other terrible things that they had to swear to keep dead secret.

World War 1 ends - and patriotism instilled

Before eight months of his year's leave had passed, Father was recalled to duty, and in June 1918 he was posted to Tharrawaddy, a notoriously criminal area about sixty miles north of Rangoon. We had to move out of Sandwith Road, and Mother and the younger children set up in Tharrawaddy in a house that they told me looked out on to paddyfields. But I never went there. I had to board again at school, but I was happy enough there by now. Being 12 years old, I was put in the 'middle girls' dormitory, next to the suite of rooms where the headmistress lived. She was called Miss Colbatch-Clark, a fine headmistress and I remember her as being much loved throughout the school because we felt she had our interests truly at heart. Anyway, I know that we trusted her, and we were proud of her. She woke us all up in the middle of the night once, switched on the lights and called out: 'Girls! Girls! THE WAR IS OVER! Isn't it splendid!', and she led us in a prayer of thanksgiving as we knelt by our beds.

Just after the war our beloved Miss Colbatch-Clark was appointed as an adviser to the Committee on Education and the 'Inculcation of the Imperial Ideal' set up by Lieutenant Governor Harcourt Butler to examine how loyalty to the Empire could be encouraged through schools. Empire Day, prize-givings, school trips to places of interest like warships and cinematograph halls were to be used to encourage imperial loyalty. The Union Jack was to be conspicuous in all schools, as were portraits of the Royal family. Miss Colbatch-Clark was an adviser on the syllabus, and on what texts should be authorised and what forbidden. Our school was a model in this. Lessons were taught from an imperial point of view, so that the prosperity and civilisation brought by Empire should be their natural conclusion. J.S. Furnivall, who, as I mentioned earlier, was to become a great friend of mine, was among three literary experts asked to compile an anthology of passages of Burmese literature which could inspire bravery, gratitude, devotion, patriotism and other virtues.

After Tharawaddy, Father was posted to Hanthawaddy Division. That really was the last of boarding school for me, for the Division's headquarters were in Rangoon. Now that he was to be officially resident in the city it was felt fitting to move to a better residential area. A suitable house was found in Leeds Road very near the Gymkhana Club and negotiations started with a Chinese broker to sell the Sandwith Road house. Mother, a born business woman, took on that sale, and I well remember the zest she put into the long drawn out negotiations. She bought the Leeds Road house for Rs 60,000 and put the Sandwith Road house on the market for Rs 40,000 and then - she gazumped and gazumped, finally selling the house for Rs 65,000! She was as pleased as Punch! Father was rather horrified at this, but in general he appreciated my mother's thrifty nature for it was a quality they both shared. Not that they were ever mean, but they were by nature frugal.

In the garden of that house there was a little Indian shop. No doubt if a proper English family had bought that house they would have expelled the shop and its family, but my mother didn't see why she should do that. Many Burmese people were hostile to Indians who they regarded as coming to the country just to make money, whether as labourers, or chettiars (money-lenders) or the owners of small businesses. But Mother made money from them. She took rent and the shop stood in a sort of feudal relationship to her. Whenever it was a Muslim feast they would give her a leg of mutton and a leg of lamb. ☞ | P 107 **LAMB BIRYANI** |

Our lovely house in Rangoon

We loved our new house in Rangoon. It was in the European residential area on a ridge slightly higher than the rest of the town at the corner of Leeds Road and Forsyth Road. Behind it was the Minto Mansions Hotel. It was built at the time of the new Government House, so pieces of woodwork salvaged from the old Government House were incorporated into our home. The heavy and ornate front door, which had two small stained glass panels set into it, head and shoulders portraits of Shakespeare and Sir Walter Scott, were taken from there, as was the beautiful openwork ornamental screen, reaching nearly up to the high ceiling, placed across the middle of the hall with an archway in its centre; the heavy, moulded bannisters had come from the same source, dark mahogany in colour like the front door and the screen. We had electric light but no piped water here; instead, there was a big well at the back of the house from which all our water supply was drawn in buckets by the paniwallah. The house itself was built of brick and had a proper ground floor not on stilts, while upstairs were four big bedrooms off a corridor that had a polished wooden floor, just like England. The front verandah jutted out on stilts making a kind of portico where visitors' cars could park, and Father used it as his private sitting room because it was covered and enclosed with venetian windows. It

From left: Freddy, Robert, Sam, Willy's son Robert and Dorothy in front of Ellesmere, Leeds Road, 1926

had an enormous table strewn with all his leisure things, periodicals, books and newspapers, and a big recliner chair made of cane with a solid wooden frame and two slats that swung out so he could rest his legs. The venetians were stained with earth oil to protect them from the white ants and when the rain fell, it hung from them in amber drops and bounced off the earth in sprays like little horses.

I loved those first days of the rains because the earth gave out a lovely smell. The side verandahs were open, and Mother used to pray there as evening was falling. She would walk up and down intoning quietly and clicking her amber beads while Father sat in his long chair, reading the newspaper with his glass of whisky beside him. I liked to read over his shoulder and play with his hair which was silky soft. Mother rebuked me very firmly for this, because for Burmese Buddhists a man has a special kind of holiness and his head is the most revered part of him that a woman should not touch, but that didn't stop me doing it.

The garden was much bigger than the Sandwith Road garden. There were so many fruit trees: mango, citron, pomelo, durian, cashew apple and roseapple and at the other end of the garden there was enough room for a tennis court and a badminton court. They were mud courts, made afresh every year after the rains when a gang of Indian coolies would come with a heavy roller to smooth the surface after it had been prepared with a mixture of mud and cow dung - the dung to stick the mud down.

Ma Than Mya abandoned

While I liked to stay up with Father, Mother and Alice retired early for the night soon after the younger ones. They did not go to sleep though because they liked to end the day with a long chat. They'd go into Alice's big bedroom and while Alice got ready for bed, Mother would be shampooed by Ma Than Mya before going back to her own room to sleep. Shampooing, unlike massage, can be done with the feet as well as the hands; there are two different words in Burmese for hand and foot shampooing. My cousins were slightly built and small, and Mother's nightly shampoo consisted of Ma Than Mya stepping slowly up and down her legs as she lay flat on a mattress placed on the floor.

It was on just such a peaceful evening that a storm blew up that disturbed us all deeply for a long time. Mother suddenly spotted that the girl quietly walking up and down her legs looked pregnant. She questioned her and refused to believe her denials. Alice took her to the Dufferin Hospital the next day and the test proved positive. There were terrifying angry scenes and she was turned out of the house. I felt desperately unhappy. Ma Than Mya, only two or three years older than me, had been my playmate for many years and I believed her absolutely when she swore to Mother that she hadn't slept with anyone.

What about the Virgin Mary? Perhaps I should tell Mother about her since she was a Buddhist and didn't know about the immaculate conception. Life for young girls suddenly seemed fraught with danger, when an innocent pregnancy could bring such appalling punishment. I remember seeing her as she left and the Muslim driver, who I recall as being a kind fellow, striding after her with a big stick. I hope he took care of her, for the memory of that pregnant teenage girl mercilessly turned out of the only home she'd ever known oppressed me more and more as time passed. I still feel shame and guilt when I remember her. It turned out that the father was the brother of Ma Tin Chi. Mother had paid for him and his older brother to go to school, and they came to stay with us from time to time in the holidays. I never liked the younger boy, he was not a nice chap. Apparently, he raped her. She told us that one time when she came to see us secretly at the back door.

Now there was only one cousin left, Ma Tin Chi. 'Tinch' we called her. She was a lovely rosy cheeked little girl, about seventeen at the time, and she was put in charge of the cooking. She was in a very anomalous position because she had to go into the kitchen, so she was neither servant nor family member. We had a male servant who kept trying to make a pass at her and he felt free to do this. She would complain about it, but Alice didn't do anything about it until I took her side and quarrelled seriously with Alice.

The end of innocence

Perhaps that was the moment that marked the end of the age of innocence when we'd all been a happy family together, throwing water at each other with roars of laughter when it was Thingyan in Bassein. None of that in Rangoon. Thingyan had become for Mother a period of various religious observances and for us a time when we ate the special dishes prepared traditionally for the festival. There was no water-throwing in the streets in our part of the town either; all the fun took place in the centre of the town where there were more Burmese people and we saw nothing of it. But Christmas became more important in our lives. We had plum pudding and York ham which was bought raw and boiled in beer and stuck with cloves on top with golden breadcrumbs round. There were lots of oranges and horrible Christmas cake. There is a special orchid that grew at Christmas time and it was called the dezimba. The small ivory flowers grew on a long spray and there was a little root in the shape of an acorn that was attached to the end. It had a lovely special smell. The smell of this, and oranges and cake and books, all was the smell of Christmas. We became aware of carols too, because we sang them at school, and I used to go to the Cathedral with Alice every Sunday. I had been baptised in Moulmein when I was five. In later years this puzzled me, for I knew that Father was not a believer though he came from a strict non-conformist family, but he told me that the best schools in Burma were run by Church of England missionaries, and only accepted children who had been baptised into their faith.

Mother became more religious when we were in Rangoon. She prayed and made offerings daily. From time to time we had pongyis in the house who came and chanted prayers in the evening until late into the night. And there would be special food made with special kinds of rice. It was called 'Hsun Taw Tin', I don't really remember what kind of thing it was. And she would make offerings in front of the altar at home, little dishes of rice, and a bit of curry and bananas and things like that. Nobody was allowed to eat those offerings. They were supposed to be thrown away and the people who ate them were the lowest of the low.

She used to visit the local pagoda regularly. Sometimes we would be expected to go with her to the Shwedagon Pagoda in a family expedition. There was a long flight of marble steps to climb up before you got to the platform round the base of the pagoda where the ring of altars stood. As you went up those wide steps on either side there were stalls selling candles and joss sticks, packets of gold leaf for gilding the pagoda, lots and lots of flowers and simple toys for small children. Mother knew some of the stall holders and she'd call at one of them and they would unroll a mat for her to sit down for a rest and a leisurely chat before making our purchases. She always enjoyed turning a shopping expedition into a small social occasion. ☞ | P 108 **SAMOSA SALAD WITH MINT AND CORIANDER CHUTNEY** |

At the bottom of the Shwedagon Pagoda stairs you had to take your shoes off. Footwearing, as entering a pagoda with one's shoes on was known, was a mark of great disrespect to the Buddha and all Buddhists, rather like walking topless into a Christian church. It had been a source of considerable tension between the Burmese and the British, who said that to take off one's shoes and socks was demeaning to Europeans. Towards the end of the war some groups started making a fuss about it and wanted to make footwearing illegal. Father was not unsympathetic. He said that if it meant that much to the Burmese then it simply wasn't worth fighting about. But, for a while, public discussion on the issue was forbidden because it was too sensitive to deal with in time of war. Then in October 1919, at Eindawya Pagoda in Mandalay, half a dozen monks attacked two Europeans and six Eurasians for wearing shoes on the pagoda platform and one of them, a police officer called Mr Robey, had his nose almost severed from his face. The newspapers were full of it. After that it was decreed that footwearing decisions would be left to the managers and trustees of individual pagodas and those visiting pagodas would have to abide by that decision. However, soldiers, police and officials who entered a pagoda to preserve public order were not bound by the decision. So when we went to the Shwedagon, next to the 'No Footwearing' notice was also another large sign detailing the exceptions.

Father was right to suggest that it was best not to fight about footwearing. These kinds of footwearing regulations were a constant reminder to the Burmese that they were not masters of their own destiny, and Buddhism was to become a focus of protest at imperialism in the following years. Under the Burmese Kings, Buddhist monks wrote the Burmese lawbooks, they heard judicial cases and could reprieve condemned prisoners from execution. Father said that in the old days this meant that monks served as a check to royal power, and if villagers could not afford to pay their taxes, it was the pongyis who would mediate for them with the king. Monks served as diplomatic representatives and were peacemakers in Burma's wars with her neighbours. After the British came to Burma, the monk hierarchy, known as the sangha, offered to support British rule if the foreigners in turn recognised and supported their authority, but this was rejected, and their institutions dismantled. Father felt they should have been treated more sympathetically. He said that the indiscipline that came from the destruction of the monarchy and the sangha, together with their traditional voicing of village concerns and the respect bestowed on them by villagers, contributed to the emergence of the 'political pongyi' meddling in mundane political matters.

U Ottama: political pongyi

One such political pongyi, U Ottama, became very famous at that time. He spent most of his time touring the districts, rabble rousing Burmese farmers with fiery speeches. They were easy to rouse. After the First World War, bad trade conditions and poor harvests had given rise to serious hardship, and even thoroughly establishment village headmen (called thugyis) were reluctant to force villagers to pay their taxes knowing their situation. U Ottama's calls for an end to British rule which had robbed peasants of their freedom, their land and their riches, found fertile ground. He really came to fame in 1921 when he wrote an open letter in *The Sun* newspaper called 'Craddock go home' (Craddock was the Governor at the time, and much disliked as an arch-bureaucrat). But really U Ottama was famed as a powerful speaker who addressed the crowd in a very colloquial way, administering the 'medicine of bravery' so that those present would not be cowed by British rule. Patricia Herbert has written a marvellous article where she quotes one of his chants:

> Who took our territory unlawfully? - The English, the English.
> Who is oppressing our race? - The English, the English.
> Who is our real enemy? - The English, the English.
> What is it that we must not fear? - The English, the English[7].

[7] Quoted in Herbert, P. (1982). 'The Hsaya San Rebellion (1930-1932) Reappraised' Melbourne: Monash University, Centre of Southeast Asian Studies. Working Papers, No. 27, pp. 1-16.

His vivid use of imagery reminded me of Mother. He said English people were like turtles that use their four short legs to gather and keep under their chests all that they can, never thinking of sharing with others. The Burmese people were like a dead cow that does not feel even if you pour salt water in its eyes[8]. But perhaps most powerful for me was his indictment of the education system as a dung heap. Three generations had trodden in it and he was shouting a warning to the next generation lest they follow in their parents' footsteps.They must act, boycott foreign goods and not co-operate with British rule. Strong stuff, and probably influenced by the time he had spent with the Indian National Congress. Indeed, when he came to Rangoon he spent some time addressing the crowd in Hindustani, as there were Indian labourers there too. Shortly after this speech he was given a prison sentence for sedition and bringing the government into hatred.

Boycott the Whyte Committee! Follow the nation's lead!

Looking back on it that was a period of some unrest. In 1919, Dyarchy had been introduced in India. This was a two-tier system of administration which made some portfolios answerable to a Legislative Council some of whose members were elected albeit by a very narrow franchise. Even though Burma was part of India, we were not to be included, but fobbed off with the Craddock Reform scheme which vested all serious power in Lt Governor Craddock, or his replacement. There were protests and eventually London set up the Whyte Committee to assess Burmese people's aspirations and fitness for self-government.

One of the reasons given for Burma's exclusion was the tiny number of Burmese university graduates which meant that there were no people to whom the British could hand over power. But there had been no university in Burma until the University of Rangoon opened in December 1920 and proficiency in English was an entry requirement. Most Burmese people could not afford to send their children to a school where they could learn English, a school which moreover, would invariably be situated in the town. Scarcely surprisingly, this requirement was deeply resented and considered to be a plot to keep down the numbers of Burmese graduates. Matters were not helped by the appointment of Lt Governor Craddock to the University Chancellorship. A few days after he opened the university, students initiated a university boycott. Originally this was to protest at the entrance requirements, but it soon broadened to include the type of education given at Anglo-vernacular schools, a 'slave education', designed to bind pupils unthinkingly to the Empire, to denigrate themselves and glorify the English. As a school student, I was struck by the focus of our education, so I had some sympathy for their call for a national university and a national education system that would teach Burmese history and Burmese literature.

---

[8] Records from British spies at the time confirm the use of this imagery by U Ottama in speeches at Dadye (3 February 1921) and Sukalat (4 February 1921).

Although I did not think of myself as a particularly political person at the time I must have imbibed some of this nationalist dissatisfaction, and when a grand fancy dress party was held at the Minto Mansions Hotel in aid of some charity, I had the idea of dressing as a nationalist in a bid to win the prize for the most original costume. I modelled myself on street demonstrators wearing pinni aingyis (jackets of homespun cotton) and carrying banners. Mother liked this idea very much and she dressed me in a yaw longyi, a sarong of black Burmese silk and a pinni aingyi and piled my long black hair on top of my head in a beautiful sadon (top knot). I made two cardboard placards to hang on my chest and my back and wrote in big block letters on the front placard: BOYCOTT THE WHYTE COMMITTEE, and on the back: FOLLOW THE NATION'S LEAD. I was rather pleased with myself when I looked in my glass, and Mother said I looked much better in Burmese clothes. I was sure that I would win the prize until I joined the parade before the judges who were to choose the prizewinners. There was a tremendous drawing aside of skirts and loud cries of protest from the assembled mothers watching their young: 'Look at that girl! How dare she come in here dressed like that? Out with her! Out with her!' Some of them stood up as I passed and made as if they were going to attack me, and I got really scared at one stage. Of course, I wasn't thrown out for the people running the show knew very well that I was my Father's daughter and therefore not to be taken liberties with. It was a terrible evening. I was wearing by far the most original costume but I didn't win a prize.

Tomorrow will soon be today...

I began to see Father differently too. He was still the great and good man and loving and friendly father - that never changed, ever - but I began to wonder what he really felt and thought behind his public face. I remember one Christmas, Mary and I had autograph albums among our Christmas presents, and of course, Father was the first person to be asked to write in them.

In Mary's he wrote:

> Dear Child, would you in full deserve
> The joys your friends invite,
> You need but faithfully observe
> The precepts they indict.

And in mine:

> At fifteen the world is a wonderful place,
> All golden and bright and gay;
> Life is a game that's just begun
> A glorious game to play.
> Make then the most of to-day,

Tomorrow may seem far away,
But time travels fast,
Present fades into past,
Tomorrow will soon be to-day.

At fifty the world, though wonderful still,
Is tarnished, and drab, and grey;
Life is a game that's nearly done,
The glory has gone from the play.
Make then the most of to-day,
Tomorrow may seem far away,
But time travels fast,
Present fades into past,
Tomorrow will soon be to-day.

I was shattered. 'Is your life like that, Father?' I asked him. He was standing looking out of a window. 'Well, I was just taking fifteen and fifty as roughly your age and mine and giving you good advice!'. I brooded over Mary's poem too. I couldn't make out what it meant at first, but I suddenly got there: 'Toe the line, mate, or you'll suffer for it!'.

By then it must have seemed to Father that he would never achieve a senior appointment. The previous years had been difficult times but no promotion. He had been passed over, not only for the senior judicial service in Lower Burma, but also the Judicial Commissionership of Upper Burma, both posts for which he was the obvious candidate, having had by then over twenty years' experience.

In 1921, it was decided to extend a version of the dyarchy system to Burma. I suspect it was a case of too little, too late. Dyarchy did not give control over key aspects of government like defence, law and order, finance, currency and transport, and the Governor could veto legislation and assume emergency powers. That was the reason behind the call for the boycott of the Whyte Committee. The eyes of the nationalists were now set on Home Rule.

I think by then Father was tired, and what started off as a vague plan about chucking it all in and moving to England which would have the added benefit of making the children's education less expensive, became a decision. We were told on the 11th May 1921. I remember the date precisely because that night, when we were washing our feet before bedtime, we were all discussing this marvellous news and were playing 'Let's guess what we shall be doing next year, this time - next year, on the 11th of May, where shall we be?' We had a guessing game. I can't remember what the others guessed, but I said I would be riding on top of a London bus - like the one on the cover of *The Strand* magazine.

I wasn't upset - I was terribly excited: I had always thought of England as my Mecca, and here we were, all going to Mecca together. The Minto Mansions had done for me. Among the mothers who had shouted at me were some Eurasians. It was an eye-opener to me that Eurasians, slighted as they were by Europeans, still found it possible to make common cause with them against the Burmese. The prospect of going away to live in England had a new attraction added to its original glamour: I thought we'd escape from all these disturbing problems of race.

We set sail for England in March 1922, a party of ten: parents, seven children: Alice, Mary, Sam, Dorothy, Freddy, Robert and me (Willy was already in England), and the only Burmese cousin left now living with us, Tinch. We had always known we were all to go to school in England and how much nicer not to have to go in batches of twos and threes but all together, and Mother and Father and all of us to live there together, happily ever after.

From left: Mary, Father, Sam and G, 1925

HOKKIEN PORK WITH GINGER

Serves 4 | prepare 20 mins + 12 hours to marinate | cook 120 mins | easy

This was one of Grandy's favourite dishes that she often prepared for us on special occasions. She would stand patiently over the simmering pot spooning off the fat as it rendered out of the pork belly leaving a wonderfully dark, salty, gingery broth with chunks of tender pork.

INGREDIENTS

To marinate the pork:

750 g pork belly

2 tbsp peanut or sunflower oil

2 tbsp granulated sugar

100ml dry sherry

6 tbsp light soy sauce

2 tbsp ketchup manis (sweet soy sauce)

6cm piece cinnamon

2 whole star anise

½ tsp cloves

To cook the pork:

2 medium white onions finely chopped

1 tbsp grated ginger

1 tbsp finely chopped garlic

1 tsp five-spice powder

2 dried red chillies

4 soft boiled eggs (page 30)

Cut the pork into slices the thickness of your index finger, then cut the slices into bite size chunks. Fry the pork in batches in a little oil, scooping them onto a plate as they brown. Keep the oil.

Heat the sugar in a small heavy pan until it caramelises. Carefully add the dry sherry and when it stops sputtering, the light soy sauce, ketchup manis, and whole spices. Pour this marinade over the fried pork and leave to rest in the refrigerator overnight.

Heat 2 tablespoons of the reserved cooking oil and pork fat in a clay pot or heavy casserole dish. Fry the onions until soft. Add the garlic, whole chillies and ginger and fry for a few more minutes until fragrant. Add the five-spice powder and the pork with the marinade and spices. Add enough water to cover the meat, bring to the boil then lower the heat to minimum. Cook for about 1.5 hours or until the pork is tender, skimming off any fat that rises to the surface. Serve the pork with boiled rice and two halves of boiled egg on top.

KHAO SWE

Serves 4 | prepare 20 mins | cook 40 mins | challenging

Khao swe is one of those dishes that reminds us that people and food have always crossed political borders. It is impossible to talk about Burmese food without talking about the gastronomic traditions of Burma's neighbours. The Chinese have had an enormous influence on the history of Burma and its food, so it's no surprise to find that this dish, whose origins can be traced to Yunnan, is a favourite in the Shan states of Burma and crops up in a slightly different guise in nearby Chiang Mai, Thailand where it is called khao soi. This recipe is a mish mash of the Burmese and Thai interpretations that we serve in Ma Khin Café. The sauce is thickened with coconut cream, but the noodles are wheat. In the Shan states, no coconut milk is used, and fermented soy bean paste gives a more pronounced depth of flavour. In Thailand, rice noodles are more commonly used.

INGREDIENTS

For the curry paste:

2 stalks of lemon grass chopped

4 shallots peeled and coarsely chopped

8 dried long red chillies, seeds removed and soaked in cold water for 2 hours

2 fresh bird's eye chillies, seeds and stems removed

2cm piece fresh galangal, peeled and coarsely chopped (can be bought frozen in Chinese supermarkets)

2cm piece of ginger peeled and coarsely chopped

1 tsp fermented shrimp paste

1 tsp Madras curry powder

½ tsp turmeric

½ tsp ground cumin

½ tsp ground coriander

To prepare the khao swe:

Sunflower oil

1 packet wonton wrappers

2 boned and skinned, free range chicken thighs

1 packet dried egg noodles

150 ml chicken stock (page 29)

300 ml thick coconut milk

1 tsp palm sugar or dark brown sugar

2 stalks lemon grass cut into 4cm lengths

6 kaffir lime leaves

Zest and juice of 1 lime

1 tbsp light soy sauce

1 tbsp fish sauce

2 tbsp chopped pickled Chinese mustard leaf (available from Chinese supermarkets)

4 soft boiled eggs (page 30)

2 tbsp chopped coriander

2 tbsp chopped roasted peanuts (page 28)

2 tbsp crispy shallots (page 27)

Put all of the ingredients for the curry paste in a food processor and purée to a smooth paste. Pack the paste into a jar and top with a film of sunflower oil. It will keep in the fridge for a week and can also be frozen.

Cut the wonton wrappers into strips about 5mm wide and deep fry for a few minutes in sunflower oil at 180°C. Drain the crispy noodles on kitchen paper.

Heat the oven to 180°C. Season the chicken thighs, drizzle them with a little oil and bake in an oven proof dish until cooked through. Slice the meat into bite size pieces.

Boil the egg noodles following the instructions on the packet. Refresh the noodles in iced water and drain thoroughly.

Heat 2 tablespoons of sunflower oil in a wok and fry a generous tablespoon of the curry paste, taking care that it does not burn. Add the chicken stock and coconut milk followed by the palm sugar, lemon grass and lime leaves. Cook the sauce for 10 minutes then add the grated zest and juice of the lime, the soy sauce and the fish sauce. Stir in the boiled noodles and warm them through. Using tongs distribute the noodles among four deep bowls. Scatter a tablespoon of chopped Chinese mustard leaf over the noodles and arrange the sliced chicken on top with the 2 halves of the boiled egg. Pour over the hot sauce. Place a handful of crispy wonton strips on top and sprinkle with the chopped coriander leaves, peanuts and crispy shallots.

LAMB BIRYANI

Serves 4 | prepare 30 mins | cook 120 mins | challenging

Thanks to Athar and Nishat in Delhi who kindly welcomed us into their home and shared the secrets of the perfect biryani. We ate this with parathas and homemade lime pickle (page 189). Nishat used a simple flour and water paste to seal the lid of the casserole to ensure no steam escaped from the pot as the rice cooked.

INGREDIENTS

To cook the lamb:
500g boned lamb neck fillet
1 black cardamom
6 green cardamoms, crushed
6 cloves
3cm piece of cinnamon
1 medium white onion, chopped
2 tsp ginger grated
2 tsp finely chopped garlic
1 tsp turmeric
1 tsp garam masala
½ tsp chilli powder
½ tsp cumin powder
200g chopped tinned tomatoes
150g natural yoghurt
500ml light chicken stock (page 29)
2 tbsp sunflower oil
Water
Salt

To par boil the rice:
300g basmati rice
1 tsp cumin seeds
1 star anise
2 laurel leaves
5 black peppercorns
Salt
1 litre water

To finish:
2 tbsp chopped mint
2 tbsp chopped coriander
4 tbsp milk
Pinch saffron
2 tbsp crispy shallots (page 27)

Cut the lamb fillet into bite size pieces. In a heavy casserole dish, heat the oil and brown the pieces of lamb over a high flame. Set the browned meat aside. Add a little more oil and fry the cardamoms, cloves and cinnamon until fragrant. Add the onion and fry over a medium flame until the onion begins to brown. Add the ginger and garlic and fry for a few minutes before returning the meat to the pan. Add the powdered spices and salt to taste. Stir well and add the tomato, yoghurt and chicken stock with sufficient water to cover the meat. Bring to the boil and then cover the pan and simmer over a low heat for about 1.5 hours until the lamb is tender. You should have about 150-200ml of thin sauce. If the lamb is too dry, add a little water. The volume of liquid is important as it will be absorbed by the rice in the final stage of cooking.

While the lamb is cooking, prepare the rice. Bring the water to the boil with the spices and salt. Add the rice and parboil for 3 minutes. Strain and set aside.

Assemble the biryani. Warm the milk with the saffron in a small pan to infuse it with flavour. Place half of the rice in the base of a heavy casserole. Add the lamb curry, and sprinkle with the chopped herbs. Finish with the rest of the rice, drizzling the saffron-infused milk on top and a scattering of crispy shallots.

Cover and cook over a low heat for 10 minutes. Turn off the heat and without lifting the lid, leave the biryani to stand for 15 minutes before serving.

SAMOSA SALAD WITH MINT AND CORIANDER CHUTNEY

Serves 4 | prepare 60 mins | cook 15 mins | medium difficulty

Our samosas are prepared using the same pastry as the curry puff recipe. The samosas are bigger than curry puffs and folded differently. This samosa salad is very typically Burmese and looks spectacular. Sev is a crispy snack made from fried chickpea flour and can usually be found alongside Bombay mix at Indian grocers. If you can't find sev, substitute with rice crispies dusted with a little curry powder.

INGREDIENTS

***Curry puff pastry** (page 75)*

For the samosa filling:
30ml sunflower oil
1 medium onion peeled and finely chopped
1 tsp grated ginger
1 small fresh green chilli finely chopped
150g frozen peas boiled
250g boiled potato cut into 5mm dice
¼ tsp chilli powder
½ tsp coriander seeds
½ tsp garam masala
1 tsp amchoor (dried mango powder) or juice of half lime
½ tsp salt
1 tbsp fresh chopped coriander

For the mint and coriander chutney:
Large handful of fresh mint
Large handful of fresh coriander
Juice of 1 lime
1 green chilli finely chopped
1 tsp sugar

For the salad:
100g cooked chickpeas
½ tsp mustard seeds
2 tbsp grated fresh coconut
½ tsp fresh green chilli finely chopped
1 tbsp fresh chopped dill
2 tomatoes peeled and chopped
½ red onion peeled and finely sliced
Juice of 1 lime
Salt
1 tbsp natural yoghurt
2 tbsp sev

In a large frying pan, fry the onion, ginger and fresh chilli. When the onion begins to brown, add the diced potato, peas and spices. Check for salt and stir in the fresh coriander.

Divide the pastry into 6 equal pieces. Roll one of the pieces into a circle with a diameter of 15cm. Cut the circle in half. Moisten the diameter and fold over to create a pouch. Fill the pouch with the potato mixture and seal the opening pressing the seam together to close the samosa. Deep fry at 170°C. The samosa should brown gradually. If the oil is too hot, it will crisp rapidly on the outside leaving the pastry undercooked. Once fried, the samosas can be reheated in a warm oven.

Put all of the ingredients for the mint and coriander chutney in a food processor and grind to a paste, adding sufficient water to make the chutney pourable.

Take two mixing bowls. In the first dress the tomato, sliced onion, and dill, with a little lime juice and salt. In the second mix the chickpeas, mustard seeds, grated coconut, chilli and salt. On a large plate, layer the chickpea mix with the tomato and onion. Place the samosas sliced in half on top of the salad then drizzle with the yoghurt and chutney. Finish with a sprinkling of sev.

BACK TO THE MOTHER COUNTRY
(1922-1927)

The sea! The sea!

Two shipping lines ran direct passenger services between Rangoon and England, the Bibby and the Henderson. The Bibby docked at Tilbury, and the Henderson at Liverpool. The Bibby Line was more expensive and had bigger ships named after British counties, while the Henderson ships were called after Burmese towns. All the Bibby stewards were European, but on Henderson liners, even the cabin stewards were Indian. Top brass travelled Bibby, smaller fry travelled Henderson. Indian Civil Servants always travelled by Bibby, but police and railway officials were Henderson people. We, of course, sailed Bibby and the ship was the SS *Lancashire*, which we thought was very appropriate because that was Father's county. We were leaving Burma for good, but I wasn't sad - I was just looking forward to England.

What a wonder it was to find ourselves out on the open sea when we woke up that first morning! The sea! I'd never imagined it was so enormous and so blue. Whichever way we looked there was nothing but sea, as far as the eye could reach. The sky was as blue as the sea and the sun danced on the waves, dazzlingly beautiful. When we were in the middle of the Indian Ocean Father called us excitedly to come and look at schools of porpoises making great curving leaps out of the sea and back into it again, and sometimes at night he would show us patches of phosphorescence in the wake of the ship, kaleidoscopes of many colours. The ship itself and its routines were things of wonder too: the ship bigger even than we'd imagined it, so many rooms down the centre between decks where people played cards, or chatted, smoked, drank tea, or did whatever adults liked to do; the wide decks scattered with deck chairs, people reading, snoozing, sewing, and knitting in them; on an upper deck, games of quoits and skittles which we soon learned to play. The whole ship seemed designed as a playground of many intriguing possibilities. And the food...! So many meals for a start, and served, to my surprise, by Whites. Early morning tea or coffee and fruit brought to the cabin, breakfast in the dining saloon: porridge, bacon and eggs, grilled kidneys, sausages, kippers, smoked haddock, potted shrimps, toast and marmalade - we'd never ever had such grand food! Elevenses, lunch, afternoon tea at four, supper for children at six, and dinner for adults at eight with ladies in evening dresses and gents in dinner jackets.

☞ | P126 **KEDGEREE** |

Our first port of call was Colombo, where we docked to refuel, before sailing across the Indian Ocean to the Red Sea. Mother was deeply impressed, indeed positively awestruck, by the jagged, reddish brown cliffs our ship passed as we sailed up the Red Sea. I remember her calling me to look at them and share her wonder and I remember how later, when we'd passed through the Straits of Messina en route to Marseille, she was delighted to see little pink and white houses clinging to green hillsides along the Italian shoreline and how lovely she thought it would be to live there. Before that we'd moved slowly up the Suez Canal, sometimes having to tie up at the side to let a ship pass on its opposite way. When the boat anchored at Port Said, we were not allowed ashore, but the shore came aboard: such a bustle, such a clamour of voices; hawkers in small boats crowding round the ship setting up stalls on deck; people buying and selling tourist goods, carpets, and glassware; the gully-gully men - conjurers whose patter began 'Gully-gully-gully' and then they'd do a trick; little boys in the water beside the boat diving for sixpences thrown down by passengers – 'Hey, Mr Mackintosh! Hey, Mr MacGreadie!' they'd call up asking for more sixpences - last sights and sounds and smells before crossing the Mediterranean into staider Europe.

Mother was a very bad sailor but thank goodness we had perfect weather until the Gulf of Lyon, where the sea turned choppy, and she was so dreadfully seasick that she was not going to remain on the wretched boat one minute longer. We all disembarked at Marseille and stayed in a hotel till she recovered. One of those days Father took me for a walk and pointing to an island way out to sea said, 'That's the Chateau d'If!'. I was thrilled to pieces. Imagination came to life: *The Count of Montecristo* had been one of my favourite books in Rangoon and the Chateau d'If was where the Count had been imprisoned. I wanted so much to go and see it, but there wasn't time for soon we were on the train to Paris.

Mother loved Paris, in fact she altogether loved France. She constantly remarked on the courtesy and consideration of the French and how different they were to the English, forgetting that there we were travellers staying in expensive hotels and not at all in the same relationship to the French as we were to our imperial masters in Rangoon. She loved French coffee and croissants. She found the bidet in the hotel bedroom a wonderful invention for the Burmese custom of washing the feet before bed, a custom Mother maintained although her feet were squeezed into shoes during the day. The bidet was a pleasant surprise after her experience of baths on the *Lancashire*.

I loved those huge tubs filled with sea water, but Mother was horrified at the idea of wallowing in your own filth, and only doused herself with the small zinc bucket of fresh water meant for the face.

☞ | P 129 **BANH MI VIETNAMESE BAGUETTE** |

Journey's end

And finally, there was London. We took the train from Dover to Victoria on a sunny May day: the grass was so green, and the sunshine so kindly, unlike the blinding glare in Rangoon. The Palace Hotel in Bloomsbury Street was a very grand place and on our first morning Father took me on an open-topped bus down Oxford Street and I was overjoyed - here was our journey's end at last, exactly where, a year ago, I'd imagined I'd be: on the top of a London bus! No matter that Father grumbled, saying these new motor buses weren't half as comfortable as the old horse-drawn omnibuses of his youth! But, I wondered, where was the England smell of Granny's Christmas parcels? And where were the daisies? However, all this excitement was short-lived, for Mother very soon fell seriously ill with pneumonia, so ill that we thought she would die. She could not be moved from the Palace Hotel for several weeks and it was staggeringly expensive. A Doctor Grant came every day to see Mother, an elderly man with white hair and a long white moustache and he was immensely kind. It says a great deal for his skill and her constitution that after three weeks she began to recover.

When she was well enough we moved to a small private hotel in the Notting Hill Gate area. That was where I saw my first daisy. How excited I was! I didn't know then that they are a curse on a lawn. I also didn't understand the full implications of moving to Notting Hill Gate. Thomas Cook's had given Father a list of small private hotels, and naturally he hadn't thought to check with them whether the places they recommended would take a family like us. Father and Alice trailed from door to door until they found a place that would take 'a coloured family'.

We were not there for very many weeks before Father rented a furnished house in Bournemouth where Mother could convalesce. Old colonials were a familiar sight in the town and the shopkeepers and the locals used to address Father as 'Captain Carr' thinking he must be Indian Army. What a joke, we thought because we knew he was not army, he was a judge. Every week he would draw out £10 from the bank, horrifying Mother who violently disapproved of a country where you paid for everything in golden sovereigns and not in nice, humble rupees. Tinch's wonder was the postman. Just imagine! He was an Englishman, not an Indian! What an indignity, that a pure Englishman with golden hair and blue eyes, should be a postman!

We did not have a maid there, and Alice taught us girls how to help with the housework. I had a handbrush to brush the carpet because there were no hoovers in those days, and I thought this was a horrible business. Tinch had learned to do English cooking by then, and she could make cakes too, but Mother preferred Burmese food. Willy came with his new wife Betty, but they didn't stay long because she said the house smelled of balachaung. Mother continued to oversee the cooking and she loved exploring her English garden to find suitable ingredients for Burmese dishes. She used the windfall apples for 'toziya': vegetables either cooked or half-cooked or grilled which you use for dipping into your fish paste. She liked adapting anything she found in England to Burmese purposes. She loved rhubarb, but she didn't use it as a sweet, but to make a kind of curry that she made with roselle in Burma. We also started to enjoy some thoroughly English combinations. Hot buttered toast, muffins and crumpets toasted with a toasting fork before the fire. And Mary made a great discovery: she ate cheddar cheese and marmalade and found it was quite delicious, and that became one of our family things, cheddar cheese and marmalade. ☞ | P 130 **SOUR VEGETABLE AND LENTIL SOUP WITH RHUBARB** |

Aunty Gertie and the spindles

Mary, Sam and I were to go to boarding school in September, so Father sent to the educational agency, Truman and Knightley, for school brochures and we spent many hours looking through them. He couldn't afford the most exclusive and expensive public schools because he had taken early retirement, so it had to be a private school. In the end, we found a place called Blackdown which was in Somerset and had a brother school for Sam in Devon. The headmistress, Miss Fitze, wrote and promised to take good care of us and see that our teeth were looked after, and both Father and I thought this sounded lovely and kind so that is the place we chose.

Before we went away to school our English Granny came down from Southport with my namesake, our Aunty Gertie, to meet us. They stayed at a hotel and came to tea one afternoon. Father and Alice acted as interpreters for Mother, and the rest of us were called one by one to meet them. I was absolutely captivated by Granny, she was so just like a Granny should be: very pink and white with bright blue eyes, snow white hair and dressed in voluminous black silk with lace at the neck and a pretty black bonnet on her hair. We all liked her, but Aunty Gertie wore a tailored suit and a fearful cross-patch expression on her face. She didn't take much notice of us and the only thing she said to me was, 'Take your feet off the spindles, Gertie', in a very angry voice. I was startled as I hadn't a clue what spindles were. Mother was full of praise for Granny after she'd gone. How beautiful she was! What perfect manners she had! How kind she'd been to the children! But I was uneasy. What a motley crew we must have looked to these two elegant ladies. They were just like the ladies from neighbouring houses I used to see going to church on Sundays, richly dressed, wearing smart hats and gloves, looking solid and comfortable. They belonged where they were in a way that we didn't, and I had an unhappy sense of not belonging.

Education in England: Miss Sparrow and Rockwell Green

Mid-September, and we were kitted out with all the clothes the two schools decreed. Father took Sam to Chulmleigh School, and the next day Mary and I were put on a train for Wellington, in which two girls from Portsmouth would also be travelling to Blackdown School. One of them was a new girl and the other had been at the school for two years. She had been told to look after us on the journey, and she did well enough, but every time she asked us a question and I answered, the other girl fell into irrepressible giggles. It was unnerving. When we got to the school I found to my relief that Mary and I were to be in a different house from our travelling companions, and what was even more gratifying we were not put into a dormitory with lots of other girls but given a double room to share. Our dream, to be educated in England, was about to come true.

There were two African girls at the school and neither Mary and I, nor the African girls, ever suffered the least racist slight, or insult at that school. After some natural initial curiosity about these strange-looking foreigners from countries that they knew nothing about, the English girls soon accepted us as very little different from themselves. I remember one of them asking me once, 'Do you feel English or Burmese?', to which I answered, 'I don't feel either, I just feel me!' Still, Mary and I were known as the Burmese Girls, which was odd to us, because in Burma we would never have been thought of as Burmese. At that time there were no laws against racial discrimination in Britain, so London landladies could turn us away with impunity, but at school no one was unkind.

I realise now that that was because we were not penniless migrant workers, but visitors well able to pay our way. None of the girls at school knew anything about Burma, but they were very interested in anything I had to say about it. They all thought I was very clever, but that was only because my school in Rangoon was so much better than Blackdown, where the lessons all had a certain impromptu character about them and there was no library. Our only access to books other than our texts was my adored gym mistress, Miss Sparrow, whom we called The Robin because she looked like a little robin redbreast. She loved Rupert Brooke and introduced him to her followers and we used to moon over him hopelessly. It was Miss Sparrow who encouraged my brief but intense relationship with the high church. She attended church in a village about three miles away and enticed some of us down there - I even learnt to wobble about on a bicycle in my enthusiasm for Sundays at Rockwell Green. The vicar was a very handsome, charismatic fellow, and I genuinely enjoyed the services, the ceremony, the incense, and the beautiful vestments. The smell and the ritual reminded me of when we would be washed and smartly dressed to go to the Shwedagon with Mother.

I think I was very happy at Blackdown on the whole. In Burma, we had no outdoor life because Mother didn't allow us to go out in the sun, and if we went to wild places there was always the fear of snakes and scorpions. In England, we went to sleep without a mosquito net, and there was no worry about dacoits and thieves. It was only when I came to Blackdown that I went to bed feeling secure. I enjoyed English country life, or parts of it - I didn't like playing hockey in winter, and the mud and people hitting my ankle with sticks, but I liked the countryside.

The greatest thing about Blackdown though was that I made friends. My best friend was a girl who was as different as could be from myself. Her name was Blanche Smith and she was a year or two older than me, staying on at school simply because she liked being there. She had bright red hair and was very good at all sports but was not at all interested in lessons. She was always my partner when we went for country walks in crocodile fashion, and she never failed to spot birds' nests in the hedges, rabbits in the fields and squirrels on the trees. It was 'Look! Look!' all the way, and her excitement helped me to forget that I was cold, and the country lanes slushy and that walking in single file was a dreary business. One weekend she invited me to go home with her to Porlock, where her mother ran a small private hotel called Lorna Doone! Imagine my delight! I had only seen the Chateau d'If in the distance, but here I was actually going to stay in a place called Lorna Doone which was right in the Doone country. Mrs Smith welcomed me warmly, but she looked reproachfully at Blanche saying, 'Oh Blanchie! What stories you've been telling me!', and Blanche, with gales of laughter, explained that she'd told her Mother that I was as black as her boots. 'She's a naughty girl, Gertrude, to tell me stories. Why, you're not black at all! In fact, you're nearly as white as I am'. I learned to love Mrs Smith very dearly, for I stayed with Blanche many times after that and was always so kindly received.

Father reclaims his career

When I came back from school in the Christmas holidays of 1922, Father told me that he had been offered promotion. There had been elections to the Legislative Council in 1922. Franchise was based on taxation, very few peasants were eligible to vote, and there was a strong boycott movement, so turnout was very low – it was, I believe, well under 10%. Despite protests, the Dyarchy reforms were going to be put in place in January 1923, making Burma a Governor's Province of India with a modicum of self-government. There had also been changes to the judicial system there and a single High Court was instituted in Rangoon in 1922. This resulted in an unforeseen need for senior and experienced judges and Father was recalled to serve first as an Additional Judge in the High Court Bench provisionally established at Mandalay, and later as permanent Chief Justice at Rangoon. He accepted in part I suspect because he had a large family to support, but also because ever since her illness, Mother had virulently taken against England. It was damp, grey and expensive and the people were rude and disrespectful. She hated it. They returned to Burma early in 1923, taking Alice, Freddy, Dorothy, and Robert back with them and leaving Mary, Sam and me at school in England.

From then on, I imagine life was less frustrating for Father. His career followed the usual kind of course until he retired in 1932: he heard appeals in the Rangoon High Court, and he occasionally went on an inspection tour of Courts in the Districts. He lectured and chaired committees, and in due course he was knighted. At home, family life continued as before. They still lived in our old house near the Gymkhana Club, but Father never joined it. He did join the Turf Club though and he used to go with Mother to the races. In the hot weather the family would go up to the hills and when he was not on duty Father would go there too, gardening, walking, and swimming in a big open-air swimming pool not far from our house. He described all this in long letters to Mary, Sam and me, regular letters sent once a week. ☞ | P 133 **SHAN FISH CAKES** |

Every two years he would come and visit and I would be counting the days for months before his arrival. He always came alone, and he enormously enjoyed those home leaves when he would spend our school holidays with whoever of us happened to be around. Mother refused to come to England, but she missed us a lot. She wanted her children to come back, and perhaps that is why she clung to Alice so fiercely.

Leaving school

I left Blackdown in the summer of 1924 and went to London. That was the time of the British Empire Exhibition at Wembley, in 1924. It cost one shilling and sixpence to get in - seven and a half pence in today's money, which is not much now but was a reasonable sum in those days! It was huge and truly impressive, and there were gardens and a lake and a bandstand. Each country had a pavilion, erected in the architectural style of that country or modelled on some famous site and containing exhibits, specimens of craftwork, and even people. I was thrilled to discover that Burma had its own pavilion. To get to it you had to go past all kinds of stuffed animals, natural wonders and products displayed in kiosks, and there was even a scenic railway and fairground. The Burma pavilion was a temple and a couple of village houses, and not really much like the Burma I knew. Like some of the other countries Burma had a 'race in residence'. I imagine she would have been a girl smoking a cheroot and was jolly relieved that whoever it was wasn't there when I went. Imagine if I had known her!

That autumn, I was coached for Cambridge Entrance. I stayed at 23 Lyndhurst Road, Hampstead, which was not a coaching establishment, but a pricey hostel for foreign girls. I made good friends at this hostel, although I'd felt so outclassed when I first arrived, a raw schoolgirl among a host of elegantly dressed young women, very sure of themselves. Some of them talked politics and economics together with passion, and it was from their fascinating talk that I learned more about the Indian National Congress and of Mahatma Gandhi.

I left when Father came home on leave in June 1925 and we had a glorious summer together. First, the two of us stayed at 'Lorna Doone' in Porlock, as Mrs Smith's paying guests. We used to go for long walks over Exmoor, and at night we could hear the waves on the shingle, whoosh! whoosh! Mrs Smith liked Father very much. He liked his tot of whisky at night but he didn't like to keep a bottle of whisky in his room without telling the lady of the house so he asked Mrs Smith's permission. She thought this was so polite and said 'You can see he's a real gentleman even though he wears an old-fashioned Norfolk Jacket'. To accompany meals, she used to go to the pub next door and get cider from the barrel. She was a wonderful cook and would roast enormous joints.

| P 134 **TANDOORI LAMB SHANKS** |

When the schools broke up, we collected Mary and Sam and went to stay at the Royal Hotel in Dawlish. There was a shop downstairs and dancing, but we weren't interested in dancing, so at night we would be with newspapers and magazines upstairs together and Father would send us down to get chocolate almonds. There was a lovely sandy beach for bathing, and Father used to dive off a rock into the sea. I loved watching him, but I was always afraid that he would drown.

G, Father and Sam, Dawlish, 1925

The summer holidays over, we took Mary to her new school, Cheltenham Ladies College. Sam, poor Sam, was to go back to Burma with Father. Mother had absolutely insisted on this, saying she wasn't going to have another son go astray like Willy. Willy had taken up with an English girl without permission. Sam was a simple soul, she said, unlike Willy who'd always had his wits about him, and if Willy had fallen prey to female wiles and married his landlady's daughter, how much more danger was Sam in, he who would surely fall for the first pretty face. Sam, soft-hearted and home-loving was ready enough to go back home after three years of boarding school, but he didn't settle down at the Diocesan Boys' High School in Rangoon, and when in 1928, Dorothy, who was younger than him, was sent to join Mary at Cheltenham, he wanted to go back to England too. Mother was adamant, and a compromise was reached by sending Sam to a big boarding school in Maymyo near Mandalay that was run along English private school lines. He hadn't been there a year before he and another fellow ran away and were missing for several days before they were found living in a village, in a villager's hut, dressed in Burmese villager's clothes. He was expelled, and the head teacher said that he was more a fool than a knave, just easily led. Not long after this escapade he was found to be suffering from TB and was sent to a sanatorium in Madras for a couple of years.

That was an end to Sam's schooling. Poor Sam was the odd one out. Freddy and Robert had each other even though they were always fighting. There was a little girl at school that Robert was rather in love with and he called her his little brown owl and Freddy used to mock him like anything. Robert used to mock him back and send Freddy into the most terrible rages – the veins would stand out in his neck, his face would go all red and he would go berserk. I remember him chasing Robert round the big dining table with a knife once. Freddy was a thin little chap and Robert was stumpy. Robert was very much Mother's favourite because he was the youngest and he had very engaging ways. He used to mock her gently sometimes because Mother couldn't pronounce words with a final consonant, so her version of 'toast' was 'to'. Every mispronunciation he picked up and imitated. He used to do odd jobs for Mother but always for a fee. Mother approved of this, but we all scorned him for it as a terrible money-grubber.

Illness

I had failed my Cambridge Entrance and so Father fixed me up at King's College where I studied English with French as a subsidiary subject. My French had been very poor when I first went to King's, but luckily, I had a good coach who helped me so much that by February I was able to take part in a debate in French, speaking from the floor on the motion that Imperialism was a bad thing. I proposed also to speak, later in the debate, in defence of Imperialism, for in truth I was somewhat apolitical at this time. My argument against Empire had been based on no great political conviction: it was simply a piecing together of notions I'd picked up from my friends in Hampstead and U Ottama. I was equally unaware of social and political conditions in Britain. I knew nothing of the miners, nor of the hardships of the working classes. The 1926 General Strike was a bit of a nuisance for getting about London, but never mind, some of the King's boys were driving buses. I didn't think of them as strike-breakers who were doing wrong. I was enjoying life at King's. I had friends of both sexes, but no close friendships and certainly there were no romances. Nobody fell in love with ugly old me. I wished someone would, of course, for although I was a university student my hopes rested more on marriage than on a career.

At the end of my first year at King's in the summer of 1926, I went to stay with Blanche for a week or two and there I had a fit. Mrs Smith thought it must be an epileptic fit and called her doctor who, not having seen me fitting, decided I was simply 'unstrung', and gave me a pep talk: 'Miss Carr, I think you've been studying too hard. You've got two courses open to you and it remains for you to decide which you take. Either let this mental strain get the better of you, which means a bad nervous breakdown and three months complete rest in consequence, or else make an effort to pull yourself together. Take a double dose of this medicine and don't let yourself be sick after it, and get up tomorrow morning and forget all about fits and things. I know it will require a terrible exertion of your will-power, don't think me brutal for suggesting it, but I don't like to see people giving in to a nervous breakdown without a fight. Now what will you do?' Well, I couldn't say 'Give in and have three months' rest', so I said, 'I'll do as you say'.

I went back to London to start my second year at King's, and I was really enjoying myself, but the fits continued. Father cabled, telling me to see the Warden and ask her to get a doctor to examine me and send him the results. I did so, and the Warden and her doctor took my case history very seriously and made arrangements for a careful watch to be kept on me. Shortly after this, I had another fit in the presence of the Senior Woman Student and the doctor advised me to give up my studies for the time being.

I had to leave the hostel and go and stay with Father's brother, Uncle Fred and his wife, Aunty Annie, in Derby until Father was able to take special leave to come to England to sort the thing out. Uncle Fred and Aunty Annie were extremely kind to me, giving me the best bedroom in their small house and every comfort they could afford. Aunty Annie worked very hard, helped by a maid who lived in. Every Monday was washing day, and Aunty Annie slaved over a big copper on the kitchen range, boiling the family linen with a big ladle to stir and turn it over, an operation that fascinated me. I wasn't allowed to do anything but go for walks and have lots of rest. When Father arrived, he took me to see Dr Risien Russell, then the authority on epilepsy. I must say I didn't take to him much: he was an ugly man with a very spready moustache. He gave me various prescriptions and a sheet of instructions, including orders never to be left alone, particularly in the bath. I needed as much fresh air as possible, and my parents decided I was to go back to Burma where doors and windows don't have to be closed.

It was a prison sentence. By February 1927, I was on my way back to Rangoon.

Forced back to Rangoon

Our boat arrived early in Rangoon so there was no one to meet Father and me at the jetty, and we made our own way back to Leeds Road. Mother and Alice were asleep and the house was silent. When Mother heard I was back she rushed down the big staircase with a whoop of joy. She had just got out of bed and her hair was all over the place. As she flung her arms round me I felt the house close in. I wept and wept, tears of utter despair but Mother thought them tears of joy.

It was even worse now. I was treated like some delicate piece of china and attended everywhere I went. I couldn't even go for a walk by myself. By this time Father had been on the High Court Bench for four years and so was much more involved in official entertainment. We used to be invited to Government House, the Honourable Mr Justice Carr, Mrs Carr, Miss Carr (Alice), and on very rare occasions, Miss G. Carr would be thrown in too. When I was younger, I had always rather admired the great and important people who dined at our house, but now, listening to their conversation it struck me it was talk about absolutely nothing. How fatuous it all was, and my god, here were people of great prestige who had risen high in the world, and what were they talking about? Rubbish. But Rangoon's dreary social life was the only activity I was allowed, visiting Mother's cronies, dropping cards, being seen and doing the right thing. 'Brainwork' was forbidden, it was supposed to be bad for my malady. Mother and Father sometimes held a dinner party for Alice and me, when they invited young people, including single young men, but they were awful evenings too. We wouldn't know the guests very well, and of course the men felt duty bound to dance with the host's daughters but were obviously no more interested in me than I was interested in them. This didn't ease Mother's suspicion that I was going to get into trouble one of these days. Not that there was much grounds for that. I was horribly self-conscious about my looks, because the course of bromide for my epilepsy had brought out enormous boils all over my face, much worse than acne, so that I sometimes refused to go to the races I was so disfigured. Mother had always told me how ugly I was, and now, in my twenties, I was even worse. ☞ | P 137 **PAVLOVA WITH RASPBERRIES** |

Mother at home

I am ashamed to say that at that time I became somewhat patronising towards Mother, perhaps in part because I was so miserable. She was so temperamentally different from Father. He was such a silent man, and how she loved to talk. She enjoyed inventing epigrams and proverbs and she had an extraordinary facility with words, though her Burmese was rather earthy and she had a strong Moulmein accent. I remember her following a series of whodunnits in one of her papers that related the exploits of a detective Maung San Sha, a rewriting of the Sherlock Holmes yarns put into a Burmese setting. 'Dear simple Mother!',

Portrait of Mother

I reflected at the time, 'What a child she is, getting so excited about stories I shared with Father years ago'. I was feeling very grown-up and sophisticated having returned from London. I felt life must be very lonely for Father with a wife who didn't share his intellectual interests. Perhaps I was over conscious of the language barrier between them because I remembered so vividly growing out of one myself. But I took for granted the fact that she was keenly interested in Burmese current affairs and an avid newspaper reader, reading *The Sun*, a Burmese language paper, every day. And I didn't always appreciate the hundred and one little tendernesses she constantly lavished on Father. At breakfast the last course was always fresh fruit, and this she always prepared for him herself, peeling, stoning, slicing, and arranging it beautifully on a dessert plate, so he could eat it trouble-free. When he ate oranges, she peeled the inside skin of the orange, and all the proper part of the orange was piled on a plate and he ate it with a teaspoon. Every day she laid out his clothes for him, and none of his bodily comforts were ever neglected. Mrs Beeton herself couldn't have shown more wifely solicitude.

When she entertained officially, she enjoyed playing the gracious hostess and did it very well too. She had beautiful taste in clothes and never loaded herself with jewels in a vulgar manner. I marvelled at how she could keep conversation flowing easily around her, sitting the right people next to each other, always with Alice on hand to translate, and tolerating any clumsy attempts to speak Burmese. She would always make sure that she was not sitting next to a Bishop though, because they could never manage anything in Burmese. The big functions however had one snag: Burmese ladies and gentlemen had to be properly shod in European shoes and stockings, and not come stockingless in Burmese slippers. How Mother hated having to wear what she called 'Lady Shoes'. They pinched her feet and were hot and uncomfortable. They were her only concession to European dress and with that single exception, she dressed all her life in the fashion of her youth. She was in a strange position on these formal occasions. While she took her status from her husband, she was not an authentic character in the drawing rooms so lovingly recreated by English wives. In general, while one might be polite to native women, it was not the done thing to be friendly with them. Meanwhile, with the growth of nationalism, the Burmese attitude towards women in her position became more hostile. They came to be regarded as traitors to their race, women who had sold out to the imperialists. Some were deeply hurt by this suggestion, but Mother was furious and only reaffirmed the Englishness of her children. She was determined that they should act in a suitably English way, particularly her daughters. I used to think that she had such an empty kind of life, doing so little, managing the servants and organising the work of the household, gardening, bathing and visiting, but I do realise now that her life wasn't as empty as I had thought it at the time. She enjoyed cooking, perhaps partly because she was saved from having to do it as a daily chore. She was very good at it and she took pleasure in preparing delicious food. She would make wonderful salads in a moment, with fresh vegetables and fruit from her garden mixed with crispy shallots and toasted chickpea flour and other tasty ingredients. ☞ | P 138 **BURMESE POMELO, CABBAGE, AND SHRIMP SALAD** |

And who wouldn't much rather have an army of servants to do the housework? Mother enjoyed gardening, growing fruit and veg as well as flowers, and it was a hobby she shared with Father. She took a great interest too in the work of the various committees she was asked to serve on by charitable organisations – Maternity Homes for the Poor was one of them, and then there was Mrs Tee Tee Luce's Home for Waifs and Strays.

But this was not the kind of life I wanted to lead. So boring! I described it all when I wrote to Mary in England, whom I missed terribly. She kept all my letters and preserved them to this day. 'Things', I wrote to her in April 1927, 'are very much as they were before we left Burma in 1922'. It wasn't Burma I was talking about. It was the kind of self-contained life our family lived, from which getting away to school in England had been a such liberating experience. Back, unwillingly, in that same old small world, older, smaller, I was too steeped in self-pity to notice that Burma had indeed changed, and was changing still, politically. It was only very gradually, over the next three years, and even then it was sub-consciously, that I became aware of heightened political tension in the air.

Political tensions, unrest, and organising

When Dyarchy had been introduced there had been a significant boycott of electoral participation. Many nationalists were concerned that, cut off from the force of Indian nationalism, the Burmese would be denied the political gains granted to India and turned into a crown colony. Moreover, there were suspicions about the Legislative Council. Not only was the franchise extremely limited but certain elected seats were reserved for special interests and minorities like the Indians and the Karens. The idea was to protect the interests of those numerically weak communities, an early example of what we would now call 'positive discrimination', but the nationalists accused the government of a divide and rule policy. They contested the existence of minority interests, opposed to the general interest of the vast majority of people in Burma, which they said was to be free of British rule.

Nationalist associations called Wunthanu Athins were springing up all over Burma. The British cracked down and police would come to villages when Wunthanu Athin meetings were taking place and round up all those present. They would take them to an administrative centre, give them a summary trial and sentence them to prison. In response to this, Bu Athins, secret organisations within Wunthanu Athins, were formed. Their members swore a terrible, binding oath. Father read me the English translation of it and it demonstrated their utter commitment to the cause: 'From today to the end of my life, so long as Home Rule is not attained, I will work for Home Rule heart and soul without flinching from duties even if my bones are crushed and skin torn. If I fail to work for Home Rule may I die on land from the dangers of land, and on water from the dangers of water, may I suffer in Hell permanently, as permanently as the stump of a tree sticking out of the ground. I will not bid for fisheries or (government licensed) shops; I will not drink intoxicating liquor or take to opium; I will not co-operate with the Government. If I co-operate with the Government may I suffer in Hell permanently. If a member of a Bu Athin is in trouble and requires my assistance I will help him, not avoiding the sun or rain, without wearing umbrella or shoes. I will not wear apparel of foreign make. I will not marry foreigners. If a member of a Bu Athin does an act and infringes the law and the Government asks about it, I shall say, "No"'. Quite terrifying. I wrote it in my commonplace book it so haunted me.

The hated Governor Craddock had been replaced by Sir Harcourt Butler in 1923, but this did little to calm the situation. A conference in Paungde, in May 1924, attended by, some said, between two and three hundred thousand people, advised those who could not afford it not to pay their taxes and an Anti-Tax campaign was initiated. The thugyi, whose responsibility it was to collect the tax, might seize livestock in lieu of payment, but the cows could not be sold on, as no one would bid. Even if someone bought them, the cattle would be maimed. Some thugyis were killed when they attempted to collect taxes and in one area people armed themselves with daggers and determined to kill any government official who approached them. Meanwhile the wunthanus were providing advice and help, giving practical support to those villagers who were jailed or fined.

The Burma I went back to in 1927 was in ferment, yet I could see little of it, in part because much of the unrest was in the countryside. But that was to change. In the end, I had insisted that, brainwork or no brainwork, I should be allowed to go to the University. Father took me to see the Principal, Dr Sloss, and I sat while they discussed my academic record. Sloss occasionally threw me a question, rather disdainfully I thought, but I was in the end admitted to the English Honours class of University College, the oldest of the constituent colleges at Rangoon University. I began to live in two worlds: one at home and one at Rangoon University.

KEDGEREE

Serves 4 | prepare 30 mins | cook 20 mins | easy

There is something quintessentially Raj about kedgeree. I imagine it steaming in a silver dish alongside kippers, boiled eggs, black pudding and racks of toast, all part of the buffet breakfast served to Grandy and her family on the journey to Southampton. But actually if kedgeree were served, it was probably to second class passengers, with only European food offered to those like her travelling 'port out, starboard home'.

INGREDIENTS

500ml milk
1 pinch saffron
250g smoked cod or haddock
50g butter
6 fresh or dried curry leaves
4 green cardamom pods crushed
5cm stick cinnamon
1 medium white onion peeled and finely chopped
1 tsp grated ginger
1 green chilli deseeded and finely chopped
1 tsp turmeric
¼ tsp chilli powder
2 tsp Madras curry powder
500g cooked basmati rice (page 24)
1 tbsp chopped chives
1 tbsp chopped coriander
Juice of a lemon
4 soft boiled eggs (page 30)
Salt

Warm the milk and saffron in a wide shallow pan. Poach the fish for 10 minutes and allow to cool. Peel off the skin and flake the fish coarsely with a fork.

Heat the butter in a wide frying pan or wok until it begins to sizzle. Add the curry leaves, cinnamon and crushed cardamom pods, and when they become aromatic, add the onion. Stir fry until the onion begins to brown. Add the ginger and chilli and continue to fry for a few minutes before adding the powdered spices and then the rice. Stir fry, tossing the rice with the other ingredients until it has heated through thoroughly, then add the flaked fish followed by the herbs. Squeeze in the juice of the lemon and check the seasoning. Serve in 4 dishes with slices of poached egg on top.

BANH MI VIETNAMESE BAGUETTE

Serves 4 | prepare 30 mins + 12 hours to marinate | cook 20 mins | easy

Since coming to live in Spain, I indulge occasionally in a mid-morning 'almuerzo' or elevenses. Typically, this consists of a 'bocadillo', a French style baguette stuffed with anything from tuna and olives, to potato tortilla or my personal favourite, deep fried calamares with garlic mayonnaise. So many things are improved by being stuffed into a crispy baguette. When the Vietnamese were finally able to free themselves of the French colonisers they wisely kept French bread, and banh mi is still the country's best known fast food.

INGREDIENTS

For the pickled vegetables:

½ medium daikon (winter radish, or white turnip)
1 medium red onion
1 large carrot
½ cucumber
1 tsp salt
70g sugar
250g white vinegar
200ml water

For the char siu pork:

1 pork fillet
1 tbsp honey
1 tbsp hoisin sauce
½ tbsp light soy sauce
½ tbsp oyster sauce
½ tbsp yellow bean sauce
¼ tsp five-spice powder
1 tbsp rice vinegar
½ tbsp sesame oil
½ tsp smoked salt
1 tbsp sunflower oil

For the banh mi:

4 half baguettes
25g butter or mayonnaise
100g smooth pork or chicken liver paté
A small bunch of fresh coriander

For the banh mi sauce:

3 tbsp Thai sweet chilli sauce
6 tbsp hoisin sauce
1 tbsp rice vinegar
1 tbsp light soy sauce

To make the pickled vegetables: peel and slice the daikon and carrot into matchstick size pieces. Slice the cucumber and red onion thinly. Place the vegetables in a mixing bowl and sprinkle on the salt. Leave for 1 hour then massage the vegetables. They should become soft and bendy. Squeeze out the excess water and discard. Stir the sugar into the vinegar and water until it dissolves. Pour over the vegetables and leave to stand for at least 12 hours before using.

To make the char siu pork, mix together the marinade ingredients and place into a zip lock bag with the pork. Massage the pork with the marinade then place in the fridge overnight.

Remove the pork from the fridge 1 hour before cooking and heat the oven to 180ºC. In a non-stick pan heat 1 tablespoon of sunflower oil and sear the pork fillet on all sides. Transfer the fillet to a metal baking tray with a drizzle of oil and 50ml water. Cook in the oven for about 12-15 minutes, basting occasionally. The water will prevent the marinade ingredients from burning and should be converted to a thick syrup by the end of the cooking time.

To make the banh mi sauce, mix the ingredients in a bowl and add any leftover juices from cooking the pork.

Slice the bread in half and remove the crumb. Spread with butter and paté. Cut the pork into slices and arrange these in the sandwich, drizzling the pork with the sauce. Now add a generous amount of pickles (you should squeeze all the vinegar from the pickles so that the banh mi isn't soggy). Finish with coriander leaves.

SOUR VEGETABLE AND LENTIL SOUP WITH RHUBARB

Serves 4 | prepare 15 mins | cook 75 mins | easy

Sour soup is nearly always served at lunchtime in Burma, not as a dish in itself, but as an accompaniment to a rice meal with curries and condiments. Roselle (hibiscus) leaves are commonly used together with tamarind paste to give the soup its characteristic tartness. This recipe substitutes the roselle leaves with rhubarb, just as Ma Khin did when she lived in Britain. If tamarind is not available use fresh lime juice. Yellow bean paste adds depth and substance to the soup. If you can't find it use light soy sauce.

INGREDIENTS

For the vegetable stock:

2 large carrots
1 turnip
1 medium swede
2 medium parsnips
1 large white onion
1 stick celery
1 leek
3 bay leaves
3 cloves garlic unpeeled and crushed
½ tsp black peppercorns
2 litres water

To finish:

50g red lentils
1-2 tbsp tamarind paste
1-2 tsp yellow bean paste (available from Chinese supermarkets)
2 stalks lemon grass cut into thumb length pieces
8 lime leaves
2cm ginger sliced
150g pumpkin in 1cm dice
150g kale, spinach or other leafy veg
150g rhubarb cut into 1cm slices
Salt and freshly ground black pepper
1 tbsp chopped fresh dill

Wash the lentils, cover with cold water and leave to soak while you prepare the stock. Peel and coarsely chop the carrot, turnip, swede, parsnips and onion. Slice open the leek lengthwise and chop coarsely. Rinse the leek in warm water to remove any mud or sand and drain. Slice the celery coarsely. Put all of the vegetables in a stock pot and cover with water. Bring to the boil and remove any scum that floats to the surface. Add the peppercorns and bay leaves and simmer gently for 45 minutes. Remove from the heat and strain the stock. Return it to the pan and boil vigorously until the stock has reduced to half its volume.

Stir the tamarind and yellow bean paste into the vegetable stock, adjusting the quantity to taste. Add the lemon grass, lime leaves and ginger and then the pumpkin and drained lentils and cook for about 20 minutes until the vegetables are tender and the lentils are completely cooked. Now add the rhubarb and kale and cook for 5 minutes more. Adjust the seasoning and serve in individual bowls sprinkled with chopped dill.

SHAN FISH CAKES

Serves 4 | prepare 45 mins | cook 15 mins | medium difficulty

Steamed rice, potato and fish cakes are served as a kind of Russian salad in the Shan states. Catfish or snake head fish would be more typical from this inland mountainous zone, but the dish works well with cod, hake or any other white fish. We have taken this dish one step further by making small patties out of the ingredients, covering them with breadcrumbs and deep frying them. The resulting crispy fish cakes may not be authentically Shan, but they are quite delicious.

INGREDIENTS

350g potatoes skin on
1 fresh plum tomato
300g hake or cod
1 tsp grated ginger
2 sticks lemon grass finely chopped
1 tsp turmeric
Salt and freshly ground black pepper
150g cooked rice
2 tbsp garlic oil (page 28)
1 tbsp chopped chives
50g plain flour
1 egg beaten
100g breadcrumbs
1 litre sunflower oil for deep frying
4 tbsp mayonnaise
1 tsp balachaung (page 185) or any hot chilli sauce

Boil the potatoes in their skins in salted water. Add the tomato for the last 10 minutes. You can test with a knife when you think the potato is cooked. Drain the potatoes and tomato and leave to stand for 10 minutes until cool enough to handle. Peel and mash the potatoes. Skin and break up the tomato with a fork and combine this with the mashed potato.

Chop the lemon grass very finely and mix with the grated ginger. Place the fish fillet skin side down in a buttered ovenproof dish and spread the ginger and lemongrass over the fillet. Dot the fish with butter, season with salt, pepper and turmeric and bake in an ovenproof dish covered with foil at 180°C for 15 minutes or until just cooked. Allow to cool, peel off the skin and remove any bones then break the fish into coarse flakes. Put the fish, potato and tomato, cooked rice, chives and garlic oil in a mixing bowl and combine the ingredients by squeezing them through your fingers with a clenched fist. Check the seasoning and divide into 12 balls. Flatten the balls between your hands to make fish cakes about 2cm thick.

Prepare 3 bowls with flour, egg and breadcrumbs. Dip each fish cake first in flour, patting off any excess, then in the egg and finally in breadcrumbs. Place the finished fish cakes on a tray lined with greaseproof paper. Heat the oil to 180°C and deep fry the fish cakes until crisp and golden. Drain the fish cakes on kitchen paper. Mix the balachaung or other spicy sauce with the mayonnaise and serve alongside the fish cakes.

TANDOORI LAMB SHANKS

Serves 4 | prepare 20 mins +1 day to marinate | cook 3 hours | medium difficulty

I adore traditional roast lamb and it's so simple to prepare. I make small incisions in a leg of lamb and stuff in peeled garlic cloves and fresh rosemary. Roasted in the oven, basted with white wine and served with roast potatoes, parsnips and a green salad, it's one of those winning dishes for a dinner party. I'm sure Blanche's mother, being a great cook, would have enjoyed this spicier alternative, though finding some of the ingredients may have been a bit of a problem in 1920s Somerset.

INGREDIENTS

For the lamb:

4 lamb shanks weighing about 400g each

For the marinade:

Pinch saffron threads
1 tsp coarse salt
2 green chillies
200g unsweetened yoghurt
1 tsp chopped ginger
1 tsp chopped garlic
1 tbsp concentrated tomato purée
Juice of 1 lime
1 tsp ground cumin
1 tsp turmeric
½ tsp crushed chilli flakes
1 tsp paprika
¼ tsp cinnamon
1 tbsp chopped fresh coriander

Grind the salt and saffron threads in a mortar. Discard the stems from the chillies, remove the seeds and chop finely. Combine the ingredients for the marinade in a small mixing bowl. Make two deep slashes in each lamb shank and rub the marinade into the meat. Leave to rest in the fridge for 24 hours.

Take the lamb out of the fridge a few hours before cooking. Heat the oven to 200°C. Lift the lamb shanks out of the marinade and place in an oiled baking dish in which they fit comfortably. Recover what you can of the marinade and add water until you have about 250ml of sauce. Roast the lamb shanks in the hot oven for 20-30 minutes after which time they should be beginning to brown. Pour over the reserved sauce. Cover the shanks with aluminium foil and return the pan to the oven. Lower the heat to 160°C and bake for 1.5 hours. Remove the foil and baste the shanks with any remaining liquid (if the pan is dry you may need to add a little water). Return the dish to the oven uncovered and roast for 15 minutes more during which time nearly all of the liquid should have evaporated and the shanks will be tender.

Remove the shanks from the oven and place on a serving dish. This goes really well with dahl (page 233), and aloo parathas and lime pickle (page 189).

PAVLOVA WITH RASPBERRIES

Serves 8 | prepare 30 mins | cook 45 mins | medium difficulty

Raspberries and wild strawberries were one of Grandy's fondest memories of her visits to Kalaw. The temperate climate of the Shan hills is ideal for cultivating fruit and vegetables that are virtually unknown in tropical lower Burma. This dish works really well with frozen raspberries. Thanks to La Torre del Visco Hotel and restaurant for the recipe.

INGREDIENTS

300g frozen raspberries defrosted
280g + 1 tbsp granulated sugar
1 tsp cornflour
5 egg whites
½ tsp salt
1 tsp white wine vinegar
1 tsp vanilla extract
2 tbsp flaked almonds
500ml double cream
100g mascarpone
1 tbsp rose water
2 tbsp icing sugar
Butter for greasing

Stir the extra tablespoon of sugar into the raspberries and put them in a sieve over the sink to drain off any excess liquid. Grease a shallow rectangular baking tin (35cm x 25cm) and line with greaseproof paper. Preheat the oven to 140°C.

Mix the 280g of granulated sugar with the cornflour. Beat the egg whites with the salt until they form stiff peaks. Continue to beat while adding the sugar and cornflour mix one spoonful at a time. When all of the sugar is incorporated, beat in the vinegar and vanilla extract. Fill the baking tin with the meringue, spreading it with a spatula to make it as even as possible. Sprinkle the flaked almonds on top and bake for 45 minutes. The meringue should be crispy on top but still soft underneath. Allow to cool.

Whip the cream and mascarpone until stiff. Stir in the rose water and the raspberries. Place a sheet of greaseproof paper on a clean work surface and dust it with icing sugar. Invert the pavlova onto the paper and carefully peel off the sticky parchment that will be attached to the base of the pavlova. Spread the raspberry and cream mixture over the pavlova. Lift the greaseproof paper nearest you with one hand and roll the meringue using your free hand to form and tuck. Place in the fridge for a couple of hours before serving sprinkled with more icing sugar.

BURMESE POMELO, CABBAGE, AND SHRIMP SALAD

Serves 4 | prepare 30 mins | cook 0 mins | easy

The neutral taste of peanut oil is ideal for cooking with spices. But when it comes to dressing salads, peanut oil offers little taste compared to the rich fruitiness of olive oil. The Burmese have overcome this problem by flavouring the oil with shallots, garlic or turmeric. Shrimp floss adds a wonderful umami flavor to this salad. You can make it with those little pink dried shrimps that can be found in the fridge at a Chinese supermarket. Look out for giant pomelo at the Chinese supermarket too. The pearls of flesh from its segments are much less acidic than grapefruit, though the latter is an acceptable substitute and the two can be combined.

INGREDIENTS

1 tbsp dried shrimp
½ Chinese pomelo or 2 pink grapefruits, or a mixture of both
1 tbsp chickpea flour
½ savoy cabbage thinly sliced
150g ripe cherry tomatoes cut in half
1 tbsp grated ginger
1 tbsp roasted pumpkin seeds
2 tbsp crispy shallots (page 27)
2 tbsp shallot oil (page 28)
Juice of 1 lime
1 tsp fish sauce
1 tbsp chopped fresh coriander

Soak the dried shrimp for 10 minutes in a little cold water then pat dry on kitchen paper and grind in a small food processor. Cut the pomelo in half then quarters. Separate the segments from the thick skin and break them into pieces with your hands, separating the flesh from the bitter and tough white membrane. If you are using grapefruit, cut off the top and base to give you a stable cutting surface then stand it on a chopping board. With a sharp paring knife cut the skin from the grapefruit working from top to bottom following the curve of the fruit and making sure you remove not just the skin but also the white pith. Once thoroughly peeled, and working over a bowl to catch the juices, slip the knife between one of the segments and the connective membrane. Cut until you reach the centre of the fruit, trying not to cut through the membranes. Repeat until you have freed wedges of perfectly peeled grapefruit.

Place the chickpea flour in a dry frying pan and warm over a medium flame. Stir constantly with a spoon until it browns. Wrap the ginger in a small piece of muslin and squeeze tightly. Catch the juice that flows out in a small bowl. Put the cabbage, cherry tomatoes, pomelo and raw shallots in a mixing bowl. Dress with the ginger juice, lime juice, shallot oil and fish sauce to taste. Stir in the crispy shallots, pumpkin seeds and shrimp powder. Arrange the salad on a wide serving dish and sprinkle with the toasted chickpea flour and chopped coriander.

MAKING DIFFERENCES: BETWEEN TWO WORLDS (1927-1932)

Rangoon University - starting again

I felt very lost that first day at the University of Rangoon, swept along corridors with a milling crowd of students in Burmese dress, and not a familiar face among them. Dressed as I was in European clothes, it was a great relief to see a number of girls I'd been to school with among a cluster of Eurasians at one end of the Women's Common Room. I almost ran to them and was puzzled to be received somewhat coolly. But you see as usual I stood out as belonging to no faction. All the students were on first name terms, but I was known as Miss Carr, that was the distinction they accorded me. Even in our small English honours class of six, they were friendly but they behaved with respect. Everyone knew who my father was, my lifestyle was different from theirs and I was driven to college in the family limousine, a very classy Chrysler.

But it was at Rangoon University that I first saw nationalist Burma at close quarters. In 1930, a Rangoon University student called Maung Ba Thaung established the Do-Bama ('We Burmese') Society to instill nationalism in the Burmese and make them 'morally, intellectually and physically strong'. One year later, national school teachers and college students formed the All Burma Youth League to work for the economic improvement of Burma, beginning with a campaign to stop smoking imported cigarettes and to appeal to students to lead more austere lives. At home, official privilege and its constraints insulated us from this kind of thing. Our Burmese mother notwithstanding, the Burmese people we met socially tended to be Government officials and their families who talked no politics. At the university, however, there were many Burmese students - though they were not, in fact, so large a majority in the university as they were countrywide.

In my first week as a student in 1927, I found my way to the University bookshop. It was surprisingly well stocked, not only with text books but also with a variety of recent publications, among them new novels and modern poetry that I had seen reviewed in the English weeklies that Father got regularly from London.

I was browsing happily when a lean, sun-tanned Englishman came and talked to me, very knowledgeably, about the books on display. He asked me what kind of books I liked to read and showed me a series of single poems published in paper covers. They were, as I remember, the *Ariel Poems*, by T.S. Eliot. I bought it and showed it to Father that evening, telling him how finding that bookshop had made my day and what a highly intelligent bookseller I'd met there. 'That was no bookseller', said Father. 'That was Furnivall - used to be Commissioner of Land Records - an ICS man - resigned not long ago'. 'Why did he resign?' I asked. 'Didn't like Dyarchy. Thought it wouldn't do'. Father was a man of few words and anyway, he was deep in a book he was reading.

It was only later that I discovered the reasons for Furnivall's resignation. Throughout his twenty-one years in the Indian Civil Service, and indeed for the rest of his life, he returned again and again to what he saw as Burma's greatest need after she lost her sovereignty: a system of education that would equip her to survive in the modern world. He felt strongly that successive British reforms had failed to provide this because, to put it bluntly, they had been directed at advancing British economic interests. No attempt had been made to develop the Burmese language as a medium of modern instruction. Instead, the teaching of English was steadily extended at every level resulting in a cleavage between town and countryside. He said a society in such a state of disarray could not possibly exercise political responsibility within a democratic constitution. He saw this political reform as a dereliction of duty in which he wanted no part and he resigned from the ICS.

Immediately after his resignation he set to work on a one-man damage-limitation exercise. The University bookshop was a part of this. Until then there had been only one bookshop in Rangoon: Smart and Mookerdum, Indian owned, and expensive, because they priced their books by simply turning shillings into rupees, and there were fifteen rupees to the pound but only twelve shillings. Furnivall went to Dr Sloss and asked for the monopoly of supplying text-books to the University in return for which he would price his books at the proper exchange rate. The deal was done, and the bookshop was eventually established as the Burma Book Club. There you could order any book published in England as well as English newspapers, weeklies, and magazines. It was at that time in a room within the precincts of the old college buildings, for the splendid new Rangoon University Estate, six miles out of town, was still under construction. Indeed, no part of the University had yet been moved to the new estate, and all teaching was still in Commissioner Road, in buildings of timber sprawling over a crowded area of the town.

At first, I only went to College for lectures and took no part in social activities because I was under strict medication for my malady. But quite early in my first term I was asked to play Mrs Hardcastle in a college production of

She Stoops to Conquer and through rehearsals got to know more students from other English classes. They were mostly Eurasians, as were most of the cast. Only one Burman had been given a role but he had been to the kind of school most Eurasians went to: an English speaking Mission school. He played Mr Hardcastle, and he and the man who played Tony Lumpkin were both so good that the play turned out a rollicking success. ☞ | P 160 **LAPHET THOKE TEA LEAF SALAD** |

G, graduation at Rangoon University, 1930

I did well at University, achieved a first and got a gold medal, and after I graduated I became a tutor in the English department with responsibilities for marking and tutorials, but not lecturing. I was also doing some writing for Furnivall's *World of Books*, a bi-lingual monthly magazine he founded in tandem with his bookshop, whose motto in English was: 'The bricks are fallen down, but we will build with hewn stones'. Its main object was to help develop Burmese into a language which could express modern concepts. I remember him turning up in the staff common room and, sitting down on the table where I was marking essays, asking me to do some book reviews. I jumped at that, and he said 'Come and choose a book now'. So off we went to his bookshop and he took down a book called *Politics and Literature* - or was it *Literature and Politics*? - saying 'This is the book I thought of for you', and ignorant as I was I turned it down for some short stories, saying I didn't really know anything about politics.

As an undergraduate, I found I loved acting, and I was very good at it, particularly the ugly old woman parts. There was at that time no dramatic society in the college and producing our play had been the one-off bright idea of one of the tutors. But after our success, interest in plays and play-acting grew. We put on several one-act plays and there was talk of founding a college dramatic society. I was keen to use my new role to support this, and so I called a meeting to discuss a prospective dramatic society. But that meeting was disturbing. More Burmese students than I'd expected came to it, among them a small hostile group, one of whom said there was no need for a dramatic society because the Students' Union already had an Entertainments Sub-Committee. When it was explained that our society was to have different functions the answer was, OK then, but let it be called the Anglo-Indian Students' Dramatic Society, so that no Burmese student would want to join it. That gave me a nasty jolt. I hadn't been aware of hostile sectarian feeling in the student community. I knew, of course, that 'Anglo-Indian Students' did organise dances and picnics to which few, if any Burmese students came or were invited, but I hadn't seen this as symptomatic of deep social division, since life outside the University was similarly compartmentalised and, I thought, generally tolerated as a fact of life. All the Burmese I'd ever met, both at home and in our English Honours class, had been unfailingly friendly. Now it was a painful shock to feel myself rejected by my mother's people.

I discussed this with my friend, Khin Zaw, a fellow Tutor in the English Department. He had really enjoyed the previous performances. It had been, he said, a revelation to him of a literary form that did not exist in Burmese writing. How was it, I asked him, that when I'd seen so many Burmese obviously enjoying that performance and turning up in force both when the three one-act plays were put on and coming to our meeting, everything had suddenly turned sour? Why so much hostility? He tried to reassure me: there hadn't been general Burmese resentment against us; the group at the meeting were a politically

The dramatic society at Rangoon University (G 6th from left), 1929

minded minority who liked to stir up trouble. Lots of Burmese students wanted to join the dramatic society - his friend Maung Nu, for example, who'd suggested at the meeting that we should encourage play-writing by inviting scripts from members. 'I'll introduce him to you', he said. And that was how I first met Maung Nu - U Nu to you, who later became Prime Minister of Burma. In 1929, he wasn't as politically active as he became a few years later as Thakhin Nu. He was set on trying to write plays, and write them he did, with Burmese characters in Burmese settings, but written in English, in exercise books which he tied together with red tape and gave me to read and criticise. I never knew what to say because I thought they were wordy and impossible to read.

Falling in love

University staff were graded as in all the imperial services. Senior academics were members of the Indian Educational Service (IES). They were Europeans with British university qualifications. Burmese staff were subordinate to them and graded according to their individual qualifications. Tutors in the English Department were usually recruited from recent Honours graduates, yet Khin Zaw, with only a Pass degree, had not only been made a Tutor but had also shared the College English prize with me. He'd been 'discovered' in his first year by the Professor of English, W.G. Fraser, an Aberdonian Scot, who was so impressed by his essays that he advised him to read for an Honours degree-advice which he didn't take because he didn't think he was good enough.

He was that rare thing: a Burman from an ordinary family in a rural area who had nevertheless made it to university in Rangoon. His family were small landowners in Gyobingauk, a small town in the Tharrawaddy district, none of whom spoke English, and he'd been to a local school where English was poorly taught. However, he'd taken to the language and read whatever came his way. Fraser, intrigued by this curious chap, had made him write the story of his life, and when I got to know him better he let me read it. I was impressed and interested. 'Do you know', I said to him one day 'I don't remember ever seeing you about until we met as tutors.' He'd seen me, he said. Apparently, I'd tried to sell him a poppy once. On my very first day my 'arrogant way of striding about the corridors like a man', smoking a cigarette through a long holder, had so riled everyone that they'd plotted to teach me a lesson by deliberately jostling me whenever they passed me in the corridors. I'd never noticed this, perhaps because London had got me so used to jostling. And as for that long cigarette holder, it had been prescribed by the specialist in London.

We saw each other in the staff room practically every day, and found we liked and disliked the same people and the same books. We talked a lot about plays, and I told him about evening readings we Honours students had enjoyed at

G and K

Gordon Luce's house. Professor Luce lectured us on Shakespeare and Elizabethan drama. Khin Zaw and I worked closely together on a production of *The Rivals*, in which I was Mrs Malaprop and he, no actor, worked hard behind the scenes on odd jobs. It was when we were discussing the design of the programme with the producer, Mack (a new young lecturer called Mackenzie), that Mack said, Let's give you a stage name', and we rambled on happily about names in general, finally agreeing that we three would henceforth be Mack, G, and K to each other. The play was produced on two successive nights in September 1929, and on the 23rd September, I wrote to tell Mary how well it had gone. A week later I told her: 'I am terribly in love! Would I could tell you all about it, sister dear. I will, one day, but it's a great secret, so you mustn't mention it in your letters'. ☞ | P 163 **MOHINGA** |

Of love and two missionary spirits

Of course, it had been working up to this in the months since I'd first met him. On the 28th July I'd written to Mary: ' Something seemeth to have happened to me, the scales have fallen from my eyes and what not, and behold Gertrude, gazing on a newly discovered world. I've decided that learning is, in itself, a vulgar thing. It is only worthwhile as a means to an end. So far learning has been the most important thing in my life, but henceforth teaching shall be the most important thing. Ain't it thrilling? I think I shall go off next year and teach at a school somewhere in the districts. I'm going to put my life and soul into learning how to teach. I shall probably grow terribly old doing that, but I'm already so old I don't care anymore.' I told Fraser I was going and he was most concerned: 'Do you mean now, forthwith, straight away, at once and this minute?' 'Of course not', I said, and when I'd given him more details he said I must come and have a chat with him sometime about it.

This missionary spirit was not only a symptom of falling in love, but also had arisen from getting to know large numbers of Burmese students through giving tutorials and learning how unequal their opportunities had been. The many from urban areas wrote English with varying degrees of ease depending on the kind of school they'd been to, the best speakers and writers being the product of English-speaking mission schools where most of the pupils were Eurasians. The very few from rural areas had to struggle hardest to get through compulsory English. K's talk, and his account of growing up in Gyobingauk made me curious about rural Burma of which I knew nothing. Kalaw, where we spent so many holidays was 'rural' of course, but it was in the Shan States, not in Burmese Burma, and anyway it was a hill station for the well-heeled classes. I learned from him how desperate the lives of the peasantry had become. K said that the Gautama Buddha's prophecy of the dreadful consequences of materialism and greed, their social destruction and the consequent decline of Buddhist values was realised in the hardship of Burmese rural life. He would quote: 'From goods not being bestowed on the destitute, poverty grows rife; from poverty growing rife, stealing increases; from the spread of stealing, violence grows apace; from the growth of violence, the destruction of life becomes common.'

Through him and his friends I got to know a whole lot more about the situation of the ordinary Burmese and the unpopularity of Dyarchy. Apparently, in Gyobingauk it had become a term of abuse – a man who lost his temper with his wife would say, 'You are a Dyarchy', meaning 'You are a fool'. After 1927, the political situation worsened: the Simon Commission was established to decide the future of reforms in India and Burma and had no Indian or Burmese to sit on the seven-man panel. The Simon Commission recommended the separation of Burma from India. This was opposed by many nationalists, not because they viewed Burma as an integral part of India, but because it would obstruct co-operation between the Burmese and Indian nationalist movements.

From K and his friends, I became aware of U Wisara, the first pongyi martyr. He had welcomed Mahatma Gandhi to Rangoon in March 1929, when he had come to Burma on a fundraising mission. In return Gandhi invited him to India for medical treatment for the bad health resulting from the years he'd spent in prison for preaching against the British. It was not to be, as the following month U Wisara was arrested for making seditious speeches and this time sentenced to six years. He went on hunger strike for the rights of imprisoned political pongyis, including their right to wear pongyis' robes, but despite massive popular support, his appeal was dismissed. He fasted to death and was given a hero's funeral. A bronze statue of him was cast but not erected for ten years because of objections from Rangoon town council, but the 19th September, the day of his death, was observed by students as a national day of mourning for the rest of the colonial period.

The 'missionary spirit' didn't last, for we were both much more interested in going to England than we were to the Burmese countryside. As we drew closer to each other K and I hatched a plot: both of us would apply for State Scholarships to study at British universities and sail away together to paradise. There was a competitive examination for those scholarships with compulsory essays to write in English and Burmese. I spoke Burmese of course, but had never learnt to read and write it, so I started taking lessons. My parents knew of my plan as I'd been agitating to get back to England ever since I'd been forced to leave in 1927, but they most definitely did not know about K's part in it. Of course, they knew who he was and what his circumstances were and so on, but he was just another state scholar like me studying to be a librarian - which was not much better than a clerk you know. ☞ | P 164 **BEIN MOTE SWEET RICE FLOUR PANCAKE** |

Mixing isn't easy

I had agonised for weeks and months before I reached this plan for abandonment, and the awful thing was that there was no one I could talk to about it except Mary. I was the prisoner of my upbringing in the artificial social set-up of my time and place. The letters between us had always been shared with Father and Alice, so it was not until May 1930 when we were on holiday in Kalaw, and Father had to get back to work in Rangoon, and Alice went with him to keep house, that I was at last able to write freely to Mary. It wasn't going to be possible for her to write back freely to me because I'd be back in Rangoon before her answer could reach me, so here was yet another thing to agonise about: What was going to be Mary's reaction to my news?

To cut a long story short, Mary was supportive but anxious and felt I should at least tell Father. She was right, so when K and I both succeeded in winning State Scholarships I made up my mind to tell Father that we meant to marry when we came back to Burma. I chose a day when Mother and Alice were out visiting so we could talk long and freely, but in the event we didn't. It wasn't in Father's nature to chew over emotional problems. He could not bear to put feelings into words. 'Hmm,' he said, looking sharply at me when I blurted out my news. At last he spoke: 'You don't know what you're taking on. A mixed marriage isn't easy. You'd have to give up a lot of things you like doing, things you've been brought up to do.' 'But Father', I said, 'whoever I married I'd be making a mixed marriage because I'm mixed myself. Anyway, ours would be different from yours, because at least we can speak the same language, and we have lots of interests in common'. Looking back, I am appalled at the cruelty of those words. How could I have been so stupid! There was a long silence, and then, 'Mother will be very upset', he said, and I answered, 'I know. I'm not going to tell her'. We said nothing more.

K and I sailed together on the Henderson liner the SS *Bhamo*. That was late in August 1930, when political unrest was simmering in Burma and had been for months. There had been terrible riots in Rangoon in May. Hundreds of Indians had been killed, almost all Coringhis, the people from Madras who provided the dock labour, shifting bags of rice from quay to ship, and bags of salt from ship to quay, for a few rupees. I sometimes came across them because in the slack season they would supplement their income by rickshaw pulling, driving themselves to an even earlier grave. These labourers had gone on strike and the shipowners and labour contractors had turned to Burmese labourers. But the Burmans were mostly displaced agricultural workers and were not used to this kind of labour. They were considered inefficient and the shipowners were forced to grant the Coringhis their increase. The Burmans were no longer n eeded and were now unemployed again, whilst the Coringhis, having been out of work and consequently unpaid for almost three weeks were easily provoked and resentful of the Burman strike-breakers. The situation was highly inflammable and as Burmans gathered on the wharf in the vain hope of work, there were bitter exchanges between them and the Coringhi gangs.

A few days later the Burmese invaded the tenements where the Indians lived and slaughtered them. It was awful. It was reported that at the Stevenson Street jetty a crowd of Burmans cornered some two hundred Coringhis, forced them to jump into the river, and threw stones at them. Corpses littered the mud between high and low water mark the next day. Indians were terrified. They hid in mosques, temples, and churches and Rangoon ground to a halt as they barricaded themselves indoors. Food was low, sewage piled up and the health of the city was seriously threatened before they went back to work.

Then in June, there was a rumour that there'd be riots again on the 24th when the second volume of the Simon Report was due to be published. In the event, this riot didn't happen, but another one did at Rangoon jail, which was not very far from our house, and the servants brought tales of bloody scenes. Thirty-six people were killed and sixty-seven seriously wounded. A colleague of Father's, Maurice Collis, then district magistrate of Rangoon, had attended the riot and was also charged with the investigation [9]. Apparently, the inmates had heard rumours that there was to be trouble on the 24th June and planned to take advantage of the disorder to kill Major Bharucha, relatively recently appointed as superintendent of the Central Jail. He had brought in a much harsher regime to improve discipline, requiring inmates to do obeisances to guards who had struck them and imposing harsh physical punishments. The prisoners took advantage of the entry of a jail lorry to overcome the turnkey and in a matter of minutes they seized the sentry post and the wall. Yet they did not jump to the ground outside the jail as, according to Maurice, their first priority was to deal with the notorious Major Bharucha, who they imagined would

[9] Maurice Collis describes the aftermath in his memoir *Trials in Burma*, first published in 1938 by Faber and Faber.

soon arrive to deal with the situation. Some seized rifles while others helped themselves liberally to methylated spirits and were very soon drunk. Maurice described the roundhouse at the centre of the jail where the hardcore were holed up. It was shot up by the police, and covered with the dead and dying, many of whom had terrible gaping wounds on their breasts. They had been shot in the back by high velocity .303 bullets and you could see the wounds because they were not well clothed, indeed many of them were naked.

England, escape, and rebellion

While all this was going on, there we were in London enjoying ourselves. Mary met us at Victoria Station. She looked so English, so smart, dressed in a little tweed coat and skirt. She was by that time at Royal Holloway College. I think it was a bit of a shock when she met K because he was very brown and wearing a pretty awful suit made in Burma, so didn't look a proper gent. She had great sympathy for me with being in love with the wrong kind of person.

When K and I arrived together in London I found it a new, unfettered world, free of the taboos imposed by Rangoon's hierarchical social structure. We were equals here, no longer princess and pauper. In fact, rather the reverse, for economically K had the edge: he had a small private income from his paddy fields to boost his scholarship income. He bought me an eternity ring, and we were engaged - unofficially, of course. We were much more part of the Burmese community in London than we were of University College London itself. We ate with our Burmese friends, we played tennis and went to the cinema and to dances with them. There was one chap called Maung Hla who was studying to be a printer. He could cope with anything. He was settled in his own flat and he did his own Burmese cooking. He improvised ingredients using anchovy paste for ngapi and getting turmeric from the chemist. We would go to his place for Burmese meals followed by poker and companionship.

Perhaps that was why I never felt at home in University College London as I had done at King's. Then I hadn't felt a foreigner in London, but now, I did. I spent Christmas with my four younger siblings, Mary, Dorothy, Freddy, and Robert. Mary had rented a flat in Battersea and she was put in charge of them. This was their home base when they came home from school, and Mary was like their mother and she had to give the orders. She conducted Father's affairs when money had to be sent for. They used to say 'MKB' Mary Knows Best! I have always felt that Sam and I were rather shut out. At the time of course, he was still in Burma, but neither Sam nor I went to public school, and I felt they rather looked down on us. At that time, I felt even more of an outsider, for rightly or wrongly I sensed a certain constraint between us. Was this because I was no glamorous big sister to be proud of? Was it because rumours of K had made them feel I had 'gone native' and was no longer 'one of them'? Bit of both, perhaps? Or was it all in my imagination? But the constraint was palpable.

In the meantime, over the Christmas period there was disturbing news from K's province of Tharawaddy. It had been visited by Sir J.A. Maung Gyi, acting Governor of Burma, the first ever Burman appointed to that role. He was very disliked not least for his treatment of U Wisara. During his visit, he refused permission to postpone the collecting of taxes for a few months despite the desperate state of the peasantry. The evening after his visit a group of Tharrawaddy villagers under the orders of a man called Hsaya San came together with the intention of capturing the jail, thereby collecting guns and new recruits from the released prisoners. However, as they moved across the paddyfields they were challenged by four men, one of them a headman armed with a double barrelled shotgun. The villagers did not want to engage with him, but he opened fire and they set upon him and killed him. This encounter was perceived as a bad omen, so they turned back and did not proceed to Tharrawaddy jail.

A small group of police were sent the next day to investigate reports viewed with some incredulity that some villages were planning an insurrection. Having come to a small watchman's hut in a paddyfield they stopped, deciding to rest there and go to the village early the next morning. But they could not sleep, and at dawn they heard the loud beating of gongs and saw two hundred men marching towards them bearing all kinds of weapons. They beat a hasty retreat, and the next day seventy-five men were sent to burn down the villages in the area and set up a post in the local monastery. On 25th of December they were attacked by three columns of two hundred men each from three directions. Troops were called in on the 26th of December, but still the trouble was taken to be purely local and it was believed that with the destruction of rebel headquarters by some seven hundred British troops at Alautaung (Flag Hill) in the Pegu Yomas, that the rebellion was over. In fact, it was only the beginning.

Hsaya San rebellion

I read a marvellous article by Patricia Herbert about this rebellion. She worked at the British Library and knows much more about all this than I do [10]. According to her, Hsaya San was a medical practitioner and an astrologer from the Shwebo district. He had risen through the ranks of the Wunthanu Athins where he was well regarded as a learned and dedicated man, in touch with the spirit of old Burma. He was also a leader in anti-tax campaigns. Frustrated with the divisions of politics and the lack of improvement in villagers' lives, he set about organising a rebel army based on the aims of no taxation and free use of forests. The myth that the peasant rebellion lasted for only a week and the British won

---

[10] See Herbert, P. (1982) 'The Hsaya San Rebellion (1930-1932) Reappraised'. Melbourne: Monash University, Centre of Southeast Asian Studies. Working Papers, No. 27, pp. 1-16.

an easy victory persists today, but according to what K heard, and Pat Herbert confirms this, after the battle at Alantaung the revolt spread quickly through neighbouring districts. We tried to follow it in the news, but it was not like today and news was difficult to get hold of. I read later reports by someone called C.V. Warren, who was trapped in Prome, that in one exchange a British commanding officer called Simpson ordered that some of the rebels be decapitated: 'Two and twenty heads were cut off, rolled into the dead monk's robe and taken to Prome. Six fell out on the journey and taught their lesson well. Sixteen heads, vacant and grisly, were laid outside the police station for all the world to see.' [11]

Later the peasants turned to guerilla type attacks and lightening ambushes. From April to August 1931 the rebellion was at its height and there were real fears that crucial towns would fall. Villages were burnt and there were wholesale arrests of suspects. Travellers on the road were searched for tattoos, which were taken as a sign of nationalist sympathies even though tattooing was a common practice in the villages of Burma. Those found with marks were arrested and many were tortured in police custody. Villages suspected of supporting the rebels were subject to forced evacuations miles from their fields with no food, shelter, or clothing provided, all in an attempt to force the rebels into unfamiliar territory.

But Hsaya San was no military commander and the local uprisings were not co-ordinated and not well armed. Many of his followers surrendered to free their relatives from concentration camps. And the British established the Shwe Pyi Aye Aphwe, the Golden Country Peace Group of pro-government pongyis, who toured the rural areas, giving talks and advice. Under intense pressure the rebellion began to falter by September 1931. The movement dissipated as members were wounded and captured and some groups degenerated into bands of dacoits. I was particularly impressed by the story told by Warren of Bo Hla Maung, a rebel leader from the Prome area who held out until the end of the rebellion. He eventually surrendered 'with kingly bearing' and when told that he would be executed he replied that his cause was lost and all his relatives taken by the British. His surrender meant that they would be freed and his fate did not matter now. Hsaya San was betrayed in the Shan States in August 1931 and hanged in November of that year. However, he left the royalties due from a medical book he had written towards the purchase of books for a library. The first books bought were by Lenin, Trotsky, and Marx.

Meanwhile back in London

K was anxious about his home province, true, but he found London unadulterated liberation. He set out to do all the things he had always wanted to do, especially music. He'd brought his Burmese violin with him and used to play it for us on

[11] Warren, C. V. (1937) *Burmese Interlude* London: Skeffington p. 64.

the boat. My Parsi friend was a good musician and she said he was good. He played classical music, Burmese and European, all by ear, for he'd never had lessons in either. Now in London, he was going to explore European music further. He bought an HMV gramophone and spent many hours at Keith Prowse listening to records and buying as many as he could afford. He loved going dancing too, forbidden fruit in Burma where ballroom dancing looked shockingly permissive to Burmese people. He even took lessons and made me go with him to learn to tango in Regent Street! He hugely enjoyed many things English, from Joe Lyons steak and kidney pie to Low and Terry in *The Evening Standard*. He loved the cinema and there was a young actress called Lillian Harvey he adored. He enjoyed Gilbert and Sullivan operas. Years later, when romantic nonsense had given way to husbandly familiarity, he liked to sing the famous song from the *The Mikado* about Katisha at me:

'I have to take under my wing, tra la,
a most unattractive old thing, tra la,
with a caricature of a face.'

I didn't resent it. It was good for a laugh.

When we arrived in London I went to live in Crosby Hall, a student residence in Chelsea. They were real bedsitters, great big rooms with lots of armchairs, and smashing breakfasts, because the people who cooked for us were students from King's College for Women, the domestic science college. They learned really classy catering, and at breakfast time there would be hotplates with very thin bacon sizzling on it, kidneys, kippers, cereals, toast and all the doings.
☞ | P 166 **EGGS FLORENTINE** |

In our residence in Crosby Hall you ate at old oak trestle tables, like in a medieval hall. Before I'd been there very long, an old friend came to stay there too. Her father, U May Oung, had been a distinguished lawyer and High Court Judge. At the Diocesan Girls' High School she'd been entered on the register as May Oung, and we called her May. She was a few years older than me and I'd lost touch with her after she left school. Now she had reappeared, grown up, and was a very important lvady under her proper Burmese name, Daw Mya Sein, the only woman delegate to the Burma Round Table Conference. The Burma Round Table Conference was held to discuss constitutional arrangements if Burma was to be separated from India. It was not allowed to discuss separation itself which was, as I said, highly disputed. Rather they had to indulge in speculations, allegedly hypothetical, though it was clear that the British Government were going to push ahead with separation despite its unpopularity.

May was made much of at Crosby Hall, and when she was at dinner the Warden and politically minded residents would gather round her to talk the politics of colonialism. At such times she was often called to the telephone and on one occasion when her meal had been interrupted one time too many, she asked me to take the call for her: 'Say I'm out and take a message. Say you're my secretary!', she said, jokingly. We took to doing this whenever she was sick of answering telephone calls, though I didn't in fact do any other secretarial work for her. She often took me to social functions when delegates were allowed to bring a guest, and it was as her guest that I went to the inaugural meeting of the Burma Round Table Conference, dressed in Burmese clothes. That was how I came to have my photo on the front page of one of the tabloids - was it *The Daily Mirror* or *The Pictorial*? I forget. After the meeting, the entire Burmese delegation went on to a smart photographer called Vandyke to have a group photo taken, and Daw Mya Sein insisted that I must be in the picture too in spite of the angry, and I must admit perfectly legitimate), mutterings of some of the men.

May Oung and G, London, 1931

turday, Nov. 28, 1931.

YES ON TO-DAY'S RACE—P. 2

Wireless on Page 14

aily Mirror

NEWSPAPER WITH THE LARGEST NET SALE

LY PICTURE

SATURDAY, NOVEMBER 28, 1931 One Penny

Registered at the G.P.O. as a Newspaper.

FREE £500 PICTURE CONTEST—P. 19

£3,000 Cross-Word on Page 16

NKLER—THE SOUTH ATLANTIC LINDBERGH

ENING OF BURMA CONFERENCE

TIVE GIRL'S SPEECH

Mr. Bert Hinkler the famous Australian airman, who, flying a British Puss Moth machine, yesterday completed the first non-stop solo flight from South America to West Africa over a distance of 2,000 miles. Mr. Hinkler, who is seen here with his mother, arrived at St. Louis, French West Africa, twenty-four hours overdue.

Miss May Oung (nearer camera), the only woman delegate to the Round Table Conference on Burma, arriving with a friend at House of Lords, where the Conference was opened in the King's Robing Room by the Prince of Wales yesterday. She replied to the Prince's speech in English, expressing thanks on behalf of the women of Burm addressing the Conference. (Right) Miss C

By the following Easter, I realised I couldn't manage on my scholarship money and I moved to a bedsitter in K's boarding house. This was a disastrous move as it turned out. One of our Burman friends wrote to his mother that K and I were now practically man and wife - shocking news which, of course, was immediately reported to my mother, who fell into a towering rage. 'Mother is extremely upset', Father wrote to me, 'she says she'd long suspected you of deceiving her and that she should have got the truth out of you. I told her you had told me about your plans with K before you left, which made her angrier than ever. She is driven almost mad, sometimes brandishing a large Shan dagger, saying she is going to take the next boat to England and carve you up. You had better write and tell her, whether it is true or not, that you have abandoned your plan to marry K. I ask this not only for her sake, but also for mine, for I am having to bear the brunt of her rage.'

I was stricken with remorse. I ought to have faced the music myself before I left instead of leaving Father with an intolerable burden to bear. I wrote at once to Mother, telling her it was all off between K and me, and gradually things simmered down. I realise with hindsight she wanted us to make good marriages without the risks that she had taken when she'd flouted all the rules. She wanted very much that the boys should become ICS men, or enter a profession and that us girls should marry such men, not a mere librarian and a Burman to boot.

Reunited for a while

My parents at this time were much preoccupied with their own concerns. Tragically Willy had died. He had gone back to Burma with Betty shortly after Father in 1923. He always had money troubles and he just couldn't make a living in England, but Father thought that he should be able to manage something in Rangoon. Willy was very kind to Sam and they became great friends. He joined Steel Brothers but he was unhappy there because while he wasn't treated quite like the Burmans, he certainly wasn't treated like the Europeans. He was quite an arrogant kind of chap. He joined the Burma Frontier Service that administered the hill tribe areas and he and Betty were always travelling around different stations in the far north of Burma. Their first son, Bill, was born in Meiktla. Willy died still in great debt. Father cleared his debts and gave Betty and the boys an allowance. They went back to England and she married a bus driver. I didn't see them again.

By that time Father was at the end of his career, due to retire with many honours, official and unofficial to his credit. He was President of the Burma Research Society, for example, and in the King's Birthday Honours, he was created a knight. How often I wish I hadn't thrown a shadow over a year that should have been one of quiet contentment, the sense of a job well done. After Christmas,

I set about trying to find a flat for them, for they were coming to England in the spring of 1932, after Father retired in February. There were five of them: Mother, Father, Alice, Sam and Tinch, our Burmese cousin. It was nearly ten years since Mother had last seen Mary, four since Dorothy had left Burma, Freddy had followed the year after, and Robert and I the year after that. Mary had left the Royal Holloway College with a degree in French and Latin, and she went to the Triangle Secretarial College in South Moulton Street. Dorothy was just about to leave school to go to King's, and the boys were still at school. Freddy's best friend was the brother of Margot Fonteyn, whose real name was Hookham. Mother used to call him Nga Le. To be 'le de' means to be spinning round like a top, a 'smart alec'. She thought he was a very bad influence and the reason Freddy always got such bad reports. Robert was 13 and always riding around on his bicycle. The poet, Cecil Day Lewis, was a master at the school, and he was much revered by the boys, not for his poetry but for his crime fiction, written under the name of Nicholas Blake. Day Lewis was a friend of my professor, Gordon Luce, and Luce told me that Day Lewis had written to him about a lovely little Burmese boy who made the most extraordinary remarks. Apparently, they were playing rugby and the ball was kicked into a tree, and this little boy had laughed his head off and said, 'That tree bears strange fruit,' which greatly struck him. It must have been Robert. It sounds just like him.

The family was soon comfortably reunited. I had found a place in Kent, and after years of dispersal it was good to have a stable family home again. All went well for a month or two. K's name was never mentioned. Bygones, it seemed, were to be bygones. Once in Rangoon, when I had come home distressed and weepy because I thought I'd made a mess of an exam paper, Mother had gone down into the garden and made me a little posy of her prettiest flowers. Now, when I was similarly distressed and anxious about my studies, she went to her jewel box and brought me a ruby and diamond ring! I was overwhelmed and felt dreadfully guilty! But alas all that sweetness and light came to an end. One afternoon Mary and I went up to London to see a film with K and Myo Min, a great friend of ours, but that part of it had not been revealed to the family. After the film, K said 'Let's go to a Chinese restaurant and have dinner,' and against our better judgement we went. We ran into some other Burmese friends there and it turned into a convivial evening from which we crept home late at night!

Next morning came the inquisition, and when it came out that Myo Min had been in our party too. Mother accused me of trying to get Mary paired off with a Burman too. There was a blazing row in the course of which I refused to stop seeing K and Mother ordered me out of the house, never to darken her doors again. 'All right', I said, 'I'll go now', whereupon Mother threw a faint. 'Brandy!

Brandy!', said Alice, and when Tinch had brought brandy Mother gritted her teeth. 'I can't make her drink it,' wailed Alice, followed by 'Here! give it to me! I need it more than she does', from Mary, exasperated, and she drank it in one gulp! Yes, it was pure farce! I dashed upstairs, packed a suitcase, and when I came down with it and made for the front door, 'Stop her' cried Alice, 'she is going to him!' 'Don't be so silly', said Mary, 'She's going to a YWCA'. That much was true. I went to a very cheap YWCA with frugal amenities, where the bath water was never more than barely tepid and stayed there for a few days until K rescued me. He'd found a family in a south coast seaside town that took Burmese student paying guests in the summer: an English rubber planter from Malaya with his Burmese wife and two or three grown-up children. The Burmese wife was fat, jolly and friendly and a bridge fiend. She kept us up till all hours every night, playing bridge, but not for money; she was simply obsessed with the game. However, this was a small price to pay for her unfailing kindness and her lavish and wonderful meals.

We stayed there about a month, and then K's term as a state scholar was up. The money from the paddy fields was not enough to do more than supplement his stay in London. With no scholarship funds he had to go back to Burma, leaving me to finish my studies for another year. I was very unhappy about this. I'd had to move to Holloway for various reasons and I didn't like it. I'd much rather go to Burma with K. We said goodbye at Liverpool. There was a very nice Burmese woman on board K's boat and she gave us good advice and said people who love each other are often separated and that if we were to trust each other and be faithful all would be well. 'Thitsa, thitsa', was what she recommended to us, that is, faith, be true.

I decided at that stage that I would like to be a journalist. Somerset Maugham's play *For Services Rendered* was being performed. I liked Somerset Maugham because he had written about Burma and he understood what English people in the Raj were like. This play was about war, and I thought it was very powerful, but it was taken off after the first few performances. I wrote to him and said I thought the critics had been very unfair and I would like to put the record straight. I explained who I was and why I was interested in his work and that I was an aspiring journalist. I warned him that I wasn't an exotic oriental lady of great beauty but a woman who thought this would be a very good start to her journalistic career. Anyway, he was very kind and wrote back and invited me to tea. He lived in a very exclusive neighbourhood. I was very excited and told everyone. My co-students were rather sneering: he was a popular novelist, not a T.S. Eliot or F.R. Leavis. Somerset Maugham, I discovered, stammered terribly badly, and it had an unfortunate effect on me because I stammered too. I wasn't mocking but it almost looked as though I was. In fact, it was just sheer nerves. We were waited on by a manservant who brought in muffins on a hot silver dish. And Somerset Maugham himself must have been in a nervous state. He took the dish from his man with his bare hands and it was so hot he dropped it on the floor, the muffins rolling everywhere, only increasing the nervous tension. We spent the rest of the time stammering through the conversation. I had no idea how to interview anyone. I just waited for him to start talking. But he started talking about El Greco of all things. He said he was one of the painters he most admired, and I had never even heard of him. So that line of conversation didn't go very well. I sent him my article and he was very polite but he said it would never be accepted. He was right. My journalistic hopes were dashed.

LAPHET THOKE TEA LEAF SALAD

Serves 4 | prepare 30 mins + 10 days to ferment | cook 0 mins | medium difficulty

Laphet thoke, a fermented tea leaf salad, is unique to Burma where it is as common to eat tea leaves as to drink from them. If you are lucky enough to have brought fermented tea leaves home after a trip to Burma, you'll have no problems turning them into this delicious salad. If not, you'll have difficulty finding this unusual ingredient and may have to make your own. Authentic laphet is made from fermented fresh tea leaves which you won't find in your average supermarket so buy the best quality green tea that you can find. In Burma the ingredients for laphet thoke are often served separately on a lacquer tray. We prefer to mix the ingredients in the restaurant and serve the salad already dressed.

INGREDIENTS

To make your own fermented tea leaves (laphet):

50g best quality green tea leaves

500ml water

2 leaves of white cabbage shredded finely

1 tsp ginger grated

1 tsp garlic finely chopped

1 small white onion chopped

1 fresh bird's eye chilli, seeds removed

¼ tsp salt

2 tbsp fish sauce

For the salad:

75g fermented tea leaves

¼ white cabbage shredded

2 tbsp roasted peanuts (page 28)

2 tbsp toasted sesame seeds

2 tbsp fried split broad beans (available at Indian grocers or may be omitted)

2 tbsp dried shrimp

1 small green chilli seeds removed and chopped finely

6 cherry tomatoes halved

For the dressing:

2 tbsp fish sauce

2 tbsp garlic oil

juice of 1 lime

If you are making the fermented tea leaves yourself, boil the water and pour it over the tea leaves. Allow to steep until cool then strain. Rinse the leaves in several changes of cold water, squeezing out the moisture each time. Pick over the leaves and remove any particularly thick stems. Repeat this procedure to remove any remaining bitterness in the tea leaves.

Place the tea with the other ingredients in a food processor and chop coarsely. Place the pulp in a bowl loosely covered with a plate and leave to ferment at room temperature for three days. Add 2 tablespoons of neutral oil and mix into the fermented leaves. Store the leaves in a sealed jar in the refrigerator and allow to mature for 7 more days.

To prepare the salad, Pour boiling water over the dried shrimp and after 5 minutes drain. Pat the shrimp dry with paper towels and chop coarsely. Make the salad dressing by mixing the fish sauce, garlic oil and lime juice to taste in a small bowl. Put all of the ingredients in a mixing bowl, add the dressing, mix well and serve.

MOHINGA

Serves 4 | prepare 15 mins + 30 mins to soak the noodles | cook 60 mins | medium difficulty

'Now I was seized with the zest for the famous mohinga. I am not ashamed to confess that I ate three helpings of it. To explain a little, ... the thickness depends on the fish-content: the special fish is ngekhu, hard to get sometimes. What even the most reputable mohinga sellers had to do nowadays is to use sea-fish; this does not pulverise well, so they add semolina to thicken the gravy. But when the apparently thick gravy is poured over the rice-vermicelli the semolina deserts the gravy to cling to the vermicelli and the gravy becomes wishy washy under your eyes. There was no such mésalliance in the gravy of the mohinga at the cafeteria. It remained thick and tasty throughout... that was why it was always sold out.'

K Canvases and Miniatures Volume II

Ngekhu is catfish, difficult to find in most supermarkets so at the risk of provoking my grandfather's ire, I'd suggest you try a white sea-fish like bass. Mohinga is typically made with banana stem, but you can substitute with water chestnuts.

INGREDIENTS

For the chana dahl fritters:

50g chana dahl soaked for 2-3 hours

75-100 ml cold water

4 tbsp rice flour

2 tbsp plain flour

¼ tsp salt

¼ tsp baking powder

¼ tsp chilli flakes

To cook the fish:

300g white fish

1 litre chicken stock (page 29)

1 stick of lemon grass cut into 5cm lengths

2cm ginger sliced thinly

1 small bunch of chives

For the soup base:

3 tbsp sunflower oil

6 shallots quartered

1 cm ginger finely chopped

1 tsp garlic finely chopped

1 tsp turmeric

1 tsp paprika

¼ tsp chilli powder

200g banana stem or water chestnuts sliced

200g chickpeas

1 stick of lemon grass cut into 5cm lengths

2 tbsp fish sauce

Salt

To serve:

1 packet 3mm wide rice noodles

4 soft boiled eggs (page 30)

1 lime

2 tbsp chopped coriander

2 tbsp fish sauce

Make the chana dahl fritters. Mix together the dry ingredients and gradually add the water to make a smooth batter as thick as treacle. Drain the soaked chana dahl and add it to the batter. Set aside for 20 minutes. Deep fry spoonfuls of the batter in sunflower oil at 180ºC. Remove from the oil when they are golden and crispy and drain well on kitchen paper. When cool, the crackers can be stored in an airtight container.

Soak the noodles in a large bowl of cold water for at least 30 minutes.

Place the fish fillets in a saucepan and cover with the chicken stock. Add the ginger and lemon grass and bring to the boil. Cook for about 10 minutes then strain through a fine sieve, catching the resulting liquid in a bowl. Separate the fish from the other ingredients and remove any skin and bones, breaking the fish into small pieces. Mix the chopped chives with the fish and set aside.

Put half of the cooking liquid in a food processor and purée with the cooked chickpeas to produce a sauce the texture of single cream.

Heat the sunflower oil in a saucepan and sweat the shallots, ginger and garlic over a low heat for 5-10 minutes until soft and aromatic. Add the spices together with the banana stem or water chestnuts followed by the sauce and the bruised lemon grass. Cook everything together for 20 minutes then add the cooked fish and season to taste with the fish sauce and salt if necessary. If you feel the sauce is too thick, add some more chicken stock.

When ready to serve, drain the soaked noodles and return to the bowl. Boil a pan of salted water and pour over the noodles, leaving them to soak for a few minutes until al dente. Drain the noodles again and divide them between 4 individual bowls. Spoon the mohinga on top and place 2 halves of soft boiled egg on each plate. Sprinkle with coriander and serve with the chickpea crackers and a quarter of lime. Don't forget to place bowls of extra fish sauce, chilli flakes and balachaung (page 185) so that each person can season the mohinga to their taste.

BEIN MOTE SWEET RICE FLOUR PANCAKE

Makes 4-6 pancakes | prepare 15 mins + 30 mins resting | cook 15 mins | easy

I bought bein mote at the entrance to a monastery in Hpa An. Rather like sweet blinis they cost just a few pennies and were handed to me in a transparent plastic bag. I wolfed them down before entering the monastery, marvelling at a pond full of water lilies and golden koi. I looked around for a wastepaper bin to dispose of the empty bag. Nothing in sight, so I approached two monks shrugging and proffering the offending item with that universal gesture: 'What am I supposed to do with this?' They took it from me smiling and tossed it into the pond.

INGREDIENTS

200g rice flour
½ tsp salt
½ tsp baking soda
250ml ice-cold water
1 ripe banana
1 egg
150g soft brown sugar
4 tbsp grated fresh coconut or dessicated coconut
4 tbsp chopped pistachios
1 tsp poppy seeds

Combine the flour, salt, and baking soda in a mixing bowl and gradually add the ice-cold water. In a separate bowl, mash the banana with a fork and beat this purée with the egg and sugar. Leave this batter to rest for half an hour before using.

Heat the oven to 180º. Warm a 12cm diameter blini pan over a medium flame and add a knob of butter. Fill the pan with the pancake batter to within 1cm of the rim. Allow the pancake to cook for a few minutes then transfer the pan to the oven and bake for 7 minutes, by which time the pancake should be fully cooked. Turn the pancake out of the pan and sprinkle with coconut shavings, poppy seeds and chopped pistachios. Serve with vanilla ice cream.

EGGS FLORENTINE

Serves 2 | prepare 30 mins + 90 mins for dough to rise | cook 30 mins | challenging

The secret to really good eggs Florentine is preparation. Stir frying the spinach and toasting and buttering the muffins during the 7 minutes while the eggs are poaching is a challenge for most home chefs, and that's before you discover that your hollandaise has split! At Ma Khin Café we serve eggs Florentine for breakfast and keep the hollandaise sauce warm in a water bath set at 57°C. You don't need to be so precise but resting your prepared hollandaise in a bowl of hot water or even a thermos flask will keep it stable and give you one less thing to worry about.

INGREDIENTS

For the muffins:

200ml milk

15g sugar

2 tsp baking powder

450g plain flour

1 tsp salt

1 egg

15g butter

2 tbsp coarse semolina flour

For the hollandaise sauce:

1 egg yolk

50g butter

1 tbsp lemon juice

Salt and freshly ground black pepper

To serve:

25g butter

½ bag washed spinach

1 clove garlic minced

4 eggs

Salt

Freshly ground black pepper

To make the muffins, heat the milk until warm to the touch and add the sugar, stirring to dissolve. Melt the butter in a small pan. In a mixing bowl combine the flour with the salt and baking powder. Add the egg, butter and milk and combine with one hand until it comes together to form a ball. The dough should come away cleanly from the sides of the bowl. If it is too wet, just add a little more flour. Turn onto a surface and knead for 10 minutes then return the dough to the bowl, cover with film and leave to rise for 45 minutes.

Knock down the dough and roll out on a floured surface to a thickness of 1cm. Cut out circles with a 7cm pastry cutter. Using a spatula, carefully lift the circles onto a baking tray dusted with flour. Cover the muffins and leave to rise for 45 minutes. Heat a dry cast iron frying pan and sprinkle the surface with semolina. Place as many muffins as will fit in the frying pan and toast them, lifting a corner from time to time to check on progress. When the muffins are a pale brown, flip them over and cook the other side. You will have about 8 muffins, so freeze any that you are not going to use for another occasion,

For the hollandaise sauce, melt the butter in a small saucepan and heat until it begins to foam. Drop the egg yolks into a food processor and switch on. Add the lemon juice and then the butter in steady stream. Scrape out the sauce, season and keep warm.

Bring a shallow pan of water to the boil and add a generous teaspoon of salt. Lower the heat to minimum. The water should be just trembling. Crack the eggs into individual teacups and slip them one at a time into the water. Start a timer for 7 minutes.

While the eggs are cooking, cook the spinach. In a wide frying pan, melt the butter and when it begins to bubble, add the garlic. Fry for a few minutes, and when aromatic, but before the garlic begins to brown, add the spinach and stir well as it wilts. When the spinach has released its water, you can turn up the heat (not too high) to boil this off but keep stirring so that the garlic does not burn. Once the spinach is dry, season with salt and black pepper. Cut the muffins in half and spread each half with butter. Toast on a ridged grill pan.

Put 2 half muffins on each plate. Divide the spinach between them. Lift the eggs out of the water with a slotted spoon touching them down lightly on kitchen paper to dry them, and place 1 egg on top of each half muffin. Add a generous tablespoon of hollandaise sauce and a sprinkling of black pepper and serve.

TENSIONS IN BURMA
(1932-1939)

A family reconciliation

I was at Royal Holloway College for my last year in England, living in college. In the Christmas vacation, I went to stay at Crosby Hall because I was still in exile from the bosom of the family, but Father soon found out where I was and came to see me. 'Your mother really loves you, you know, in her own way. She has been very upset since you left us.' In the end I went home for Christmas and at Easter and again in the summer before I went back to Burma in August 1933. It was tacitly accepted now that I was going back to marry K. Mother, Father and Alice never talked about the dreaded prospect. Mary and I did though: 'Do you want a boy or a girl, for your first baby?' 'A girl, I'd much rather have a girl', 'What will you call her?', 'Rosemary', I said, very firmly. She helped me with my dressmaking and we went shopping together for my wedding trousseau.

At last Mother decided to have a talk, sitting on my bed when I was recovering from gastric flu. 'When are you getting married?', 'As soon as I get to Rangoon', 'Has he got a job and how much does he earn?' 'He is the University Librarian on Rs 400 a month'. 'Do you imagine he will be able to keep you on that? It's a clerk's wage. A librarian is no more than a clerk after all. Do you realise that when you marry, your station in life will drop to his level? You will no longer be treated as a High Court judge's daughter, with respect, but as a social nobody - a clerk's wife'. She went on and on, deploring my ingratitude to a father who, unlike so many Englishmen who deserted their Burmese wives and abandoned their children to the care of Christian missionaries, had been true to us all, sending his eight children to England to be educated so that they would be English in all their ways. And now, here I was, disgracing Father, disgracing the whole family, by marrying not only beneath the station in life that Father had given me, but marrying a Burman. Did I know, she asked, that Buddhist Law countenanced lesser wives and that many Burmans did indeed have concubines, living in the matrimonial home? I bit my lip as she went on and on, as much for Father's sake as for my own.

However, when I was up and about again she took me shopping for her wedding present to us which was to be household linen. We went to Robinson and Cleaver's in Regent Street, and when I looked longingly at fine linen sheets, she firmly said they wouldn't do for my future station in life. 'The Burmese prefer good stout cotton - ask for the stoutest they've got'. Unbleached cotton sheets were displayed, coarse and yellow. She gave me a wicked look and pronounced, 'That's the kind of thing you want in a Burmese household'. I rejected them, and we ended up compromising on plain white cotton, not unduly thick. Thereafter, Mary, Tinch, and I had lots of fun with my 'station in life' in our private chats.

Late in August 1933, I sailed from Liverpool. Mother and Alice came as far as Victoria Station to see me off, but Father came all the way and saw me onto the boat. When we parted, I wept inconsolably as I had always done in childhood whenever he left us to go home on leave, but now my tears were as much tears of remorse for all the pain I'd brought him as tears of grief at parting. I wanted so much to say how truly sorry I was, but we neither of us said anything. I just hugged him tight, he patted my shoulder from time to time and kissed me good-bye.

An emotional return

'Burma was ever so exciting to get back to this time', I wrote to Mary two weeks later. 'When we reached the pilot brig somewhere near the mouth of the river it was about two o'clock and intensely hot, with a sort of heat haze veiling everything. There was nothing whatever in sight except muddy water and the pilot brig, so I went into my cabin and finished reading my Turgenev. At about three-thirty, I managed to summon up enough energy to peer out of the window, and darling, quel beau spectacle, we were passing by flat plains of an unbelievably brilliant emerald green, and there were lots of round, flat little trees, and here and there a mud hut, and occasionally a whitewashed pagoda. It all looked most joyously fresh and luscious - not at all like the miserable burnt-up country I'd arrived in last time in March. Ever so thrilled, I went out on deck and behold more green plains on the other side, and passengers scanning the horizon for the Shwedagon Pagoda'.

The police launch was the first to come and meet us, and quite a long time later came the Customs launch, and soon after came the Port Health Officer's launch, with K at the prow in purple suit and white sola topi, looking like nothing on earth and waving wildly to the Burmans on our boat, telling them to fetch me because he hadn't seen me for a year! Then he saw me and I just waved and dashed into my cabin. A minute later the boat was in an uproar - customs officers, police sergeants, port health officers all running around looking for me, did you ever! Then K - 'We're going to be married at once', says he, 'Got to be at the University at five forty-five - it's five now - hurry - everyone else will look after your things, just bring a suitcase'. I was all of a dither. The policeman snatched my passport from my hand, the Customs man dragged me to the smoke room for a bit of customs business, the Port Health man said, 'Come along, hurry, we'll never get there!' - All I can remember is a whole lot of passengers gaping in amazement, me completely bewildered, answering questions feverishly to all and sundry - thin policemen and fat policemen, and black and coffee-coloured and white men in all kinds of clothes. Then flung on to the Port Health launch and borne away to Rangoon.

K's car was garaged by the wharf, so we got into it plus suitcase carried by a large bearded policeman, and then to the Htin Si's house on the University Estate, and we sat in the drawing room waiting for the magistrate. When it was almost six o'clock and he hadn't turned up K got excited, rang him up and came back looking dashed, and said with an air of terrific indifference that the magistrate had been called away on urgent business and couldn't marry us till the next day. Instead we had cold drinks, and then Mrs Htin Si and K took me round to his flat, and then K took me to the de Glanvilles' where I spent the night. I realised then it was Mother's last attempt to prevent my marriage. The de Glanvilles both tried to talk me round, and Sir Oscar was very stern, while Lady de Glanville held my hand from time to time. In the end he said, 'I've got no power to stop you getting married, if you must', and I realised it had all been set up when he called the magistrate and said, 'It's alright, old boy, you can do it tomorrow'.

Husband and wife

I woke up at five and couldn't sleep again, so at about six o'clock in the morning I got out of bed and discovered, to my joy, a sort of balcony-like verandah leading out of my room. I went out on it and looked right down into Lady de Glanville's garden and said how do you do to all the flowers I used to know. There were a lot of little Burmese children running along the road going somewhere to bathe, very excited. Outside the house there was a pond and two Indians came down to it with a cow which they proceeded laboriously to bathe, and while I was enjoying it all a girl turned up with tea and toast and two boiled eggs, good and fresh. I got dressed for my wedding, wore a bamboo orchid Mrs Htin Si brought me to pin on my dress, and carried a great bunch of pink chrysanthemums just arrived from Kalaw, a present from Lady de Glanville. The magistrate came, and getting married was quickly done, and about six o'clock we went for a long drive by way of a honeymoon. K had a little two-seater Fiat and after the service and the tea party which included delicious spicy sausages on sticks and a wedding cake made by Mrs Htin Si ☞ | P 182 **SPICY SAUSAGES AND OYSTERS** |, he took me for a drive round Inya Lake. It was the end of the rains and we had such lovely sunset colours in the sky, gold and pink and red. Unfortunately, the car broke down and I had to board a bus (my first bus in Burma!) in all my wedding finery. I moved into K's flat that evening. He was Assistant Warden of Pegu Hall, one of the hostels for men students, so he had a rent-free flat there, and of course all the students were very interested in this notorious marriage. K put one of our favourite dance tunes on the gramophone player and we danced round the room by ourselves, with dozens of pairs of eyes peeping in at us through the window!

It was not only my family who opposed my marriage to K. Many of his friends objected to it too. His family were split on the matter, as they were split on all things, because the two sides of his family did not get on well. By this time, both his mother and father were dead, but the relatives continued to fight over what was appropriate for the children. Having been to England he was, after all, a good catch, and his mother's side of the family were good business people. They had ideas that he should marry one of his distant cousins, a very young and pretty girl. The woman who was particularly pressing for this match was a sister of his mother's, an aunt who ran a very successful rice and sesame oil shop in Rangoon. She employed Indian workers to grind sesame seeds on the premises, and she sold it in tins herself, sitting at a little desk. In later years, we used to go to her shop and buy a bag of rice and a tin of oil, but she would never give a relative a concessionary price. Her husband spent the whole day in a deckchair in front of the house. He was the man about the house, but all he needed to do was be a man and from time to time be her chauffeur. She gave him enough money to amuse himself at night, playing cards, or going to the bawdy house, but that was alright. Venereal disease in Burma is known as Children's Disease, the kind of thing you can expect from a man. She was very hostile to me even before we met and apparently, she warned K that if he married me he'd have to be able to keep me in silk knickers! When he finally introduced us she just set her mouth and turned her back.

On the other hand, K's paternal relatives were always very friendly towards me and visited us quite often in Rangoon. Pe Thaw, who was an adopted cousin of his, was particularly kind and ended up being one of my closest friends. After we had married, K told me firmly that he was a Burman and there were to be no birthdays, or Christmases in his household. I think that this was a result of the general hostility of his friends and relatives, and his determination to act on the Burmese maxim that when you marry a wife you must first kill a cat. But Pe Thaw turned up on Christmas day bringing me all kinds of little presents.

The card-dropping fraternity that I'd met in my parents' houses, both British and Burmese, entirely ignored me and my marriage. But I had felt absolutely no sense of loss, for I was not at all the social outcast Mother had prophesied I would be. All our university friends rallied round us, junior and senior staff,

Burmese and British alike, making me feel warmly welcome, and Gordon Luce even wrote a wedding poem for us written in a mixture of English and Burmese:

'We send with this a little cheque
Intended, if you will, to deck
A corner or a cubby-hole,
Or comfort your immortal soul
With peppered parsnips, scented tea,
Or bundled fish, or noni fruit,
Twelve kinds of ginger salad, golden rice,
Neat's tongue, pigs trotter, or shark's fin.

Poets must live: on ngapi* you,
As Waley's bard on badger stew;
Our Habibullah rats embraces,
And strictly meditates back drainage spaces -
Each Buddha has his peculiar carriage:
Oh may you ride to heaven on marriage!'

*Ngapi is fermented fish paste and a key ingredient of balachaung.
☞ | P 185 **BALACHAUNG** |

I think he was rather pleased that I had dared to marry K and he imagined a lovely Burmese household and the nice Burmese meals we'd have with fish baked in the leaves of the yeyo tree, ginger salad and balachaung.

When the opportunity to move into one of the small bungalows for junior staff arose, we seized it. Friends dropped in for pot-luck dinners, for tennis, for long cold drinks after long hot walks round Inya lake - and talk, talk, always talk, for there was nothing K liked better. We had to pay rent now, so I took a job tutoring at the University. Many of our Burmese friends were our contemporaries, staff or post-graduate students living on the Estate, among them the poets, Maung Wun (Minthuwun), Thein Han (Zawgyi) and Htin Fatt (Maung Htin). They were beginning to write experimental verse and prose, inventing simpler, more direct forms of expression and outraging scholars of classical Burmese and their literary establishment. K had fun translating the poems of Zawgyi and Minthuwun into English. He never wrote in Burmese - said he didn't know it well enough, while he was fascinated by the rich vocabulary of English.

Nationalist organizing: Dobama Asiayone and Thakhins

The university students had become more politicised since I had been away. The Do-Bama Society and the All Burma Youth League merged in 1934 to form the Dobama Asiayone to work along Gandhian civil disobedience lines, not for dominion status, but for the complete independence of Burma, as well as for wage increases for the working class, and the protection of the people from official oppression. The organisation's nationalist ideology allowed it to embrace royalists, fascists, and Fabian Socialists alike. Members called themselves Thakhin and Master or Thakhin Ma, the female equivalent, rather than the humbler prefixes of Maung or U meaning brother or uncle, and Ma or Daw meaning sister or aunt. Thakhin was the equivalent of the Hindi, 'Sahib' and usually used by Burmese when addressing Europeans. It quickly gained fashion among the young nationalists as signifying the new generation's determination to be the masters of their own country. Many of the older generation considered the title very arrogant. In 1936, the Thakhins won three seats in the Legislative Council as a 'wrecking party'.

As the Dobama Asiayone gained popular following, it moved away from the university to recruit peasants and workers, and the students formed their own nationalist group. This soon gained control of the Rangoon University Students' Union. It was led by Maung Nu and Aung San, both of course soon to be important nationalist leaders. They were among the earliest Thakhins and continued to maintain close personal ties with the Dobama Asiayone. Aung San was a self-possessed and charismatic young man - though he was so late in beginning to speak that he was believed to be dumb – he was as a student already widely loved, though regarded as a difficult character. K and I were responsible for discipline in Pegu Hall where he lived. His room was always in a mess. Books everywhere, on the table, on the bed, on the floor, and his bed always unmade. Grubby and surly, he was also clear thinking and practical, broadminded, above factionalism, honest, and deeply religious. K had a very strict 'lights out' policy but Aung San refused to comply. The third time K went to his room about it he told him that he had either to switch the light off or come out and fight him. Aung San did neither, and later K went into his room and removed the light bulb.

Aung San was editor of the student magazine *Oway 'Peacock's Call'*, and he was expelled for refusing to divulge the writer of an article called *'Hell Hound at Large'*, the Hell Hound being the bursar of Rangoon University. Maung Nu, then President of the Rangoon University Students' Union had also been expelled a few days earlier. The students went on strike in support of their leaders just three days before the college exams began. Then the school students came out on a sympathy strike, and this was only a matter of days before the High School exams were due to start. I was very irritated because all the exams were called off, and I lost Rs. 450 in exam fees alone. Such a nuisance as I'd been planning to buy a refrigerator with it.

Rosemary (with Jane and nanny behind), 1937

Against this background, K and I lived our private family life, but both of us very much part of the University: K as University Librarian, and I teaching at the University as well as managing my menage and having my three babies - Rosemary in July 1935, Jane in December 1936, and Susan in August 1939. When I found out about my first pregnancy my family sent me condolences! Father said his feelings about 'my news' were mixed, and K retorted that his were positively kaleidoscopic. Unfortunately K wanted a white baby too, but he was sure that it was going to be a brown one. In the event my first daughter, Rosemary, was indeed very brown, but he loved her just the same. She was such a determined little girl, refusing help when putting on her shoes and saying sternly, 'I do it myself!'

We had a half and half life. I had to start keeping house, and I had a number of Karen nannies. You sent a contact who knew people in the Karen village and a girl came. We were quite friendly with them. They didn't eat with us, but they ate the same food as we did, only after us. The exception was an Indian boy who wanted to eat his own food. We had a low Burmese table for them, round which they all sat and ate in the Burmese way. We would eat round that table too unless we had guests, when we had a proper dining table. K would also eat his breakfast at that table. For chota hazri he had bacon and eggs. There was one grocer in Rangoon that bought cold store food from England and you could get proper bacon not in a tin. I would go to Barnet Brothers and buy number one slice (the thinnest). I had to teach our Burmese cooks how to make steak and kidney pudding because he liked that too. At one stage he had tennis elbow and the doctor said it was vitamin deficiency and he ought to take Marmite. K got very addicted and it had to be put in everything. 'Marmi' our Burmese cook used to call it. ☞ | P 187
MAHOGANY BEEF PIE |

K and I had our ups and downs. He was dynamic, passionately interested in a great many things and quick to respond warmly to anyone sharing those interests and, indeed, quick to respond to congenial personalities who didn't share any of them. He was always good company because he was a cheerful bloke and had a ready wit. His sense of fun had a streak of cruelty in it, but he was never aggressively violent. He did like to hold the floor, his friends indulged him, and he had a great many of them. He truly loved his family and his home, but he preferred life to revolve round himself. He had little self-discipline and was notorious for getting up very late in the morning and spending a lot of money. But chiefly, he was lovable, and I loved him. Even Mother grew to like him.

Mother and Father return to Burma

My parents had decided to come back to Burma for good in 1934. Mother just didn't settle in England and they decided to come back to live in Kalaw. When K finally agreed to visit them, it was a tremendous success and he became great friends with Mother. They sat next to each other at meals, and vied with each other in telling funny stories, making witty conversation. She made sure that Burmese food was served alongside the rather drab European dishes, eating large quantities of nan gyi thoke with K. He said he liked Mother very much and had great respect for her brains and character. Until that visit he had claimed a noble and chivalrous pity for Alice which I found highly irritating, but by the time we left he said he hated her more than any other woman in the world.

Father with Sally and Puppy at The Grey House, 1938

I think she was jealous because he got on so well with Mother, but whatever the reason Alice behaved appallingly. She sulked mysteriously at him and was often most insultingly uncivil to him with no provocation whatever. When visitors called she would introduce me but not him, or say: 'Oh, you haven't met my sister, have you? This is my sister, and this is... murmur, murmur...', inaudibly with a look of shame and disgust on her face, turning away from K! I felt like sulking too and making scenes on such occasions, but they'd have been no good so I would just be cold with her for a few days. But that aside it was a highly successful visit and we both enjoyed it.

Mother too was pleasantly surprised when they came to visit us in Rangoon and found us living in a neat little bungalow with polished woodblock floors (very European), and not a concubine in sight! But she still couldn't get over the poor match I'd made and would needle me from time to time: 'My poor daughter! How hard you have to work! What it is to be a wife - a slave by day and a harlot by night!'

In those early years of motherhood, I was helped by my cousin, Tinch. My parents' return had been a devastating blow for her. She wanted desperately to stay behind in England. Whether she ever said so openly I don't know, though it seemed, from the dark hints dropped by Mother and Alice about her shocking and ungrateful behaviour, that some kind of confrontation had taken place. She was very sick on the boat back to Burma and complained to me that she had no one to talk to in 'everlasting first class', and she wished she could be in a different class so she could mix with the people who wanted to mix with her instead of having to sit next to Mr Percy Pottinger. I suppose like me, she too just didn't fit in naturally anywhere.

Meanwhile K was very busy learning to play the piano and read Western stave notation while at the same time examining Burmese musical instruments and discussing them with Burmese professional musicians and scholars. Minthuwun had written a series of Burmese nursery rhymes that delighted K now he was surrounded by babies, and he had fun translating them into English. The big sitting room was soon filled with his collection of musical instruments: a full set of Burmese drums, a Burmese xylophone, a piano, a new oboe he had ordered from London which he was now teaching himself to play, a Burmese oboe to compare it with, cymbals, bamboo clappers - the lot. What with K's musical triumphs and my promotion to a lectureship, life seemed good.

Indian separation and violence

However, after Jane was born in December 1936, the political situation in Burma became much more fraught. Separation from India was instigated on

1st April 1937, and there were mass protests outside the High Court organised by the Thakhins, and U, now Thakhin Nu, was one of those who stepped out and burned the British flag! There were strikes and unrest all over the country and they lasted until the outbreak of what we called the 'European war'. Most of them were strikes by people like sugar workers and saw mill workers and they did not have a direct effect on us, but we were worried by the oil strike which went on for over a year, and of course we felt it when the rickshaw pullers and bus drivers came out on strike.

The Prime Minister at the time was Dr Ba Maw who had been Hsaya San's lawyer and I was quite sympathetic to the aims of the party he led, the Sinyetha or 'Poor Man's Party'. It called for changes like tax reduction, lower rent, village reconstruction, and compulsory free education. But Dr Ba Maw was not popular. He was an urbane chap and I remember seeing a newspaper cartoon of him split down the middle, half European, half Burman and thinking he was like me! It was impossible for him to implement most of his radical policies, though he did legalise the (now toothless) Wunthanu Athins.

Then there was more anti-Indian feeling whipped up by the press, and riots and massacres and looting. Indians and Muslims were considered more or less the same people and they were all called 'Kala' which means Black, and is rather derogatory. The trouble began with the publication of some extracts from a pamphlet allegedly written by a Burmese Muslim, Maung Shwe Hpi. It turned out later that it had been originally published seven years previously in response to a tract written by a Burmese Buddhist that was offensive to Islam, and at that time had attracted no attention [12]. In July 1938, Mother was visiting us in Rangoon, and I remember well her commenting on a piece in *The Sun* newspaper which was very anti-Muslim and referred to Indians as people who have 'taken possession of the wealth of the Burmese people and also their daughters and sisters'. *The Sun* was owned by an opportunistic opposition politician called U Saw, the leader of the nationalist Myochit Party, and it began a sustained anti-Indian campaign. A few days later I had to send K out to rescue Mother. She had gone to the Shwedagon Pagoda in her usual devout fashion, but there was a mass meeting there to protest at Maung Shwe Hpi's pamphlet. K said that speakers were openly supporting the massacre of Indians. Afterwards a hardcore of around a thousand Burmans marched to the Rangoon's Indian bazaar. 'Kala-kala Yaik-yaik' (Indians! Beat them up!). 'Bama-ma-dwe. Bama-pyi-hma-in-sha-lo-la!' (Burmese women with Indians - aren't there enough husbands in Burma?). Arming themselves along the way with bricks and bamboo, sticks and stones they attacked any Indian they happened to meet: they tore down their stalls, destroyed their rickshaws, forced them from trams to beat them up. As the mob reached the Sootee Bara Bazaar, Indians

[12] Further details about the background to the riots can be found in the Final Report of the Riot Inquiry Committee, published in Rangoon in 1939. Available from https://ia801609.us.archive.org/22/items/in.ernet.dli.2015.206317/2015.206317.Final-Report.pdf

were frantically dismantling their stalls while trying to protect themselves from a hail of stones. It was chaos, and poor Mother was absolutely terrified. The riot was eventually broken up by a police charge, and several rioters were wounded including a pongyi.

The next day the newspapers including *The Sun* were full of the story, but it was cast in a very anti-Indian light. Prominent on their pages were pictures, not of the dozens of Indians wounded, but of the pongyi, lying on the ground. He looked dead but he wasn't, and the coverage only inflamed the situation. Not only were the Indians ruining the country, they were being protected by the wretched imperialists. The next day was even worse. One of Mother's friends visited and started claiming that the Indians were setting up a secret army and were selling poisoned parathas and roasted peas. Well we had an Indian cook and he had not joined a secret army and his parathas were absolutely delicious. ☞ | P 189 **ALOO PARATHAS AND LIME PICKLE** | The problem was that he was not able to go out and buy food as Indians on the street were attacked and killed. The upheaval was not confined to Rangoon. As the newspapers arrived in the districts the disturbances spread. Indians and Burmese Muslims who had inhabited the same village for years, if not generations, were murdered by friends and neighbours, their homes burnt down, their possessions destroyed.

I felt the newspapers should take a lot of the blame. U Saw had played the populist card to further his own political ambitions and a few weeks after the disturbances he tried to unseat Dr Ba Maw with a vote of no confidence, but the Europeans would not support him. It was alleged U Saw had connections with a section of the new generation of pongyis who had lost the leadership of the popular nationalist movement but were continuing to assert Buddhist values and riding on a Buddhist revival.

The troubles spread to the University

The University campus was not free of the disturbances. There was a row right outside the University Library when a posse of police with two Burmese boys under arrest passed by just as students were leaving one of the lecture rooms. The students started shouting, 'Shame!' and demanded the boys' release. In the middle of all this a car exhaust went off with a terrific bang and there was panic in my English lecture rooms and the students rushed out. The trouble was that the university authorities had been rather absurd in the way they treated the students. All information about the riots had been kept from them and they were virtually imprisoned in the hostels. So they all got excited as rumours spread that awful atrocities were being perpetrated on the Burmese. Later that evening a mass meeting of students was held and there appeared at the doorway, most miraculously - Dr Ba Maw. He spoke to them calmly with great sense and tact. What was all this fuss about? Burmans massacred? Not a bit of it. Quite the contrary. Government and police unable to cope with the situation? Come, come! And then he went on to say how mob-minded, sub-intelligent, hysterical, and totally venal were those who took part in the riots. University students would see that the only useful service they could render their Motherland was to go out as rescue parties, rescuing with magnanimous indiscrimination Indians and Burmans alike. 'Now how about choosing some delegates among yourselves – I'll take them round the town in my car to show them that all I say is true and just'. And so the delegates were chosen, went off, and the next day the university was crawling with Red Cross cars driven by students.

The students continued to agitate though and by the end of the year some students were even in jail for the support they offered the oil strike leaders. The student body and schoolchildren went on strike again, demanding the release of their companions and the cancellation of repressive law and order measures. On the 19th December, they decided to picket the Secretariat, the nerve centre of British administration in Rangoon. This huge Victorian, yellow building shaped like a square U was surrounded by extensive grounds and bound by an iron fence with nine gates. On December 20th about two thousand students blocked these gates and withstood all police attempts to move them. They began to congregate in one corner right opposite *The Sun* Press building, to listen to speeches before leaving. At this point, the students were rushed, unprovoked, by the police. Eighty people were injured, many of them children, three of them very seriously. Members of the House of Representatives and the press watched from the balcony of *The Sun* building screaming at the police to stop. The unedifying spectacle of European police officers beating girls with wooden batons two feet long and two inches wide was recorded. There was no denying the witnesses' descriptions of students lying in pools of blood, of blows to the stomach, face and chest, of police pulling away those trying to help the injured to continue their beatings, though the police raided *The Sun* offices and seized the negatives of photographs. As K pointed out, it was easy enough to disclaim charges of police brutality in the districts – which he claimed was a fairly routine state of affairs - but against unarmed young people outside a press building in Rangoon, before so many distinguished witnesses, was rather more difficult.

The Sun of course reported it in detail and they had been given a key item of evidence. A young student called Aung Gyaw had been hit twice on the head by a European sergeant, the second time so hard the stick snapped in two. One of the broken pieces of the stick flew to the feet of another student who, horrified by what he had seen, picked it up and gave it to *The Sun* newspaper. Three days later Maung Aung Gyaw died of his injuries and the Governor declared a state of emergency in the city before Maung Aung Gyaw's funeral on the 27th December. The ceremony attracted hundreds of thousands of mourners. A feeling of general insecurity began to hang over our lives. Police were given the right to commandeer public vehicles for police and military use without the owners' consent and there was a public outcry, buses and trams went on strike, leaving only pony carts and rickshaws on the road. There was talk of a general strike to add to the chaos, and several Thakhins were arrested.

I agreed with Furnivall that the neglected educational system was the source of a lot of the problems, but there were also problems with the bickering in the Legislative Assembly, and ongoing disputes about separation with India. Anti-separationists clung to India, desperate to learn from her greater maturity in political organisation and ideas and fearful of not sharing in any constitutional advancement she may gain from HMG. Separationists clung to national identity, resenting Indians as foreigners in their country, who always got the better of them because they are so much cleverer at making money. Rabble-rousing demagogues were ordering strikes with no organisation for maintaining strikers and their families while the strike lasted, but setting the masses shouting slogans learnt from India. One of the slogans was 'Wreck the Constitution!'. A group of Burmese women who held a meeting at the Shwedagon Pagoda came to a weirdly assorted set of resolutions including:

1. They will see to it the country devoutly observes the practices of the Buddhist religion.
2. They will have no more inter-marriage with foreigners.
3. They will wreck the constitution.

College had closed early because the strike made teaching impossible and university exams, usually held at the beginning of March, were scheduled for the end of the month which meant my long vacation would be late starting.

Then a demonstration was fired on in Mandalay, leaving seventeen people dead, and Dr Ba Maw resigned. He was replaced by U Pu who did not command much support. Really the whole situation was a mess.

SPICY SAUSAGES AND OYSTERS

Serves 4 | prepare 45 mins | cook 20 mins | medium difficulty

Called sai long phik in the Shan States and sai ua in neighbouring Chiang Mai, these sausages are not to be confused with the no less delicious fermented pork sausages from Isaan province in Thailand. I suspect the Valencian health inspector would throw her arms up in horror if we were to ferment pork sausages at Ma Khin Café, so we opt for this safer option where the pork is flavoured with aromatic herbs and red curry paste. It was the great Alastair Little who married these spicy sausages to oysters. Surf and turf has never been better than this.

INGREDIENTS

For the red curry paste:

8 long dried red chillies
2cm piece galangal
6 shallots
4 cloves garlic
1 stalk lemon grass
½ tsp turmeric powder
Zest of 1 lime
1 tsp fermented fish paste
1 tsp palm sugar

For the sausages:

400g fatty ground pork
6 kaffir lime leaves
1 tbsp ginger grated
2 stalks lemon grass
2 tbsp chopped coriander
1 medium onion
4 tbsp fish sauce

For the shallot relish:

4 finely sliced shallots
100ml white wine vinegar
¼ tsp sugar
¼ tsp salt
1 tsp white pepper

For the oysters:

16 oysters, loosened from their shells (shucked)

To make the curry paste, break the stems off the chillies and shake out the seeds. Soak them in cold water for two hours. Peel and coarsely chop the galangal, shallots and garlic. Remove any discoloured outer leaves from the lemon grass and chop coarsely. Put all the ingredients in a small food processor and mix to a paste.

To make the sausages, chop the lemon grass finely. Carefully tear the tough central vein from the lime leaves and chop them as finely as possible. Put all the ingredients in a mixing bowl with a generous tablespoon of the curry paste and blend well by squeezing the mixture through your fingers. Roll spoonfuls of the mixture into golf ball sized pieces and form into a fat sausage. Place on a baking tray until ready to use.

In a lightly oiled frying pan, seal the sausages over a medium flame, turning so that they brown on all sides. Transfer to a baking tray and cook for 12 minutes in a preheated oven at 180°C.

Mix together the ingredients for the shallot relish and serve in small dipping bowls alongside the sausages and shucked oysters.

BALACHAUNG

Makes 1 small jar | prepare 15 mins | cook 30 mins | medium difficulty

If I were to choose one recipe from this book that sums up Burmese food it would be balachaung. The pungent smell of fish paste, with the fiery heat of chillies and the crispy texture of garlic and shallots make this my relish of choice. The secret to good balachaung is to get the ingredients as crispy as possible without any bitter hints from burnt ingredients. The frying process needs your full attention so switch off your mobile phone and make sure you have everything ready before you start cooking! The finished balachaung keeps well in a tightly sealed jar in the fridge as does the oil used for frying the ingredients which is great for dressing salads.

INGREDIENTS

500ml sunflower oil
30g dried shrimp (page 26)
100g shallots
6 large cloves garlic
1 tbsp ginger grated
¼ tsp chilli powder
¼ tsp turmeric
1 tsp fermented shrimp paste (available from Chinese supermarkets)
1-2 tsp chilli flakes

Peel the shallots and garlic and slice them as thinly as you can. Boil the shrimp for five minutes in 500ml of water to remove some of the saltiness. Drain and dry on paper towels. Whizz the drained shrimp in a small food processor.

Have ready 2 suitable pans for deep frying. In one of the pans, heat the oil to 160°C. Place the second pan nearby with a metal sieve on top ready to strain the ingredients the moment they are crispy. Deep fry the shallots in the hot oil. Stir occasionally at the beginning and frequently as they start to colour. The initial colouring takes a while to appear, but once this starts, the shallots quickly turn brown, so keep an eye on them or they will burn. Carefully strain the shallots through the sieve, recovering the hot oil in the second pan. Shake the sieve to remove any excess oil and spread the crispy shallots on a tray lined with kitchen paper. Now reheat the oil in the second pan and fry the sliced garlic in the same way, straining the oil again to recover the crispy garlic.

Reheat the oil for a third time and deep fry the ginger and shrimp floss for 5 minutes. Add the fermented shrimp paste, chilli powder and turmeric and strain immediately. Recover the ginger and shrimp mixture and dry it on kitchen paper.

Put the crispy shallots, garlic and the savoury fried shrimp in a mortar and pound lightly to break up the pieces. Stir in the chilli flakes to taste. I like to sprinkle this crispy, dry mixture onto rice, but if you prefer you can stir a few tablespoons of the savoury oil into the dry ingredients and serve a spoonful alongside your favourite curries.

MAHOGANY BEEF PIE

Serves 6 | prepare 45 mins | cook stew 120 mins, pie 30 mins | medium difficulty

Steak and kidney pudding has a bad name in my book. School dinners are to blame, as I remember gristly trimmings of meat floating in a watery gravy that smelt vaguely of ammonia, with the whole horrid mess wrapped in a soggy suet pastry. Our mahogany beef pie is as rich as the names suggests: its wonderful colour and depth of flavor enhanced by the addition of hoisin sauce. You can buy dried mandarin peel in Chinese supermarkets (it sometimes comes in a mixed bag of spices with star anise, cassia bark and fennel seeds). Alternatively add freshly grated orange zest.

INGREDIENTS

700g stewing steak
1 tbsp plain flour
½ tsp salt
4 tbsp sunflower oil
1 large onion peeled and finely chopped
4 cloves garlic peeled and finely chopped
2 star anise
8 cloves
5cm piece cinnamon
200ml red wine
460g tin chopped tomatoes
500ml chicken stock (page 29)
2 tbsp hoisin sauce
1 piece of dried mandarin peel
2 medium carrots peeled and sliced
150g baby onions
150g button mushrooms
1 packet puff pastry
1 egg

Cut the stewing steak into 4cm chunks. Mix the flour with the salt and dust the meat with this, shaking off any excess. In a heavy cast iron casserole dish with a lid, heat 2 tablespoons of the oil and brown the meat in batches over a high flame. Set the browned meat to one side and heat the remaining two tablespoons of oil in the casserole. (If the casserole dish has not burnt while browning the meat you don't need to wash it). Sauté the chopped onion until it begins to brown. Quickly add the garlic and whole spices and continue to cook for a few minutes. Now add the tomatoes and continue to cook, stirring frequently. Return the meat to the pan and add the red wine. Boil vigorously until the wine has reduced and there is only a little liquid left. Pour in the stock, bring to the boil then cover the casserole and cook for 1.5 hours in a preheated oven at 160°C.

Meanwhile blanche the carrots in boiling salted water for 3 minutes. Lift the carrots from the water with a slotted spoon and refresh in iced water. Repeat this process with the baby onions. Peel the onions leaving enough of the root to hold the onion together. Trim the roots from the button mushrooms and wipe off any soil. Heat a tablespoon of oil in a small frying pan and sautée the mushrooms for a few minutes until they begin to soften and brown. Set aside.

Remove the casserole from the oven and stir in the onions, carrots and mushrooms together with the hoisin sauce and the mandarin peel (or orange zest). Return the casserole to the oven for a further 30 minutes by which time the meat should be tender. Allow the casserole to cool and store the stew in the refrigerator or freeze.

When you are ready to make the pie, reheat the stew and pour into a prepared pie dish. Cover with the defrosted puff pastry, trimming it to fit over the pie and allowing a 2cm overlap. Pinch the edges of the pastry to form an attractive pleat. Beat the egg and glaze the pastry. Place the pie in a preheated oven at 180°C for 25 minutes. Allow to rest for 10 minutes before serving with a simple green salad and some boiled new potatoes.

ALOO PARATHAS AND LIME PICKLE

Serves 4 | prepare 45 mins + 30 mins resting | cook 15 mins | medium difficulty

This has to be one of my favourite breakfast dishes. I learned to love it on a holiday in Himachal Pradesh, Northern India. The mornings were crisp even though it was summer, and a cup of chai tea with aloo parathas and lime pickle was our daily breakfast, just the thing to prepare us for another day's ascent - though in truth nothing could have prepared us for the extraordinary scenery we witnessed on that trip through the peaks of the Himalayas.

Amchoor powder is made from dried mangoes and gives a delightful tang to the parathas. If you can't get hold of it from an Indian grocers, try substituting with a teaspoon of liquid tamarind or lime juice. Ghee is clarified butter, easily made by heating unsalted butter and skimming off the white scum that forms on the surface. The clarified butter remaining is ghee.

LIME PICKLE:

To make the lime pickle, cut the limes in half and then each half into four pieces. Put the pieces in a tray with the pieces of fresh green chilli and sprinkle with the turmeric, paprika, chilli powder, salt and sugar. Heat the oil in a small frying pan and fry the cumin, mustard and fenugreek seeds until the mustard seeds begin to pop. Allow the oil to cool then pour the mixture over the limes. Mix everything well and pack the limes into a sterilized 2 litre Kilner jar. Seal and place in a window where they will receive lots of sunlight. Invert the jar every day so that the spices and juices mix thoroughly. After about three weeks the pickle will be ready.

INGREDIENTS

For the lime pickle:
12 limes
1 large fresh green chilli chopped with seeds
1 tbsp turmeric
1 tsp paprika
½ tsp chilli powder
60g coarse sea salt
30g sugar
3 tbsp sunflower oil
1 tsp cumin seeds
1 tsp mustard seeds
1 tsp fenugreek seeds

ALOO PARATHAS:

INGREDIENTS

For the potato stuffing:

1 medium potato (about 200g)

1 small fresh green chilli

¼ tsp red chilli powder

½ tsp garam masala

½ tsp amchoor (dried mango powder)

1 tbsp chopped coriander

Salt

2 tbsp ghee

For the dough:

300g wheat flour

½ tsp salt

1 tbsp melted ghee

100ml water

To make the potato filling, boil the potato in its skin, then peel and mash with a potato ricer. Add the rest of the ingredients and mix well.

For the parathas, put the flour in a mixing bowl. Make a well in the centre and add half the water, the ghee and salt. Mix with your hand, gradually adding more water until the dough comes together to form a ball. Knead gently on a lightly floured surface for a few minutes until smooth and elastic. Return the dough ball to the bowl and cover with a damp cloth. Set aside for 30 minutes.

Pinch two small balls from the dough about 3cm in diameter. Roll out each ball on a floured surface to a diameter of about 12cm. Place a spoonful of potato stuffing in the centre of one of the rounds and spread it out leaving about 3cm around the edge. Place the second piece of dough on top and press the edges together. Working gently, roll out this 'sandwich' of dough to a diameter of about 18cm.

Heat a wide skillet and place the paratha on top. When the base is partly cooked, flip it over. With a pastry brush, spread some ghee on the partly cooked surface. Flip the paratha again, and paint ghee on the second side. When the base is cooked, flip the paratha for a third time and finish cooking. You should see crisp brown spots on the surface and the whole process should take about 3 minutes. (If it takes longer the pan may not be hot enough, and the paratha will be dry). Serve with lime pickle.

WAR
(1939-1943)

'Colonialism's difficulty...'

A few months later in September 1939 World War 2 broke out. It seemed far away and something that would touch us directly only because of our brothers and sisters in England. Indeed, I felt terribly conscience-stricken because we were so safe and luxuriously provided with a million things while they were in constant danger of air raids and having to put up with so many shortages. Still, political tension was growing and K and I felt growing sympathy for the nationalist cause. This sympathy was fuelled by the outrage we shared with many people in Burma after the Governor's speech to the Senate and Legislature on the outbreak of war. There, he claimed that, 'Smaller states are just as entitled as larger states to live and enjoy their independent national rights in peace and not under continual menace,' and 'The resort to force destroys the security on which only peace and prosperity can be built'. I mean, really, wasn't Burma a 'smaller' state too?

'Colonialism's difficulty is Freedom's opportunity!' was the new slogan. About the streets there were red and blue posters showing a Burman leading Burmese troops waving the Dobama flag about to spear a gorilla labelled with a Union Jack and underneath a warning to the 'deceitful monkeys' to leave the country. There were rallies with slogans like 'May the British be Bombed and Defeated,' and 'Long Live Revolution'. The rallies included Indians, and the Governor proscribed Hindus and Muslims from taking part in processions. K opined that the Brits would rather the Burmans were burning Indians' homes than marching with them. The press continued its hostility to U Pu and his ministry for kowtowing to the British as he supported the war effort unconditionally. His position was becoming more and more untenable and he lashed out. Many of our students were by now on the run or in prison and Maung Nu was in Insein Jail. In September 1940, U Pu's Ministry was defeated on a no-confidence motion when U Saw, who had been U Pu's Agricultural and Forestry Minister, changed allegiances. U Saw who had, if you asked me, long harboured the highest political ambitions, was at last Prime Minister of Burma.

U Saw in government was far less radical than U Saw out of government. He agreed to enter into as full a co-operation as possible with the British, downgrading his call for independence to a request for Dominion status. The new Governor thought he was a splendid fellow and his reputation flourished among the British as a loveable rogue. To the Burmese he was considered even more repressive than U Pu. He revived traditional Burmese practices towards royalty, with himself standing in as King, which was regarded as blasphemy by many Burmese. It was, they said, only a matter of time before some terrible evil would befall him in punishment.

Burma was strategically importantly positioned and we were flooded with 'goodwill missions' from Thailand, and particularly from China. The Burma Road, linking Northern Burma to Kunming was by 1939 the only remaining land supply route to Chiang Kai-shek. Burma was being used to send armaments into China with no customs duty! Burma was too noble to want to profit from China's troubles by exacting customs duty on them. But some argued that Burma's interests were not at stake, so why should she forego her rightful dues? The purpose of the goodwill missions from China was to touch Burmese hearts so that they wouldn't insist on customs duties, and to teach the Burmese in speeches up and down the country that China and Burma were bound by close racial and cultural ties - brothers in the sight of God. Anyway, the customs' impasse was broken by Britain promising to make good the losses suffered by Burma not charging the duties.

This was in the context of the Second Sino-Japanese war, as well as the rise of Mao Tse Tung's Communist Army. The British, while supporting the Kuomintang against the Japanese invaders, were not confident of the former's capability to crush the growing Communist army. They were increasingly anxious to support negotiations between Japan and Chiang Kai-shek, believing Japan to be the more efficient anti-Communist force. At one point, they even closed the Burma Road and cut off supplies to the Kuomintang in an effort to wean Japan from Germany and avoid a Japanese attack on their forces in Southeast Asia. The Road was reopened in October, when the Japanese, with the collaboration of the Vichy Regime, entered Indo-China.

At the time, the rumour was that Japan was going to step across from Indo-China via Thailand into Burma and I thought it, quite honestly, ridiculous. Plans were made to evacuate University College to a safer place - guess where? A little way up country on two hundred acres of scrubland with not a hut to be seen with the Irrawaddy for water supply! I had visions of my three little girls carrying buckets of filthy Irrawaddy water to a bamboo shed where I cooked a pot of rice over three bricks and a bunch of wet sticks. In September 1941, I wrote in a letter to Mary: 'I don't know the truth about Burma's defences: it is alleged that they are impregnable, but I'm not bothered, and you mustn't bother either because war is not likely here. Japan is a dainty stepper when she walks among great powers.' ☞ | P 207 **CHA CA VIETNAMESE FISH** | & | P 208 **MUSSELS IN GREEN CURRY** |

Aung San slips away

In the confusion, Aung San had slipped away, and it turned out later he had left for China disguised as a Chinese crewman on a Norwegian boat. Nationalists maintained that when he left he carried with him an introduction to the Chinese Communist Party, seeking their support, but Dr Ba Maw claimed that the escape was planned by him in collaboration with the Japanese with the help of Ba Maw's Japanese doctor. Bluff, double bluff, error, or a rewriting of history, the fact remains that Aung San ended up in Japan. In February 1941, he returned briefly to Burma to collect thirty Thakhin volunteers for military training in Japan. They became known as the Thirty Comrades and, aided by a Japanese Colonel, Colonel Suzuki, they hatched a Burmese revolution.

Then in early September 1941, Churchill announced that the Atlantic Charter's recognition of the right of people to choose their own government did not apply to any part of the British Empire. One law for the white people and another for the rest, was the accusation. U Saw went to London to visit Churchill and the Secretary of State for India, Mr Amery. He was clear that he was not going simply to kiss Mr Churchill's hand and would return with a promise of Dominion Status, but Churchill and Amery barely found time to meet with him and were not prepared to entertain any serious discussion on Burma's status. U Saw left Britain insulted and disappointed. The Japanese option in these circumstances could only become more attractive. U Saw was arrested for making contact with the Japanese and offering collaboration in return for independence and he spent the rest of the war in detention in Uganda. And he was behind the curve. On December 29th 1941 Colonel Suzuki and Thakhin Aung San's party had reached Bangkok and organised the Burma Independence Army (BIA) with Bo Mogyo (Colonel Suzuki) as commander-in-chief.

The beginning of upheaval

'Do not listen to rumours. Here is the news', was how every news bulletin from Rangoon Radio began in those weeks and months before Pearl Harbour, and the news was designed to comfort and reassure us, so not interesting at all. The rumours were much more exciting, and there were lots of them: Aung San had disappeared! He'd been arrested and thrown in jail! No, he hadn't - he'd gone to Japan! He'd taken a lot of his friends with him! Can't be - how could they have got to Japan? Don't you know? Rangoon is full of Japanese agents - that dentist, he's a spy; and that shoemaker - he's a spy too! In the autumn of 1941, the government announced a 'Stay Put Policy': Burma was to be defended and, as the chief port, Rangoon was to be kept open at all costs. But the Japanese bombing of Pearl Harbour changed everything.

I wrote to Mary on the 8th December 1941: 'Well, sweetie, it's come, and what a relief. Thank goodness I have neither a new-born baby nor a baby on the way. I think we shall be safe enough in Rangoon. The latest notion is that there should be the minimum of evacuation which seems to me sound enough. Disorganisation is the chief danger: we suffer in this country from a complete inability to lead orderly lives (K would say "Speak for yourself, untidy woman. See how methodical I am" - and he's got something there). I am not depressed. Our house is an ARP post, so there's lots to do, and even if College closes I shall have no lack of occupation. The family is very fit and ready for anything.'

Of course, I was not as serenely cheerful as I made myself out to be. I distinctly remember going into College, the morning after Pearl Harbour and talking to a very excited Myo Min who was cock-a-hoop at the thought that here was Burma's opportunity to throw off the hated colonial yoke. 'Yes', I said 'but think of all the slaughter before that happens. It's all very well for you, you've got no children, but I have'. However, I remember too, that vaguely fearful though I was I hadn't the remotest idea of how great an upheaval war was to bring about, not only in our lives but across the world.

Things moved fast from then on. For a week or two we went on lecturing, but it became known that college would not reopen after Christmas. At night, air raid wardens came to our house to report after their rounds. Gordon Luce was one of them, and he'd sometimes bring a page or two of his 'work in progress' at the time, his magnum opus, a history of Burma and of Pagan, so it was fun when he came. Not that we took the prospect of air raids lightly, for we knew well enough that now when sirens sounded they'd be for real and no longer just for practice. We'd got an air-raid shelter in our garden and as I remember it was always in the very early hours of the morning - about four or five o'clock that the sirens would sound and we'd have to rush to get the children up and into the shelter. I always put on my after-tennis jacket to go into the shelter. That was because I'd sewn into its lapel all the money we had left in the bank.

One hundred bombs

The Japanese stepped up propaganda broadcasts in Burmese from Tokyo and promised Rangoon a Christmas present of one hundred bombs - which they duly delivered, causing havoc in the city. I remember on the 23rd of December driving back from the railway station, where I had gone to collect a Christmas hamper of vegetables which Mother had sent down from Kalaw, when suddenly bombs began to drop. Indian coolies and labourers ran out of buildings and into the streets and cars driving madly ran them over because it was every man for himself. I had taken a student with me for companionship, and it was lucky that I had for he directed me to the house of a friend of his who had an air-raid shelter, and we stayed there until the all-clear sounded. The worst thing was listening to the bombs and not knowing where it was they were landing or if one was going to drop on you. We were lucky. There was silence, the all clear sounded and back we drove with our precious hamper of vegetables. I also slipped into my after-tennis jacket pocket half a dozen hand-made silver coffee spoons I'd got in my Christmas basket from Kalaw.

There was another air raid on 25th December, and in both, it was mostly Indian coolies who were killed. There was panic and a breakdown in law and order. I think that the Indians were terrified that the Burmese would also start attacking them again and thousands of them left the city for Prome, en route to India. But Rangoon could not function without them and British officers rode out to dissuade them. They informed them of the dangers along the way, of the lack of food and water at the Taungup Pass, and the government ordered that all supplies to Taungup should be halted and people at Prome be stopped from crossing the river. The labourers were promised work, accommodation in safe camps outside the city, and free food. By the end of the week most of those who had left had turned back. The government had also issued an order forbidding Indian men to travel as deck passengers from Rangoon unless they were accompanying six women and/or children. This effectively meant that all male Indian labourers had to stay because the deck passengers were the cheap tickets. The wealthy maistries, the gangmasters who were the only contact between employer and labourer and who could afford more expensive tickets, were able to leave however, and it was difficult to co-ordinate the return to work. The city was grinding to a halt.

Evacuation and retreat

For many weeks, ever since the British warships the *Repulse* and the *Prince of Wales* had been sunk by the Japanese, I had been writing agitated letters to Father begging him to get out of Burma while there were still ships sailing to India, so that he and Mother and Alice could travel in relative comfort and take a few precious things with them, for I was sure now that Singapore would fall and sea traffic to India would become more and more dangerous. Father was angry that I should even speak of Singapore falling, and declared he wasn't going to run away. But by mid-February Singapore had fallen and the Japanese were well into south-eastern Burma. I took the children up to Kalaw and kept up the pressure on Father to leave for India, with little success until an army officer was sent to Kalaw from Taunggyi to tell residents of a plan to evacuate the town 'very soon', but when exactly he didn't say. Frantic plans were made to rent the house to the Sawbwa of Hsipaw. People who wished to be evacuated should start packing, the officer said, but would only be allowed thirty pounds of luggage each. Mother buried all the silver and precious things we had in the garden, as she didn't want it looted by the Japanese or anyone else come to that. A week later we heard a rumour that we were to leave at noon in two days' time. We hurried to finish our packing and to make arrangements and on Friday, 13th March 1942, we were at the railway station to board the evacuee train that was to come from Taunggyi at midday. ☞ | P 211 **SHAN NOODLE SOUP** |

Retreat from Burma

The military retreat from Burma has been extensively documented of course, but apart from Hugh Tinker's *'A Forgotten Long March'*[13], the movement of more than half a million Indians across the border to India has been forgotten. Even on the easy, first leg of the journey up to Prome, where there was enough food and water, they were exhausted. Cholera broke out, weakening them further, and the Prome-Taungup route was littered with corpses. On March 7th, the Rangoon garrison left the city, demolishing the port, the electric power station and the Syriam oilfields. The prison and asylum had been opened to free the inmates, the animals in the zoo had been shot. On March 8th, Rangoon was in the hands of the Japanese, and the Lower Burma route was effectively closed. The way out was now via Mandalay and the exhausted refugees turned north and were joined by Indians from all the major towns they passed through. Tinker describes truly awful scenes, where Indians were effectively pushed out of the way to facilitate the passing of the British army which laid hands on all supplies and transport. Yet this march of 600,000, of whom between 50,000 and 100,000 died, has been forgotten, no personal testimonies were collected or written, despite official admiration for their brave conduct.

I read the description by Tinker with horror when it was published in 1975. I remembered our own experiences leaving Burma, which were far milder but still awful. Indeed, I am still angry when I remember that dreadful journey across Burma westwards to Shwebo from where we were to fly to India. It took two whole days, with long stops at some intermediate stations when we'd get out of the train to wash and fill water bottles. I said goodbye to K at Thazi junction, not knowing when or if we would ever see each other again. Indeed, shortly afterwards Thazi was subjected to a horrendous bombing and for several weeks I had no idea whether K was living or dead.

---

[13] Hugh Tinker's 1975 journal article, 'A Forgotten Long March: The Indian Exodus from Burma, 1942' published in the *Journal of South East Asian Studies*, is available free online at https://www.jstor.org/stable/20070108?seq=1#page_scan_tab_contents

K in uniform

When we said our goodbyes, he was sad, but I could see also excited in his army gear, ready to fight the Japanese. I shared no such feelings. The carriage had nothing but hard wooden benches to sit or lie on, and it was filthy; the lavatory adjoining it had neither basin with running water nor WC; instead it had a hole in the wooden floor, and it stank. I was angry - furiously angry - that my father, an old and sick man who had served the Raj with devotion and distinction for more than forty years should have been treated so scurvily. I looked out at scenes of devastation. Trains, vans and trucks were left, twisted skeletons, strewn along roadsides, marked by blackened tree stumps and ash; oil wells blazing and pumping thick, black smoke into the air, cranes and bridges crashing down. Allied and Japanese bombing flattened the landscape; all cities and large towns were reduced to rubble. I later learned that Mandalay burned for a month and the beautiful great palace of the Old Kings of Burma was destroyed.

Arrival in India, 1942

Of our flight from Shwebo and the journey from Chittagong to Calcutta I remember little in detail, but a few vivid pictures stand out: Jane, sick all the way and crying all the time in the plane (a Chinese troop carrier). Excited crowds of Indians peering in at us refugees through the windows as our train stopped somewhere on the way to Calcutta. Herded into army buses by British soldiers and driven to Fort William. The indescribable filth of our crowded quarters. Susan, who was a toddler at the time, developed the most awful diarrhoea and I decided I needed to leave Fort William and stay at the Grand Hotel and pay for a doctor as I feared she might die. I paid for it all with money from my jacket lapel.

Susan was not yet recovered when a British Tommy suddenly turned up with 'Tomorrow you will entrain for Dehra Dun.' That first night in the Gurkha barracks at Dehra Dun the children cried all night, and mothers' flashing torches discovered enormous bugs in the beds - like torpedoes! Baths in tents, food in tents, Susan still ill. Again, the order 'Tomorrow you will entrain for Ranikhet' - where was Ranikhet? Wherever it was, we were met at Ranikhet by a bevy of beautiful army ladies who handed out directions to the drivers where each car load was to be taken, and to each family a number of big gunny bags and small blankets. We were dropped at a small stone cottage and there we stayed for a few months. Rosemary and Jane went to the garrison school and began to lose their Burmese. A soldier came one day to ask if I was 'desirous of embarking for the United Kingdom' and I said no. I was waiting for K as he had got news to me that he was coming out of Burma having been seconded to the Government of India Department of Information and Broadcasting.

K follows us to India

After K left us in Thazi he returned to Rangoon and he found his unit temporarily stationed at the university. They did not stay in Burma. He arrived in Delhi in 1942 and started work as the supervisor of Burmese broadcasts at All India Radio (AIR). He settled very happily into the job for which he had been generously recommended by the previous incumbent, our old friend Ma Than Aye, the singer and educationalist, who had come over to India with WAS (B) (Women's Auxiliary Service, Burma), which she had joined when Japan entered the war. She continued to work in the Unit, together with three young Burmans, Win Pe, Sein Win and Thaung Khin, who all got on well with K. He was, as might have been expected, much more interested in devising entertainment programmes than in purveying war news and set about this part of his work energetically. He got new pressings of records of Burmese music from HMV, wrote songs and scripts for special occasions such as the Thingyan festival and enjoyed himself so hugely that he decided he'd like to stay in broadcasting after the war.

But not quite all was sweetness and light: from time to time he suffered minor irritations owing to anomalies in the administrative set-up within which he, and all the foreign language units had to work. Reorganisation of AIR's news services had included formalisation of relations between themselves and those provided by the Far Eastern Bureau (FEB) of the British Ministry of Information. British journalists employed by FEB occupied a large newsroom near the office of AIR's Director of News and External Services (DNES). The Director had overall charge of this newsroom as well as the bigger newsroom on the ground floor where AIR's original Indian news staff prepared bulletins for the home services. There was not a great deal of liaison between the two newsrooms, but the FEB supplied European supervisory editorial staff to oversee the work of the native translators in the foreign language units. This placed the latter in a somewhat ambiguous position: their immediate supervisor was an FEB man, but their ultimate boss was the DNES who, like themselves was paid by the Government of India. The sense of having to serve two masters was tiresome enough, but K was aware too, of a third master in the background though very present. This was the ex-British Burma Government in exile, based in Simla, its officers invested with military rank as members of the CAS (B) (Civil Affairs Service, Burma). It wasn't that they interfered with his work, but he knew that his future in the post-war world rested with them, indeed, he was, in a sense, himself one of them, for he, too, wore the uniform of a Second-Lieutenant, and had been seconded to AIR by them.

Work at the Counter-Propaganda Directorate

In the meantime, Ma Than Aye also recommended me for a job, the post of Monitoring Officer at the Counter-Propaganda Directorate based in Simla, my role to monitor and translate into English broadcasts in Burmese from Japanese-occupied Burma. It meant living apart from K, but the children had a good school in Simla and I enjoyed living there. It was such an elegant spectacle: the ladies dazzlingly well-groomed, top memsahibs of the Raj no doubt, and even the monkeys on Jakko Hill incredibly elegant, sleek, silver grey fur and jet-black faces. Nor was I lonely there, for Mr and Mrs Htin Si, in whose house K and I had been married, were in the hotel where I stayed. We used to have dinner together and Htin Si thought Susan was a sweet little thing. He used to sing to her at night, a little Hindustani song and it went: 'Ni ni baba ni ni/ roti makinchini/ roti makin hodiya/ hamara baba so gi ya'. 'Child/bread, butter sugar/bread and butter finished/my baby's gone to sleep.' A nice little song.

The Governor of Burma, Sir Reginald Dorman-Smith, had set up his exiled government in Simla with a number of senior government officials, Burmese and British, all busy planning the reconstruction of Burma after the war had been won. The Independence question was central to all this, but London's appetite for granting self-government was limited. Everyone agreed though that at a minimum a period of direct rule would be necessary to enable reconstruction. I found my job very interesting and a real change from lecturing. I had to listen to enemy broadcasts in Burmese and translate them into English, and I was given a 9-valve HMV radio for the job. My day would start at about six o'clock in the evening which was when the programmes came out. I would listen to them on these great old cylinders and translate them into English, type them out and disseminate them to various information bureaux. I remember monitoring a report of the budget speech made by the wartime Chancellor of Burma which had been misreported by another department as some kind of instruction for housewives. I had to go to the police station and prove it with the police breathing down my neck. This caused quite a stir. Shortly afterwards I made an equally important discovery: I monitored a speech calling in all shortwave radio sets in order to change their frequency so that they could no longer receive broadcasts from India. This was a big surprise as in June 1942, the British government committee that supervised anti-Japanese propaganda had stated that radio broadcasting was not a particularly effective tool in Burma because there was a shortage of sets. Better, they thought, to go for 'whispers and pamphlets'. It was then that I first spoke to Charles Barns, who was the Director of News and External Broadcasts. He telephoned me to tell me that he was going to lay a landline to the eastern border of India with Burma so that All India Radio could broadcast there on medium wave. I had imagined him being thin and blue eyed with a blonde moustache, and I was right, but maybe that's because K had described him to me. He was K's boss and K liked him very much.

Political machinations and espionage

The political situation in Burma was ever more complicated. At first, despite the destruction, there were many who regarded the Japanese as not a bad thing: not only did they chase out the British, they brought with them the Burma Independence Army led by Aung San, with the Thirty Comrades at its core. The BIA marched ahead of the Japanese as they made their way up through Tenasserim. They set up administrations in each town, believing that this was the beginning of an independent Burma. The exception to this collaboration were the Communists who had strengthened their membership very considerably, particularly among Indian labourers in Rangoon. They refused from the outset to join the Japanese, denouncing them as fascists, and declaring that collaboration with them would only worsen Burma's predicament.

One of my former students, Thein Pe, had become very active in the Communist Party. He told me that on April 29th 1942 the Communists met with other nationalists at a well-side in a village just outside Mandalay. They agreed that those like U Nu who were less suspicious of Japanese promises of independence would remain in Burma making a temporary alliance with the Japanese but keeping in close contact with the resistance forces. Thakhins Soe and Thein Pe, both communists, were to leave to contact the retreating Chinese Nationalist Army and look for support from the Allies, so they had feet in all camps. In the event, Thakhin Soe decided to remain and organise the anti-Japanese underground. It was left to Thein Pe to contact the British. Arriving in India with another young man who said he had been one of my students, though truth be told I didn't remember him, they both made their way to Simla, and before they did anything else they tried to see me.

They sent me a note and then I talked to them over the telephone and apparently that was tapped because soon after the phone call a police officer turned up at the office. Mrs Barrington, the wife of Major Barrington and therefore above suspicion, was compelled to ask me questions. Had I just received a note from two young Burmans? Yes. Was it something about a letter from my husband? Yes, it was. Had I talked to them over the telephone afterwards? Yes, I had. What had I said? Well, they had asked me in their note to come to their hotel at one o'clock to see them, so I had telephoned to say that I was too busy to see them at the moment and couldn't they have tea with me at Davico's later in the afternoon, and they said no we can't because we are followed about by a policeman. I had said well, what's wrong with that? Bring the policeman to tea - he can have tea too. At this, Mrs Barrington just collapsed with laughter because she thought this police fuss too silly anyhow. And the policeman seemed to think the time for apology had arrived and he said 'Oh Madam, the gentlemen are not under surveillance; they have been given a policeman as a guide because they are new to Simla. It is purely for their own convenience'. Mrs B and I thought that funny too, and then I went on to tell the rest of the story: that I'd suggested, since they wanted to see me immediately, they'd better come to my office, and I asked Mrs Barrington if she minded. Of course not, was her answer, and that was the end of the questioning.

When Thein Pe and his friend arrived, they came bringing a document full of very exciting revelations about Burma under the Japanese which would be useful counter-propaganda and a grand press scoop. They'd come to me as their old Sayama, so I could vet it and sent it quickly to K who had promised to give it to Edgar Snow, the American who wrote *Red Star Over China* and *Scorched Earth*, and who had said he would help to get it published.[14] After they had gone, poor Mrs B had to come and ask me who my father was. And how lucky for me that I had such an eminently respectable father and that he was available for reference so near at hand as Dehra Dun. The little book was published in 1943 by Kitabistan of Allahabad with a striking cover design in mustard, scarlet, and black and with a brief foreword by Edgar Snow. Thein Pe used to come quite

---

[14] Marxism and Resistance in Burma 1942-1945. Thein Pe Myint's *Wartime Traveler*. Translated and Edited by Robert H. Taylor. Athens: Ohio University Press, 1984.

often for dinner in my flat, and I remember how he fell in love with a very beautiful Indian girl. Apparently, I discouraged him because I said she was too tall for him, but I don't remember that! ☞ | P 212 **MALABAR FISH CURRY** |

Thein Pe stayed in Simla for a while and became of genuine value in anti-Japanese propaganda, writing plays, articles, and pamphlets, including *'Lay-nat-tha'* 'Spirit of the Wind', a popular paper distributed in Burma by bazaar women, who used it as a wrapping for foodstuffs. But he was still highly critical of the British. In one infamous tract (that was not circulated) he wrote:

'The government trod upon the people of Burma, and when the Japanese came, its leaders fled without their trousers so as not to be noticed but they still wore their spiked shoes. Now at Simla they put on their trousers again and they also wore great coats. And they were repairing the iron spikes on their shoes which had worn off when they were in flight.'

I thought that was rather good!

Life in Delhi

I had moved to Delhi in early 1943 and was living with K and working as Assistant News Editor in the Central News Organisation of All-India Radio, but before I'd managed to properly settle in I'd had an accident. I found Delhi the worst town in the world to live in. The only possible form of transport for people like us was the push bike. Distances were terrific and streets filthy, with rubbish piled high in among shops and houses, beggars innumerable, lots of animal-drawn vehicles, and among the beasts so used were mangy, sick-looking and filthy camels. Taxis were ruinously expensive and tongas nerve-wracking, because the tongawallahs were rude and crude, their horses miserable and cruelly whipped and the passenger sat right over the pony's backside, defenceless against the poor beast's foul wind.

I had therefore bought a bike, and spent a long time searching for one which was made in England. I eventually purchased one that had the assurance 'Made in England' printed on the frame in large letters, but when I got it home I saw it had 'As good as' in tiny, tiny letters, before the 'Made in England'! Anyway, I was knocked down, by a bus no less, and the bike was wrecked. I was quite seriously injured and lost a baby. I was whipped into hospital, and they said I might as well be sterilised. I wasn't very sure about whether it was a good thing or not because I still hadn't had a son, but I was thirty-five and beginning to get too old. In war, you don't want to have children. I thought, well let's be sterilised and have an end to this. I took leave on no pay and went up to Simla for two months to recuperate.

By the time I came back there was a new post available. A Reference Officer was needed to take charge of the Central News Organisation's collection of books, most of them scattered among various borrowers, and the large number of newspapers and journals it subscribed to. I applied successfully for this post and busily set about tracking down the many books out on indefinite loan and cataloguing them. K had managed to get quarters in Katawdi House. There were big houses in Delhi where the Indian princes used to stay when business brought them to Delhi. Each house was named after the Prince, and this was the house of the Maharajah of Katawdi. There were hutments within the grounds which were taken over by the government and used as hostels for staff, military and civil, that had suddenly to be brought into Delhi for war purposes. Meals were in the dining hall, but we lived in our little huts.
☞ | P 215 **MUSHROOM KORMA** |

It was clear from what I was hearing that the nationalist splits that were apparent when I was in Simla had not healed. Just as the Burmese nationalists were divided about whether to support the Japanese, the British establishment was divided as to its trust of the Burmese, and the Japanese were divided as to the extent of political freedom to be granted Burma. Bo Moegyoe (alias) Minami (alias) Suzuki was genuinely supportive of independence, but the 15th Army, under General Shojiro, was anxious to preserve Burma as a source of supplies for the Japanese army's push into India. This would obviously be very difficult under a Burmese civilian administration and in July 1942 Suzuki was sent home and the BIA was reorganised by the Japanese into a much smaller force. However, by early 1943, Japan began to experience serious military reversals, in the light of which on 1st August 1943 the Japanese, with much pomp and circumstance, declared Burma independent, and Dr Ba Maw was appointed 'adipadi', leader of Burma, and U Nu became Minister for Foreign Affairs. Dr Ba Maw later wrote: 'One had to recognize the "Made in Japan" stamp on one's forehead. Otherwise, with flattery on every side, one might easily have mistaken our pine-wood independence for real solid teak.' Ba Maw did handle the Japanese with some skill. I don't think you could say that he was simply a puppet: he challenged Japanese economic monopolies and political interference, and he forced them to lower their demands on the Burmese farmers. But by the end of 1943, six months after the declaration of independence, the tide was beginning to turn against him, and the Thakhins were increasingly discontented both with Japanese independence and Dr Ba Maw, who had consistently outmanoeuvred them and excluded many of them from government.

CHA CA VIETNAMESE FISH

Serves 4 | prepare 20 mins + 2 hours to marinate | cook 30 mins | easy

This recipe comes from Cha Ca La Vong in Hanoi, a restaurant that has been serving cha ca for three generations. It's the only dish on the menu so I was rather surprised when the owner approached and asked us what we would like to eat! The marinated fish was brought to our table in a frying pan and placed on top of a small gas burner. With neither instructions nor experience, we followed the example of our Vietnamese neighbours who added dill and spring onions to the pan, and after a few minutes fished out aromatic chunks of fish using chopsticks, depositing it in a spoon held in their left hand. Fresh herbs, peanuts, noodles and a spicy dipping sauce were deftly added to the fish before the whole combination was wolfed down in a single mouthful.

INGREDIENTS

To marinate the fish:

400g filleted white fish (sea bream, cod, or sea bass)

4 tbsp natural unsweetened yoghurt

1 tsp chopped garlic

2 tbsp finely chopped dill

1 tsp turmeric

1 tbsp galangal, peeled and finely chopped

1 tsp Madras curry powder

3 tbsp fish sauce

2 tsp sugar

To cook and serve:

4 tbsp sunflower oil

1 handful fresh dill

4 spring onions (green and white part) cut into fine julienne

Salt

1 packet of rice noodles (preferably the round variety and not too fine)

1 lime cut into wedges

4 tbsp roasted peanuts coarsely chopped (page 28)

1 small bunch of coriander

Nuoc cham sauce (page 71)

Remove the skin and any pin bones from the fish and cut the fillets into bite size chunks. In a mixing bowl large enough to contain the fish, combine the yogurt with the garlic, galangal, sugar, fish sauce, chopped dill, turmeric and curry powder. Season with salt and reserve in the fridge for at least 2 hours or overnight if possible.

Lift the fish out of the marinade. Heat the oil in a large non-stick frying pan and fry the chunks of fish, turning them as they begin to brown. This shouldn't take more than a few minutes, so if you feel it's going too slowly you probably need to turn up the heat. Now add the julienne of spring onions and the dill, turn down the heat and allow the herbs to wilt and impart their flavour to the fish (this takes about 10 minutes).

Cook the noodles according to the instructions on the packet. Serve the fish in the pan surrounded by bowls containing peanuts, nuoc cham sauce, coriander and wedges of lime.

Each guest should have their own bowl of noodles, chopsticks and a Chinese soup spoon.

MUSSELS IN GREEN CURRY

Serves 4 | prepare 30 mins | cook 15 mins | easy

This is one of the most successful dishes in Ma Khin Café though it first appeared on the menu of my earlier restaurant in Valencia, Seu Xerea back in the 90s. Valencian mussels (called clòtxinas) are deliciously sweetand have been longing for the arrival of homemade green curry!

INGREDIENTS

For the green curry paste:

2cm ginger, peeled

2cm galangal, peeled

6 shallots peeled and coarsely chopped

3 cloves garlic peeled

2 lemon grass stalks coarsely chopped

2 tbsp chopped coriander preferably with roots

250g long fresh green chillies

¼ tsp ground white pepper

½ tsp ground coriander

½ tsp cumin powder

½ tsp turmeric

1 tsp fermented shrimp paste

Zest of 2 limes

For the mussels:

1 kg mussels, scrubbed and with beards removed

2 tbsp sunflower oil

100ml coconut milk

8 lime leaves

1 stick lemon grass cut in batons about 4cm long

A few slices of galangal

1 tsp palm sugar

Juice of 1 lime

1-2 tbsp fish sauce

Fresh coriander and Thai basil leaves

To make the curry paste, put all the ingredients in a food processor and pulse to a smooth paste. Add a little water if necessary. Unlike shop bought curry paste, this much more delicious fresh version does not keep for more than a few days, but what you don't use will freeze very well.

Heat the oil in a wok and fry 1 tablespoon of the curry paste for a few minutes. Take special care that the paste does not burn. Add half the coconut milk, the lime leaves, lemon grass, galangal and palm sugar. Once everything is boiling, throw in the mussels. Cover and cook for three minutes by which time the mussels should have opened. Scoop out the mussels and pour off about half of the liquid. Add the rest of the coconut milk and fish sauce and lime juice to taste. As soon as it boils pour the sauce over the mussels.

Serve sprinkled with fresh coriander and torn basil leaves.

SHAN NOODLE SOUP

Serves 4 | prepare 30 mins | cook 30 mins | easy

This is a breakfast dish and a kind of soupy version of nan gyi thoke (page 51). Fresh Shan noodles combine rice flour and glutinous rice flour and have a correspondingly sticky texture. In Spain we use Thai cellophane noodles made with rice flour.

INGREDIENTS

For the chicken curry:

1 tbsp sunflower oil

1 medium white onion peeled and finely chopped

1 tsp grated ginger

1 tsp chopped garlic

1 tsp Madras curry powder

½ tsp turmeric

½ tsp five-spice powder

¼ tsp chilli flakes

1 tbsp tomato paste

250g minced chicken

150ml chicken stock (page 29)

Salt

To serve the soup:

250g of cellophane rice noodles about 5mm wide

4 green Chinese or white cabbage leaves

400ml chicken stock (page 29)

50g roasted peanuts, coarsely chopped

2 tbsp crispy shallots (page 27)

2 tbsp chopped coriander

40g Chinese fermented cabbage (available from Chinese supermarkets)

Extra roast chilli flakes

Prawn crackers

For the chicken curry, heat the oil in a heavy based pan and gently fry the onion until it begins to brown. Add the ginger and garlic and continue to fry until it becomes aromatic before stirring in the spices followed by the tomato paste. Add the minced chicken and the chicken stock and cook everything together for about 20 minutes until it is quite dry.

When you are ready to serve the soup, bring a large pan of salted water to the boil. Briefly blanch the cabbage leaves in the boiling water until tender but not soft (about 2-3 minutes). Refresh the leaves in a bowl of iced water. When cold, lift the leaves out of the water and chop them coarsely. In a medium pan, bring the chicken stock to the boil and check for salt. Bring the large pan of water back to the boil and cook the noodles following the instructions on the packet. Divide the noodles between four bowls, topping them with the cabbage and a large spoonful of the chicken curry. Pour the remaining chicken stock over the noodles.

Sprinkle with roasted peanuts, crispy shallots and coriander and serve with fermented cabbage, more roast chilli flakes and prawn crackers.

MALABAR FISH CURRY

Serves 4 | prepare 40 mins | cook 25 mins | easy

Southern Indian curries often include coconut milk, and this dish from the Malabar coast is no exception. Cod and hake are perfectly suited, as are red mullet and sea bream too. I've included a savoury version of kheer rice to serve with the curry. (Kheer is better known in India as a delicious rice pudding). It's best to cook the kheer rice the day before you stir fry it.

INGREDIENTS

For the Malabar fish curry:

½ kg white fish fillets
½ tsp mustard seeds
¼ tsp fenugreek seeds
1 tsp cumin seeds
1 tsp coriander seeds
6 fresh or 12 dried curry leaves
¼ tsp turmeric
1 tbsp clarified butter or ghee
1 medium red onion
1 tsp grated ginger
1 small green chilli, finely chopped
200g tinned chopped tomatoes
1 tbsp tamarind paste
100ml chicken stock (page 29)
400ml coconut milk
Salt

For the savoury kheer rice:

200g basmati rice
110ml milk
110ml water
1 tsp salt
6 cardamom pods crushed
1 pinch of saffron threads
1 tsp brown sugar
2 tbsp mixed sultanas and raisins
2 tbsp unsalted peanuts chopped
2 tbsp unsalted cashews chopped

To serve:

2 tbsp chopped fresh coriander
2 tbsp freshly grated coconut or desiccated coconut

To make the kheer, wash the rice and bring to the boil with the milk, water, salt, cardamom, saffron and sugar. Cover tightly and cook for 10 minutes. Turn off the heat and leave covered and undisturbed for 10 more minutes.

Toast the fenugreek cumin, coriander and half of the mustard seeds in a dry frying pan together with the dried curried leaves if using (do not toast fresh curry leaves!). Grind to a powder in a coffee grinder together with the turmeric.

Cut the fish into eight pieces. Heat the ghee or clarified butter in a frying pan. Fry the fresh curry leaves (if using) and the remaining mustard seeds for about 30 seconds until they begin to pop. Add the chopped onion and sauté until it is translucent then add the ginger and chilli and continue to fry until the onion begins to brown. Add the ground spices and mix well before adding the tomatoes and tamarind.

When the oil begins to separate from the sauce add the chicken stock slowly followed by the coconut milk. Allow to cook together for 10 minutes. Add the fillets of fish and cook for a further 5 minutes.

When ready to serve, heat a splash of sunflower oil in a wok or frying pan. Stir fry the rice with the dried fruit and nuts until the rice begins to crisp. Divide the rice between four dishes and place a portion of the fish fillets on each. Spoon the sauce over the fish and sprinkle with grated coconut and chopped coriander.

MUSHROOM KORMA

Serves 4 | prepare 20 mins | cook 25 mins | easy

Korma may be considered a lightweight for more competitive curry fans. The spices are sweeter and less earthy than in the other curries you'll find in this book. This makes a korma ideal for the delicate flavours of wild mushrooms though you can also make this with cultivated varieties.

INGREDIENTS

400g mixed mushrooms, wild or cultivated
2 tbsp sunflower oil
1 medium white onion, peeled and finely chopped
1 tsp chopped garlic
1 tsp grated ginger
½ tsp green cardamom pods crushed
1 stick cinnamon
4 fresh curry leaves or 2 bay leaves
½ tsp cloves
¼ tsp ground white pepper
¼ tsp freshly grated nutmeg
1 stick cinnamon
150g unsweetened natural yoghurt
A pinch of saffron threads
Salt
1 tsp garam masala
50g unsalted almonds
2 tbsp chopped fresh tarragon

Brush any earth off the mushrooms and remove the ends of the stalks. Break larger mushrooms into bite size pieces. Roast the almonds in a hot oven and grind to a coarse powder in a food processor. Grind the salt in a mortar with the saffron threads and add this to the yoghurt, which will turn a lovely yellow.

Heat the oil in a heavy based casserole and briefly fry the curry leaves, cloves, cinnamon and cardamom. Add the onion and sauté until it begins to turn golden. Stir in the ginger and garlic and continue to fry until aromatic. Add the pepper and nutmeg followed by the mushrooms. Allow to cook for ten minutes until the mushrooms have wilted. Remove the pan from the heat and stir in the yoghurt, almonds and garam masala. Serve immediately sprinkled with tarragon and accompany with basmati rice.

ENDINGS
(1943-1949)

Blueprint for Burma

Planning for what was going to happen in post-war Burma had started when I was in Delhi in January 1943. It was decided that upon reoccupation Burma should be ruled by a military administration. The Civil Administration Service (Burma) was established in Simla to organise that. Many of its staff were not civil servants but employees of British companies as there was a shortage of administrators because of the number of Burmese second-liners who had remained in Burma. One of the major disputes at this time was 'Blueprint for Burma'. It was a document that outlined the future of Burma as imagined by Conservative and business interests: self-government after a suggested reconstruction period of six years and the establishment of monopolies for rice, timber, mining, and transportation. It was proposed that these would be run by private companies but funded by the British government. It also proposed that the Frontier Areas - where the hill people lived - should continue to be governed by HMG unless they stated they preferred to be ruled by the Burmese. Father thought the document was dreadful. He wrote to me: 'Have you read Blueprint for Burma? The advertisement describes it as, "A bold and comprehensive plan". I call it a most depressing and distressing document - sketchy and superficial, and pretty certain to alienate every Burman who reads it or comes to know of it'.

This Blueprint had been welcomed by Governor Dorman-Smith who was the leader of the Government in exile in Simla. Dorman-Smith was fanatically anti Aung San and what he called the 'Burma Traitor Army' and he was not popular with many of the Burmese in Simla. As early as August 1944, they were openly disagreeing with him, claiming that the country would reject financial assistance and reconstruction under direct rule, in favour of immediate self-government. Dorman-Smith was belligerent and talked about the Burmese having to 'take the consequences' if they resisted.

By then my parents had moved from Dehra Dun to Bangalore, where they took a sheltered flat at St Martha's Hospital, an institution run by Catholic nuns of a nursing order. They settled very comfortably there and Alice lived close by. Father enjoyed the Botanical Gardens and the public library, and went for many long walks with Mother, discovering interesting local plants and trees - lifelong botanist and bookworm that he was. He was active in an organisation set up by Anglo-Burmese evacuees to promote the interests of members of their community. Many of them were minor civil servants, for whom the august HQ of Burma Government had little time, so busy were they in drawing up grand plans for post-war reconstruction. Father's letters to me told of the many frustrations he faced in dealings with Simla on his organisation's behalf, but more often it was family news - news of my siblings and their spouses in England, for, as always, he was in close touch with all his children. It was he who told me that my brother Sam was with the 14th Army in Arakan in 1944, and early the following year that Robert, now an engineer officer in the RAF, would soon be arriving in India en route for the war zones further east.

Things were moving very quickly now. Between March and July 1944, the Japanese attempted to invade North East India, with an attack on Imphal, but they were driven back and suffered heavy losses. We were personally also caught up in the plans for the future, as there was a rumour that McCoy, the Anglo-Indian Posts and Telegraphs man who had run broadcast news in Rangoon before British withdrawal in 1942, was about to be sent to the BBC in London for training so he could be better equipped to take up the same post when Rangoon was recaptured. K was deeply upset: he'd coveted the job himself. Working at AIR had shown him the exciting possibilities broadcasting could open up, and he wanted to exercise his musical and literary talents. He badly wanted to be the man sent to the BBC to learn the tricks of the trade. We did a lot of letter-writing, we went up to Simla to lobby influential persons in Burma Government, and eventually, early in October 1944, K flew to London to take up a post in Burmese broadcasting at the BBC.

I have to say I was relieved that he had left, for personal reasons. I had started to feel that some vital spark had gone from our relationship. I didn't want to feel this, and tried to reason myself out of it. I was worried about the children - how they would feel, already unsettled by war. K being in London left me freer to straighten out my troubled thoughts and feelings.

Splits and allegiances

In mid-1944, the Burmese nationalists had regrouped to form the Anti-Fascist Organisation (later known as the Anti-Fascist Peoples Freedom League, AFPFL). This was a broad coalition, with the Communist Thakhin Soe as its political leader and Aung San as its president. The BIA, now renamed the Burma National Army (BNA), began to prepare for an uprising against the Japanese. There was some ambivalence in attitude to the British but in December 1944, after a series of British offensives into Burma, the BNA contacted the British to indicate their preparedness to ally with them to drive out the Japanese. The British in turn were split in their response. Dorman-Smith and the CAS(B) people continued to be hostile to Aung San and the 'traitors' and to make the case for the loyal hill peoples to be central to the British reconquest of Burma. Involvement with the British army and security forces from early on in the imperial project, the divisive politics of the Legislative Council, not to forget Burman chauvinism and desire for revenge on imperial collaborators, had brought atrocities and massacres with the Japanese invasion. Included among those killed by the BIA were many Karens who had figured prominently in pre-war attempts to establish unity with Burman neighbours. Moreover, during the British retreat the tribal people, but particularly the Karens, had played an important part in harassing Japanese supply routes and protecting the retreating army. This obviously entailed direct confrontation with the BIA, who had often exacted terrible reprisals.

Mountbatten, now head of South East Asia Command, was more supportive of Aung San than was Dorman-Smith and in March 1945 the War Cabinet in London gave him permission to ally formally with the AFO (now renamed the AFPFL) which had the Burma National Army as its armed wing - though with the caveat that their alliance with the Japanese earlier in the war had not been forgotten. Mountbatten ordered 4,000 arms to be issued to them and 12,000 to the Karens. These were released two days after the BNA openly declared war on the Japanese on 27th March. This date was named 'Resistance Day' but is now the 'Tatmadaw (Armed Forces) Day'. Then in the Spring of 1945, there was a race to recapture Rangoon before the onset of the rains and when it was recaptured in May it seemed to be only hours before the monsoon burst.

Trusting Charles

After K left, an American called Colonel Coffey had come round talent hunting at All India Radio, recruiting for the Office of Strategic Services - the secret service. He invited me to take a job based in Calcutta interviewing people who had been brought out of Burma. I was offered much more money than at AIR, free passage to Calcutta in air-conditioned, first class train, and it all seemed very grand and well paid. I submitted my resignation, but when Charles Barns found out where I was going he was very worried. He came to see me and advised me not to do it. He indicated it would be terrible and that I had no idea what life in a service like that would be like. He made it clear that nobody would trust me, that it would be one man's word against another. He warned me that anybody who disliked me for the most frivolous reasons could stick a knife in my back. If I was suspected of being any kind of traitor or untrustworthy

I'd be killed. Anyway, he put the fear of God into me. And so I stayed where I was. They had already made arrangements and part of me was disappointed because there was a lot of spy mania in the air and it seemed a glamorous life, but Charles said that he would find me a safer job more suited to my talents.

Early in 1945, I was moved to the post of Editorial Assistant to Charles, who was Director of News. I enjoyed the more stimulating work of this post, for once the library service had been sorted out and with new routines established, there was little else for the Reference Officer to do but see it running smoothly. In my new job, there were meetings every morning in Charles' office called 'political warfare meetings' and one of my duties was to take the minutes. Representation at these meetings was at a very high level - the top brass and all the senior news editors working at Broadcasting House in both the home and external services participated. We discussed news policy for the day, which items were to be given prominence and which not. Those meetings were really interesting. I found it instructive and amusing to see how large a part pride and prejudice played in the daily tussle between groups with different interests in their efforts to reach a consensus. I was much busier in my new post, and more closely involved in each day's news output, which was all to the good.

Political Warfare meeting AIR. Charles 1st right, G 3rd right, 1943

I was becoming closer to Charles too. I had first got to know him through K, who liked him very much, even though he was his antithesis. Unlike K, Charles hadn't got much conversation. He wasn't ICS, he was a journalist, a cut below, and he wasn't public school, but K could see that he was golden-hearted, and that meant a lot to him. When K left for London, Charles drove him to the airport and K told him to look after me. He put me in his care. He didn't realise how well he'd look after me! Not long after he went I fell ill and I couldn't go to work so I wrote in sick and Charles' personal chaprassi turned up with three books for me to read from his library. I wrote to him and thanked him very much. When I went back to work he said: 'It was very important for me to have your letter yesterday because it was my birthday'. I thought, 'What a lonely man', and my interest was piqued.

Peace – but what next?

It's strange, I can't remember what I was doing when peace was declared, but I do remember when the bomb fell on Hiroshima. I was horror-struck to think that such a thing had been done. They described the kind of suffering that it had caused, and then they dropped another on Nagasaki. I was horrified, just as I was always horrified when I heard about a troop ship being sunk. To think of all those young men, hundreds of them, sometimes thousands, sinking and being killed like that, whichever side they are on. Bad enough being shot in war, you become hardened to that, but to have complete destruction. War is terrible.

Anticipating victory, on 30th May 1945, Lord Mountbatten held a meeting in Delhi with Governor Dorman-Smith and high ranking military officers. The main purpose of the meeting was to determine how the Burma National Army should be handled. The group were generally agreed that the BNA should be used for 'mopping up operations' and then collected in holding centres where they could be interrogated and unsatisfactory members disarmed. There was disagreement on what to do about Aung San, self-styled commander-in-chief of a Provisional Government of Burma. Indeed, an ambivalent attitude, both to Aung San and to the AFPFL was to continue for well over a year. One of its most prominent voices was Governor Dorman-Smith who preferred to deal with the old pre-war politicians. He warned of deep resentment if HMG passed over those who had been loyal to the British throughout the war in favour of timeservers and traitors, but Mountbatten was clear that there was no choice, and when the Japanese surrendered on 12th September 1945, Aung San was in a powerful position.

Significant disagreements between the British on how to handle Aung San and the AFPFL continued and were also bound up with different positions on ethnic minorities in Burma. Dorman-Smith promoted the role of former Prime

Minister, U Saw, who returned to Burma in January 1946. Both Dorman-Smith and U Saw were keen to have Aung San prosecuted for the alleged murder of a village headman during the Japanese occupation. The AFPFL in the meantime was determined to prove that they represented the country. They held their first All Burma Congress in the precincts of the Shwedagon Pagoda between 17 and 23 January 1946. This called for complete independence from Britain without Dominion Status and the formation of a Provisional National Government.

Mother and Father starting again

Meanwhile Mother and Father were planning on returning to Burma and setting up house again in Kalaw. Father said he felt there was no knowing what was going to happen in India, the atmosphere was explosive and that they might find it desirable to get away as soon as possible. He made enquiries and found that they could return whenever they liked, but they had to pay their own fares and arrange their own passages. They also had to have accommodation, temporary or permanent, in Rangoon, and could not rely on the Government for food. If they wanted to go beyond Rangoon they had to provide their own transport and this last was a snag: trains had begun to run to Kalaw again, but according to reports in the newspapers there was practically no passenger rolling stock in Burma and people had to travel in cattle trucks. The journey from Rangoon to Mandalay took two days, so to Kalaw it was likely to take even longer. Added to that, it sounded as if conditions in Burma were still very bad in every way. The decision was to stay in India until after the monsoon and try to move in late October or in November when things should have improved a bit.

I did not get leave until August 1946, when I flew to Madras and then took the train to Bangalore. Father was just the same as ever and I was so pleased to find him so. And strangely, I was pleased to find Mother and Alice unchanged. But I seemed to have changed myself! For while in the past I found their ways infuriating, on this visit I found myself automatically adjusting myself to them instead of being harshly critical. And the result of my different behaviour is that I found myself liking them. I realised I had misjudged Mother in some ways. I thought her cruelty and her harsh injustices arose from a hard and cruel nature. But I realised in fact she had an excessively sensitive nature, and when she felt herself injured her instant reaction was cruelty and injustice. She was capable of love and tenderness. They had little stupid squirrels and crows, as we had in Delhi (only Father said these were called tree-rats and were not squirrels), which used to run all over the wide verandah outside their row of rooms. These squirrels were fat and very tame because Mother fed them constantly. She had a great friend in an old grandfather crow who hopped to our door when we sat down to a meal and waited for his food. If Mother pretended not to see him he put his head down and cawed very gently - she thought it quite charming, and she invited me to appreciate his good breeding. She said he was most intelligent. He liked to carry away all her crumbs, but when they were hard he dipped them in water to soften them before he swallowed.

One evening I was very touched to catch Mother tidying my room - emptying ashtrays, turning down the bed and letting down the mosquito net over it - a service I'd always thought the maid had done. I told Mother she was like Me Htwe in the story. Mother liked the comparison and was pleased with me because I not only bought her a new longyi, but I sewed it! I rather liked being at home again, though it was the same annoying kind of home - no beauty of setting, rigidly punctual meals and extreme thrift, but I felt at home and with my own people - very peaceful and soothed. ☞ | P 233 **DAHL** |

Mother also responded much better than I had imagined to some important news. I told them that I was planning to go to England with Charles and the children. I had decided that K and I must part, and had written to him telling him that I was no longer happy in our marriage, and had been learning to care very much for someone else – Charles of course. He cabled back immediately that he felt no bitterness, and that he was happy I was still fond of him. It was all very amicable. I think Mother was quite glad that now at last I was going to hitch up with a white man. I also said that I wanted them to meet Charles and he arranged to come up and meet them for the weekend. He was terribly nervous. Mother always received people very graciously and knew the right thing to say, but Father and Charles were both inarticulate chaps, just stammering at each other, that's all they did. Anyway, Mother's verdict was that he was better looking than K, but you mustn't give him pumpkin in the evenings. He looks delicate. ☞ | P 235 **MASSAMAN BEEF CURRY** |

When I kissed Father goodbye in Bangalore tears streamed down his face. It was the first time I had ever seen him weep and the last time I was ever to see him well. Early in November they heard that their passages had been cancelled because the Government had requisitioned their boat. And on 28 November he wrote to me: 'It was annoying to have our passages cancelled, but perhaps it was all for the best.' He little knew how right he was, for four weeks later he had a massive stroke and was left severely disabled. They did not leave India for Burma until February 1948, when Father was well enough to be moved in a chair.

I meet Aung San in Delhi

When I came back from Bangalore I met up with Aung San again in Delhi. He was passing through on his way to the Independence talks in London. He was to broadcast from All India Radio to Burma, and when he arrived the Burmese wanted to receive him in a suitably nationalistic way, so we all met him at the airport. Susan was a dear little thing then, so they dressed her up and gave her a bouquet of flowers to present to him while we wore traditional Burmese dress and shouted 'Dobama!', 'We Burmese!' which was the Burmese nationalist slogan.

I liked Aung San. I thought he was honest and above corruption, a true nationalist. I don't know what he thought of me. Probably not very much. We met in the AIR editor's office. He was going to broadcast in Burmese and he had to check the English translation of his paper and approve it. As he signed he looked up at me and said, in Burmese: 'Mrs Khin Zaw, when are you coming back to Burma?' This was very double edged because by this time it was notorious gossip that K and I were intending to part. He was going to go back to Burma to take up the post as Director of Broadcasting and I was going to England. I've always done the wrong thing: during imperialist times I went and married a Burman, and then, come nationalist days, independence and all that, what do I do but ditch the Burman! But I was concerned for the children, and particularly their education. I thought that the country would be in chaos for several years at least. There wouldn't be any good schools and I knew how disadvantaged I felt compared to my brothers and sisters because of my education. And besides, what would be my position as a Eurasian? I think K felt that too. Although he told me that I could always come back, and I think that he meant it, he knew too that being saddled with this wretched imperialist judge's daughter wouldn't do him any favours.

The talks in London were successful and on January 27th the London Agreement was signed which set out the path to self-government and the unification of the frontier areas and lowland Burma. This continued to be a live issue in Burma, particularly for the Karen who had suffered at the hands of the BIA during the Japanese occupation. I remember Aung San used the parable of the Two Muzzled Oxen. While the cattle are treading out the grain, the cultivator muzzles them to stop them from eating it. They can see the grain but cannot eat it because they are muzzled. Then in due course the cultivator gathers up the grain in his barn and turns the cattle loose. And all they do is to begin goring one another. In Burma, he said, the soil is so rich that there was more than enough to eat and more than enough to wear. But like the oxen, the Burmese had been muzzled and so also had the Karens, Shans, Chins, Pa-os: they could see a large fat ham, but their bellies remained empty. And when they were set free they went for one another like fighting cocks. The Second Panglong Conference, held in February 1947 and attended by Aung San and by many of the minority groups, ended with an agreement that they would co-operate in the formation of a 'Union of Burma', but not all groups were present, and the Karens sent only four observers.

From left: Charles, Ma Khin, Rita (Charles's first wife), Alice, Father and Susan, 1944

During my last month in Delhi I attended the Inter-Asian relations conference. It was hosted by Nehru and was very exciting. There was a lot of talk about what the future was going to be. I remember one conversation about the adjective for Asia, because the old adjective was 'Asiatic', but Nehru said, 'Why do we stumble over this adjective and this ugly expression. A man of Europe is called a European, and a man of Asia should be called an Asian'. Aung San was not able to attend as he was on the campaign trail. I was chosen as a delegate over Daw Mya Sein, whose 'secretary' I had been at Crosby Hall. She was felt to be not a good enough nationalist, and there was I, a good nationalist, and already in India. I featured in the delegates' photographs, wearing a skirt. Thereafter, I put on Burmese clothes for all the official functions. At the same time as the Inter-Asian conference, Mountbatten arrived as the new viceroy of India, and that is the reason that in the photograph of me with Mountbatten I am wearing a longyi.

I had to give a speech about women and say polite things about the Indians our hosts. I talked about the great example of Mahatma Gandhi and what the Indian Nationalist movement had meant to the Burmese nationalist movement and so on. I said beautiful things about Gandhi whom really I was a bit suspicious of, but as a result of that I was asked to have lunch with Nehru and a few select persons. I was the token woman and I sat at his right hand. I thought he was such a handsome man and half wished he would fall in love with me. But he didn't!

Inter-Asian relations conference. G meets Mountbatten, 1946

Charles and I set out for England

In Spring 1947, Charles the children and I took a train to Bombay and from there we boarded a ship, the *Asturias*, and left for England. When we got to the end of the railway journey we found that some of our luggage had been left behind, but luckily among the things we had held on to was a small metal box which contained our passports. Wartime travelling conditions were very chaotic, and everybody just grabbed things. We arrived with only one trunk and three children. All the clothes I had made for them for England were left behind. At first, we had to stay in a bed and breakfast. We were appalled at the food we had to eat, sausages the thickness of a finger which tasted of sawdust. We had to eat out every night which was quite costly, and we began to worry because Charles didn't have much money. He had accumulated a lot of leave in the many years he was in India, and had pay in lieu, but in the meantime, India became independent so the money took a long time to come through. I had a little money from Father, and we lived in Wandsworth with these horrible people who were friends of Charles' sister, Adelaide's husband. They were army people. We had to share a bathroom and a lavatory which was on their floor. They were not at all friendly and there were constant rows. We were leading a hand to mouth existence. I was learning to cook – I knew how to make cakes but I didn't know how to cater from day to day so I was learning that. And I had to be up in time to give the children breakfast before they went to school, the kind of thing I had never had to bother with before because we had had help at home. ☞ | P 237 **FLAPJACKS** | & | P238 **APRICOT AND FRANGIPANE TART** |

Assassination and independence

In the meantime, disaster struck in Rangoon. On July 19 1947, Aung San held his usual Saturday cabinet meeting in the Secretariat building in Rangoon. A number of men in army uniform burst in shouting, and as Aung San stood up and faced the intruders he was shot dead. [15] Seven councillors were killed: Aung San, Thakhin Mya, Mahn Ba Khaing, Abdul Razak, U Ba Choe, Sao Sam Htun, and U Ba Win. Also killed were U Ohn Maung, Deputy Secretary in Transport and Communications Department, who was in attendance only because of a particular item on the agenda that day, and eighteen-year-old Ko Htwe, a personal bodyguard of Mr Razak. There were four alleged gunmen and a fifth, U Ba Nyunt, who claimed he was charged with killing U Nu, but could not find him, so instead he had a cup of tea.

The perpetrator of this crime was Dorman-Smith's protegee, U Saw. Apparently at eleven-thirty, a blood-stained jeep had screeched into his yard containing four men carrying firearms shouting Victory! Victory! U Saw had greeted them

---

[15] For more details see the BBC documentary, aired on 19 July 1997, *Who Really Killed Aung San?*

extravagantly, welcomed them into his house, where they were found drunk with their guns some hours later. I always found this a bit suspicious. Not that I didn't think U Saw was responsible: a large stolen arms cache was discovered in the lake at the back of his house so it looked as if he had been planning to take advantage of a destabilised Burma. But what I find difficult to believe is that he would have done something like that acting on his own without feeling he would have some British support. The guns were stolen with the connivance of a British officer who was an Arms Adviser to the Burma Police. We'll never know though. He complained that he did not have a fair trial, but he was hanged for murder.

On hearing the news of the assassination, the British Governor who had replaced Dorman-Smith, Governor Rance, immediately called our old friend U Nu to his office, appointed him Prime Minister, and instructed him to form a cabinet. It was to be my old student, U Nu then, not Aung San, who would lead Burma finally to independence on 4th January 1948, but the country really was a mess by then and I was really concerned when Mother and Father insisted on returning to Kalaw in February. They thought that life would be easier in Burma than in India or England, but they were thinking of Burma in the old days. There was fighting in Kalaw when they returned, the sound of gunfire all the time. The house was in a terribly hacked about state. All the teak doors had been taken off their hinges and used for firewood. The English baths had been taken out and put in the garden. The house was in a state of utter ruin. They had to try to put things together again and make it habitable. Father couldn't do anything because he was bedridden, so they had the problem of having to care for him as well as having to put the house and garden in order.

Mother and Father return to England

They soon realised that they wouldn't be able to manage. They were in Kalaw for getting on for a year, but finally left early in 1949. Mary went to get them. She had a lot of trouble getting a plane to Kalaw and then a plane to Rangoon again, but K helped out a lot. They stayed for a while in Rangoon, but Mother was distraught. She felt that life had fallen all to pieces around her and she threw all sorts of strange fits, tearing her hair and raging against her fate. The doctors said that Father might not survive the journey he was so frail, so we were wondering the whole time if they would make it back to England.

They docked at Tilbury and Charles hired a car to go and meet them. We had been able to buy a house in Wimbledon by then which was big enough for all of us. It was on the side of a hill, and there were steps up. When Father was put on a stretcher to be carried up I noticed something. All his life he had a habitual nervous twitch which caused his left leg and right shoulder to jerk.

As soon as he was put on that stretcher and I went down the steps to see him, I noticed that this twitch was going on all the time, whereas in the past he only had it when he was telling you something excitedly.

Mother was in a real state. She had developed a psychological symptom which was an unceasing hiccup, all the time, twenty-four hours a day, seven days a week. The first morning after they arrived, I went in to see her and to ask her how she was, and she said, 'Well the rain was leaking through the roof all night. I didn't want to disturb anybody so I just turned on my side and kept away from the leak'. Sure enough there was a leak. This was not the fiery mother I had known. ☞ | P 241 **WONTON PICK-ME-UP SOUP** |

People came to visit, including Uncle Will, the husband of Father's sister Alice, from Blackburn. I remember him bursting into tears when he was shown into the bedroom and Father said brightly: 'Well, I'm a sorry old crock aren't I?', something like that. And Uncle Will talked about growing old. I had all these people on my hands and everything was very untidy. I felt very self-conscious. I thought, well here are these English relatives who didn't approve of the marriage and they are going to see a sloppy, dirty, slovenly Burmese family.

The end of an era

Father read *The Times* every day and we kept him supplied with all the books he wanted. All his children visited him in turn. Two days before he died, on a Friday, he didn't seem to take much notice of *The Times* so I read it to him, but on the Sunday he wasn't interested in the papers at all, he just lay there looking at the clock on the mantelpiece and I was sure he was thinking, 'What time will it be? What time will it be?' At that stage, the nurse was giving him oxygen. Whenever he went pale she would put the mask over his face and the colour would come back into his cheeks. Then he would look up into my eyes and laugh like a happy child. But at about one o'clock she put the mask on his face, and after a long time she just took it away... but I could see the moment when he died... it was like a light going out... as though you'd shelled a pea and only the husk was left. I have always wondered, what is it that has gone out? Where's the pea?

The next day the undertakers came. Mother was weeping, she was at a complete loss. But when they started to take his coffin away from the house, she stopped them and made them open it again, and she carefully placed a cheroot and a box of matches next to him.

When he died I think Mother lost her mind. After the funeral she went to stay with Alice, who had recently married. Mother would get up in the night, convinced that he was coming home, or try to get out of the house to get to the railway to meet him, shouting or moaning. She was so distressed, but she was also determined to find him. On 4th August, she got up early in the morning. Alice and her husband were sitting in the kitchen drinking tea, and Mother heard the sound of water in the bathroom. She asked if this was the sound of Papa's arrival. 'I'm coming, Papa, I'm coming', she said. She turned to Alice and said that she bore no ill will to anyone. Alice said that she thought at the time that this was a strange thing to say, and only later did she realise that Mother was saying her goodbyes. She retired to her bedroom for the rest of the day.

The next morning, Alice rose early and when she opened the kitchen door she heard a hissing sound. All four gas taps on the cooker were open, and Mother was lying on the floor near the stove. She had put two shawls along the bottom of the door and along the bottom of the bedroom doors to make sure that no one else was affected by the gas. She had found her own way out of an intolerable status of exiled widowhood but left us behind.

I underestimated Mother for many, many years. She had started from the Daingwunkin bazaar and had managed her bifurcated life with both rage and grace. She and Father were separated by a gulf of language and culture, and yet she loved him passionately and with unwavering loyalty.

I underestimated my mother.

But perhaps most of us do.

From left: Father, Sue, Mother and Alice, 1944

DAHL

Serves 4 | prepare 10 mins | cook 40 mins | easy

Dahl is the ultimate comfort food, and it's a dish that reminds me of home. Mum's dahl, served up with rice, balachaung and meatball curry, 'going slowly, coming nicely...'

INGREDIENTS

300g split orange lentils
1.5 litres water
2 tbsp sunflower oil
4 fresh or 8 dried curry leaves
½ tsp cumin seeds
½ tsp fennel seeds
½ tsp fenugreek seeds
¼ tsp whole cloves
4 green cardamom crushed
1 medium white onion
1 tsp chopped garlic
1 tsp grated ginger
1 tsp turmeric
¼ tsp chilli powder
100g tinned chopped tomatoes
1 medium potato peeled in 1cm dice
2 tbsp chopped coriander
Salt

Heat the oil in a large pan and fry the curry leaves and whole spices until aromatic. Add the onion and continue to fry until it is soft and translucent. Add the ginger and garlic, stirring and frying for 2 minutes before adding the turmeric, chilli powder and salt. Stir in the tinned tomato and lentils followed by the diced potato and the water. Bring to the boil and simmer until the lentils are soft and mushy (about 20-30 minutes). Sprinkle with chopped coriander.

MASSAMAN BEEF CURRY

Serves 4 | prepare 30 mins | cook 120 mins | medium difficulty

Massaman curry has its origins in Thailand's Muslim community. It is wonderfully aromatic and earthy, and quite different from the more citrus flavours of a green curry. We always make our own curry paste. It's so much better than shop bought. If you have any paste left over it freezes very well.

INGREDIENTS

For the Massaman curry paste:

1 tsp fermented fish paste

2.5cm piece cassia bark or cinnamon

1 tsp cloves

1 tsp cardamom

1 star anise

¼ tsp nutmeg

1 tsp cumin seeds

1 tsp coriander seeds

6 shallots unpeeled

5cm piece galangal

6 cloves garlic unpeeled

2 stalks lemon grass coarsely chopped

Zest of 1 lime

6 kaffir lime leaves

12 dried red chillies seeds removed and torn into pieces

A small bunch of fresh coriander with stalks

First of all, make the massaman curry paste: wrap the fermented fish paste in aluminium foil and place it on a baking tray together with the shallots, garlic, galangal and lemon grass. Bake in the oven at 180°C, removing the fish paste after 5 minutes, the garlic, galangal and lemon grass after 10 minutes and the shallots after 15 minutes. When cool enough to handle, peel the garlic, galangal and shallots and unwrap the fish paste.

In a dry frying pan, gently heat the whole spices until they begin to smoulder but taking care that they do not burn. Now dry fry in the same way the shredded dried chillies. Put the spices and chillies into a coffee grinder and grind to a fine powder.

Now put all of the curry paste ingredients into a food processor and process to a fine purée.

continue to the next page...

MASSAMAN BEEF CURRY

(continued)

INGREDIENTS

For the curry:

1kg of beef stewing steak cut into large chunks

salt and pepper to season the meat

2 tbsp massaman curry paste (see previous page)

4 tbsp sunflower oil

50g palm sugar

1 tbsp tamarind paste

6 tbsp fish sauce

1 tsp cardamom lightly crushed

2.5cm stick cassia bark or cinnamon

2 star anise

8 lime leaves

300g baby new potatoes skin on

1 small courgette

100g small shallots

2 tbsp chopped coriander

1 litre coconut milk

300ml water

In a heavy pan over a high heat, fry the seasoned chunks of beef in half of the sunflower oil until browned. Remove from the pan and set aside. Do this in batches so as not to crowd the pan. If the pan has not burnt, you don't need to wash it before proceeding. Heat the rest of the oil and fry the curry paste for a few minutes until aromatic but taking care that it does not burn. Add 800ml of the coconut milk, the water, whole spices, palm sugar, and half of the fish sauce and tamarind. Return the meat to the pan and add enough water to cover by about 2cm. Simmer covered for 1.5 to 2 hours in the oven or over a very low heat, making sure it does not burn. Stir occasionally and be patient. The meat is cooked when a fork pushed into it slips out easily without clinging to the meat. Add a little extra water if you feel the curry is becoming too dry.

While the meat is cooking, put the potatoes in a pan and cover with cold water. Add salt and bring to the boil, then simmer until the potatoes are tender. Drain and set aside. Heat the oven to 170°C. Place the shallots on a tray or in an oven proof dish and roast for about 15 minutes until soft. Allow to cool then peel and set aside. Cut the courgette into thick batons.

When the meat is cooked, add the raw courgettes and the cooked potatoes, shallots, and lime leaves. Warm gently and stir in the remaining 200ml of coconut milk. Allow everything to cook together for ten minutes by which time the courgettes should be tender. Now taste the sauce, and if necessary add a little more of the reserved fish sauce and tamarind until it has just the right salty/tangy balance. Serve the curry sprinkled with chopped fresh coriander and accompany with jasmine rice.

FLAPJACKS

Serves 4 | prepare 15 mins | cook 15 mins | easy

This was probably one of the first dishes I was allowed to cook. As Grandy kept a watchful eye, I melted the butter and enthusiastically mixed the ingredients together making sure there was plenty of raw mixture left clinging to the bowl for me to scrape out with a grubby finger. Best served with fudge and shortbread!

INGREDIENTS

250g porridge oats
125g butter
125g soft brown sugar
3 tbsp golden syrup

Heat oven to 180°C. Melt the butter in a small saucepan and stir in the golden syrup. Put the oats and brown sugar in a mixing bowl and stir in the melted butter and syrup. Mix really well then press the mixture into a 20cm x 30cm baking tin using the back of a spoon. Bake in the oven for about 15 minutes until golden.

APRICOT AND FRANGIPANE TART

Serves 6-8 | prepare 30 mins | cook 90 mins | medium difficulty

A classic example of French patisserie, I can imagine Ma Khin enjoying a slice of this tart at a pavement café during her brief sojourn in Marseille. I'm not too keen on very sweet desserts, and I love the sharp contrast of the cooked apricots with the sweet pastry. The quantity of frangipane and pastry is enough to make two tarts, so freeze half. Thanks again to Alastair Little for sharing this little gem with me.

INGREDIENTS

For the filling and topping:
600g apricots
2 tbsp sugar
2 tbsp toasted flaked almonds

For the pastry:
150g sugar
500g flour
100g ground almonds
350g diced butter softened
½ tsp salt
2 egg yolks

For the frangipane:
200g sugar
200g flour
200g ground almonds
200g butter softened
4 eggs
1 tsp salt

Cut the apricots in half and sprinkle with the sugar.

Put the dry ingredients for the pastry in a bowl and rub in the softened butter. Once this has formed a soft crumb, mix in the egg yolks and gather the pastry up into a ball. Divide into two pieces, (you only need half the pastry to make one tart). Wrap the pastry in cling film and refrigerate for at least half an hour. Roll out the pastry and use it to line a 28cm tart tin with a loose bottom. Bake at 150°C for 20-30 minutes until cooked, then allow to cool.

Put the ingredients for the frangipane in a food processor and blend briefly until mixed (again, you will have double the quantity you need). Spread half of the mixture over the cooked base. Do not attempt to do this if the tart base is still warm as it will break up. Arrange the apricot halves cut side down on top of the frangipane. Bake in the oven for 45 minutes at 150°C. The frangipane will have risen and should be brown and crispy. Sprinkle the tart with toasted flaked almonds and serve.

WONTON PICK-ME-UP SOUP

Serves 4 | prepare 40 mins | cook 20 mins | easy

When we were children, as a special treat on our birthdays, Mum would prepare our favourite dish. A typically difficult child, I always insisted on snails in garlic butter and beef Wellington. My brother, Mike was much easier to please, requesting what he called 'bone soup', a transparent peppery chicken stock prepared with the left overs of the roast bird and served with boiled vegetables and chunks of meat salvaged from the carcass. Bone soup was given to us when we were ill. It's the perfect pick-me-up. I wish I'd been able to prepare this version of bone soup for Ma Khin in her final days when she'd lost her appetite for food and tragically for life itself.

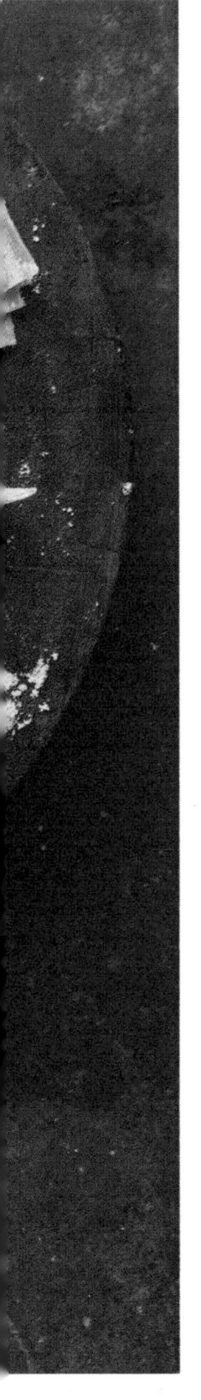

INGREDIENTS

For the wonton:

1 packet wonton wrappers defrosted

200g minced pork

50g defrosted peeled prawns finely chopped

1 tsp sesame oil

2 tbsp light soy sauce

1 tbsp Chinese black vinegar

6 tinned water chestnuts finely chopped

1 tsp garlic, finely chopped

1 tsp ginger, grated

½ tsp cornflour

1 tbsp chopped coriander

2 spring onions finely chopped

For the soup:

1 litre light chicken stock (page 29)

2-3 tbsp light soy sauce

2 spring onions

1 tbsp chopped coriander

Slice the spring onion for the soup into julienne strips and place in cold water to crisp.

Prepare the wonton. Place all of the ingredients in a mixing bowl and combine well. The best way to do this is to squeeze the ingredients with your fist so that the mixture oozes out between your fingers. Separate a sheet of wonton from the packet and paint the edges with a finger moistened with water. Place a teaspoon of the mixture in the centre of the wonton. Bring opposite corners of the wrapper together, pinching the edges to seal. Place the prepared wonton on a lightly floured tray lined with greaseproof paper. If you are not going to use the wonton the same day, they freeze very well.

To cook the wonton, bring a large pan of salted water to the boil and drop them in. Cook for 7 minutes then lift out and place in individual serving bowls. Warm the chicken stock and season to taste with soy sauce before pouring it over the wonton. Sprinkle with a little chopped coriander and crispy spring onion.

EPILOGUE: NEW BEGINNINGS

Bridget Anderson, Bristol, July 2018

In 2006 I went with Steve, my partner, Rob, and our four children to Kalaw. Rob had found The Grey House. It was like most of the colonial buildings in Burma at this time, dilapidated and run down. Poverty and tropical climate had done their work. Inside there were lots of people sleeping on bare earth floors: the son of the Sawbwa had just died, and they were relatives who were visiting for the funeral. There was a magnificent house on the opposite side of the valley and we were told that it was owned by Percy Maung Hla, who had also just passed away. We were so disappointed: Percy was the student who had come across Grandy and K in London. He reported it to his mother who immediately told Ma Khin who was still in Burma. She had no idea G & K were together. This resulted in huge conflict between Grandy and Ma Khin and the shan dagger incident. We were told that the family had built the house after the war and no one knew where they had got the money from. This could explain why Grandy always suggested that it was Percy's mother who had dug up the silver her mother had buried in the grounds of The Grey House!

Arriving at Heho airport ten years later, in 2016, we were surprised to see a huge poster of The Grey House on the road to Kalaw. It had been turned into a boutique hotel. The original house had been slightly garishly restored, and new buildings put up in place of the old servants' quarters and dotted around the garden. But Ma Khin's lemon trees were still there, and there were roses just as she would have liked. We stayed there for four days, re-reading our Aunty Mary's letters written to Grandy when Mary was staying in Kalaw, and Grandy was in Rangoon with her little girls. We talked about our family history. How much we missed Grandy, what it must have been like for her and Charles coming back to England, living in sin with three Burmese daughters. She used to tell me how our mother, Rosemary, was initially refused entry to Putney Girls' School when she first arrived because the school claimed she didn't speak English properly. 'What a lot of nonsense. And the first year that she was there - she won the English prize!'. They all did well; Susan, the youngest, went to Cambridge and studied Philosophy; Jane went to Oxford and studied

Philosophy, Politics and Economics (PPE), and our mother stayed in London and trained as a doctor. Charles was employed at the Central Office of Information, and Grandy found a job working at an English language school in central London. I can still remember the parties she held for her students.

We talked about Burma too. How much it had changed in the past ten years. In 2006 we had visited an Aunt who had just moved home as she 'couldn't stand to live next door to Muslims'. In 2016, even to privileged tourists that everyday hostility to Indians and Muslims was more in evidence. We talked about the Rohingya, colonialism and division, about racism, exclusion, and the ongoing injustice of borders.

We planned: Steve wanted to bring his customers to The Grey House as part of a gastronomic tour of Burma in the footsteps of Ma Khin. He encouraged me to return to the book I had started writing in 1989 when Grandy was still alive. Life, work and children had got in the way and it was still unfinished when she died in 1996. Steve proposed we do it as a joint project. So I sat down to finish this book, looking out at Ma Khin's garden.

Ma Khin, The Grey House garden

GLOSSARY

Adipadi - Head of State in Burmese (naing-ngan-daw-adipadi).

Alastair Little - a chef and owner of the eponymous restaurant in London's Soho. It opened in 1985 and won The Times Restaurant of the Year Award in 1993.

Anti-Fascist People's Freedom League, AFPFL - the AFPFL was a broad alliance that grew out of the Anti-Fascist Organisation (AFO), that had been formed to resist the Japanese occupation. The AFPFL aimed to resist the British colonial administration and achieve independence.

ARP post - Air Raid Precautions' local control centre.

Atlantic Charter - drafted by the USA and the UK, the Atlantic Charter defined the allied goals for the post World War 2 world. It recognised self-determination as a key goal and became the basis for the founding charter of the United Nations.

Aung San - the charismatic leftist student and nationalist leader of pre-independence Burma. He was assassinated shortly before independence and was the father of Aung San Suu Kyi.

Aung San Suu Kyi - daughter of nationalist leader Aung San, Suu Kyi ('Suu' to her familiars) was in Myanmar visiting her mother at the time of massive popular unrest in 1988. She became the General Secretary of the opposition National League for Democracy (NLD) and was held under house arrest from 1989 to 2010. In 2016 she became the country's first State Counsellor, effectively the Prime Minister.

bael fruit- the bael tree is native to India and Southeast Asia. The fruit resembles a very large pear and it has an extremely hard shell like a coconut.

Burma Independence Army (BIA) - the first Burmese National Army that entered Burma led by Japanese Colonel Suzuki (Bo Moegyoe) with Aung San as Major General.

Burma Research Society - this was founded in 1910 by J.S. Furnivall, Gordon Luce, J.A. Stewart, and Pe Maung Tin to encouraging research on all aspects of Burmese culture and science.

Burma Round Table Conference - the BRTC was held in London from 27th November 1931 to 12th January 1932. The outcome was limited by disagreements about Dyarchy and Separation from India. Burmese nationalists were generally anti-separation from India at this stage, as they saw it as a means of dividing nationalist movements which would weaken Burma's anti-colonial position.

Chateau d'If - a fortress island off the coast of Marseille featured in the Alexandre Dumas novel *The Count of Monte Cristo.*

Chiang Kai-shek - a military leader who as an influential member of the Kuomintang (KMT). When he lost the civil war with the Chinese Communist Party he retreated to Taiwan in 1949, where he was in power until his death in 1975.

chota hazri - a very light first meal of the day served at dawn. In Hindi it means a 'small thing/presence' and is often just a cup of tea and a biscuit.

Coringhi - people from Southern India who migrated to Burma to work as labourers.

dacoit - this derives from the Hindi word for 'bandit' and was the term commonly used in Burma for armed robbers.

Dobama Asiayone - the 'We Burmans Association' was established in 1930.

Dr Ba Maw - Burmese political leader and Prime Minister of Burma.

Dyarchy - the system of government introduced to India in 1919 by the Government of India Act, and later extended to Burma. Areas of administration were divided into Reserved Subjects (e.g. Law and Order) that were governed, as before, by non-elected Executive Councillors appointed by the British government, and Transferred Subjects (e.g. public health) that were governed by elected Indian/Burmese members.

General Strike 1926 - called by the Trades Union Congress in the UK in support of miners, the General Strike lasted between 3rd May and 12th May. More than one and a half million workers walked out, mainly in transport and heavy industry.

Gilbert and Sullivan operas - W.S. Gilbert and Arthur Sullivan, a dramatist and a composer respectively, collaborated to produce 14 comic operas between 1871 and 1896. One of the most famous was *The Mikado* which features the character the Grand Pooh-Ba, a man of inflated titles and limited authority.

Highland Fling, Irish Jig, and the Hornpipe - these are all traditional dances. The Highland Fling is a solo dance from Scotland, the Irish Jig is a Celtic dance to fiddle music, and the Hornpipe is a dance form that came to be associated with sailors.

HMG - short for 'Her/His Majesty's Government'

Hokkien Chinese - Hokkien speakers largely have their origins from Fujian Province in Southern China.

Home Rule - Government by nationals (as opposed to government by colonizing powers).

Htin Fatt (Maung Htin) - a famous writer and journalist, famed for his 1947 novel Nga Ba.

Hugh Tinker - historian of Burma, born 1921, died 2000.

Indian Civil Service - the elite civil service that implemented British rule in India under the British Empire.

Indian National Congress - an Indian Nationalist political party founded in 1885 that strongly influenced nationalist movements across the British Empire.

Inter-Asian relations conference - this took place in New Delhi in March-April 1947. Its objectives were 'to bring together the leading men and women of Asia on a common platform to study the problems of common concern to the people of the continent, to focus attention on social, economic and cultural problems of the different countries of Asia, and to foster mutual contact and understanding.'

Joe Lyons steak and kidney pie - J Lyons & Co owned a chain of tea shops in London throughout the 20th century. Known as Lyon's Corner houses, the larger establishments, spread over several floors, included restaurants where steak and kidney pie was always on the menu.

J.S. Furnivall - John Sydenham Furnivall was an ICS officer, historian of Burma and founder of the Burma Research Society. He is credited with formulating the concept of 'the plural society' in which different ethnic groups live parallel lives.

kanazo - a tree native to Southeast Asia that grows up to 50 metres tall and is found on tidal rivers and mangrove swamps.

Karens - an umbrella term for heterogenous groups of people living in the North East of Burma and in the Delta.

Kipling's 'whackin' white cheroots' - from Rudyard Kipling's poem Mandalay, written in 1892. A cheroot is a cigar with both ends cut rather than tapered, and so cheaper and easier to make.

Kuomintang - the Chinese Nationalist Party, founded and led by Sun Yat Sen, and later led by Chiang Kaishek.

London Agreement - agreement signed by British Prime Minister Attlee and Aung San on 27th January 1947. It committed to integration of the Frontier Areas with lowland Burma, national elections within four months, and Burmese Independence within a year.

longyi - a sheet of cloth wound round the lower body and tucked in at the top that is worn by both women and men.

Lorna Doone - *Lorna Doone: A Romance of Exmoor*, is an English novel by Richard Blackmore set in the 17th century set in the remote Doone Valley.

Low and Terry - David Low was a political cartoonist who was published in the London daily newspaper *The Evening Standard* 1927-1950.

Ma Khin Café - located in Valencia's modernist Mercado Colon and named in homage to his great-grandmother, Ma Khin Hnyaw, this restaurant was opened by Stephen Anderson in October 2014. The restaurant prides itself in serving authentic South East Asian food produced with locally sourced ingredients. **www.makhincafe.com**

Mahatma Gandhi - a famous Indian nationalist who led the Indian National Congress from 1920.

Mao Tse-Tung (Mao Zedong) - a Communist Revolutionary who founded the People's Republic of China following the Communist victory over the KMT in 1949. He ruled the country as Chairman of the Communist Party until his death in 1976.

Maung Wun (Minthuwun) - born in 1909, he was a student of Pe Maung Tin, an accomplished short story writer and one of Burma's most famous poets.

Mrs Beeton - Mrs Beeton wrote a best-selling guide to household management in 1861.

Mrs Tee Tee Luce's Home for Waifs and Strays - this was a school and orphanage for boys on Inya Road. Tee Tee Luce was the wife of University of Rangoon English Lecturer, Professor Gordon Luce.

Nehru - Jawaharlal Nehru was a prominent member of the Indian National Congress, working closely with Gandhi in the struggle for Indian Independence. He became the first Prime Minister of independent India.

Palaung, Kayan and Pa-o - Burma has an extremely diverse population. There are more than 130 ethnic groups recognised by the Burmese government. There are three different ethnic groups that live in the area of the Shan States: the The Palaung, Kayan and Pa-o.

Pearl Harbour - on 7th December 1941 the Japanese launched a surprise attack on Pearl Harbour, a US naval base near Honolulu Hawaii. More than 2,400 Americans died in the attack. The following day President Roosevelt asked the US Congress to declare war on Japan.

Pongyis - the name given to Buddhist monks in Burma, from *phun* - glory, and *gyi* - great.

Queen Supayalat - the last Queen of Burma, married to King Thibaw. Both were children of King Mindon by different mothers. They were forced to abdicate in 1885 following the British conquest of Upper Burma.

Rangoon/Yangon - This was the capital city of colonial and post-independence Burma until 2006, when the capital was relocated to Naypyidaw.

Repulse and *Prince of Wales* - HMS Prince of Wales and the battle cruiser HMS Repulse were sunk by the Japanese Navy on 10th December 1941, north of Singapore.

Retreat from Burma - the retreat from Burma to India by the British-led 14th Army was a fighting retreat, and the longest retreat in British Army history. It began on 26th April and ended just as the monsoon broke in the middle of May.

Sawbwa of Hsipaw - 'Sawbwa' is a title used by hereditary rulers in the Shan States.

Second Sino-Japanese War - the War between China and Japan between July 1937 and September 1945 in which millions of Chinese civilians and some four million Japanese and Chinese military died. After Pearl Harbour this conflict became incorporated into the Pacific Theatre of World War 2.

Seu Xerea - opened by Stephen Anderson in Valencia, Spain in 1996, Seu Xerea was the first restaurant in the city to offer a fusion of Mediterranean and Asian food.

Shan States - now known as the singular 'Shan State' this refers to the highlands of the North East of Burma, bordering Thailand, China, and Laos.

Shwedagon Pagoda - situated in Rangoon, this is the most sacred Buddhist temple in Burma. It is believed to contain relics of four buddhas and its main stupa is gilded in gold.

simnel cake - a fruit cake eaten during the Easter period in England. The cake is decorated with eleven or twelve balls of marzipan representing the apostles (with or without Judas).

Simon Commission - The 1919 Government of India Act committed to a review of the system of government after ten years. It was comprised of seven British MPs and no Indian or Burmese representatives. It provoked considerable protest. Its report was published in 1930.

spindles - the horizontal rods that can run between the legs of wooden chairs to stabilise them.

Thakhin - the term used to address Europeans in colonial Burma, it is an honorific term of address signifying 'Master' and was the equivalent to 'Sahib' in India. It was claimed by anti-colonial nationalists who designated themselves Thakhins and established a Thakhin party.

The Count of Monte Cristo - a French novel by Alexandre Dumas set in 1815-1839. The main protagonist, Edmond Dantès, is falsely accused and imprisoned in the Chateau d'If, a fortress on an island off the coast of Marseille.

Thein Han (Zawgyi) - Zawgyi, or 'Alchemist', was a leading poet and literary critic.

Thirty Comrades - the thirty Thakhin volunteers, led by Aung San, who were trained by the Japanese and formed the core of the Burma Independence Army. Among them was Bo Ne Win, who later headed the military junta that ruled Burma.

U Nu/Thakhin Nu/Maung Nu - born in 1907, U Nu was the first Prime Minister of Burma 1948-1956. His second term of government ended in 1962 when he was overthrown by General Ne Win. He died in 1995.

U Ottama - a Buddhist monk from Arakan who was an early nationalist leader.

U Pu - U Pu replaced Prime Minister Ba Maw when Dr Ba Maw resigned in 1938. He later joined the AFPFL.

Vichy Regime - headed by Marshal Pétain during World War 2. It represented the unoccupied 'Free Zone' in the southern part of France, and the French colonial Empire. Pétain signed an armistice with Nazi Germany in 1940.

Whyte Committee - Burma was omitted from the 1919 reforms to the government of India, instituted by the Government of India Act. In response to Burmese political agitation, a committee led by Sir Frederick Whyte was formed in 1921 to discuss how reforms to the government of India could be applied to Burma.

William Golding - A twentieth century British novelist, poet and playwright, perhaps most famous for *Lord of the Flies*. *Pincher Martin* was his third book.

Wunthanu Athins - Patriotic Associations (sometimes translated as 'racially faithful ones') including the General Council of Burmese Associations and the General Council of Sangha Sammeggi, the national organisation of political pongyis.

YWCA - the Young Women's Christian Association was founded in London in 1855 as a home for nurses travelling to or from the Crimean War, offering housing, education and support.

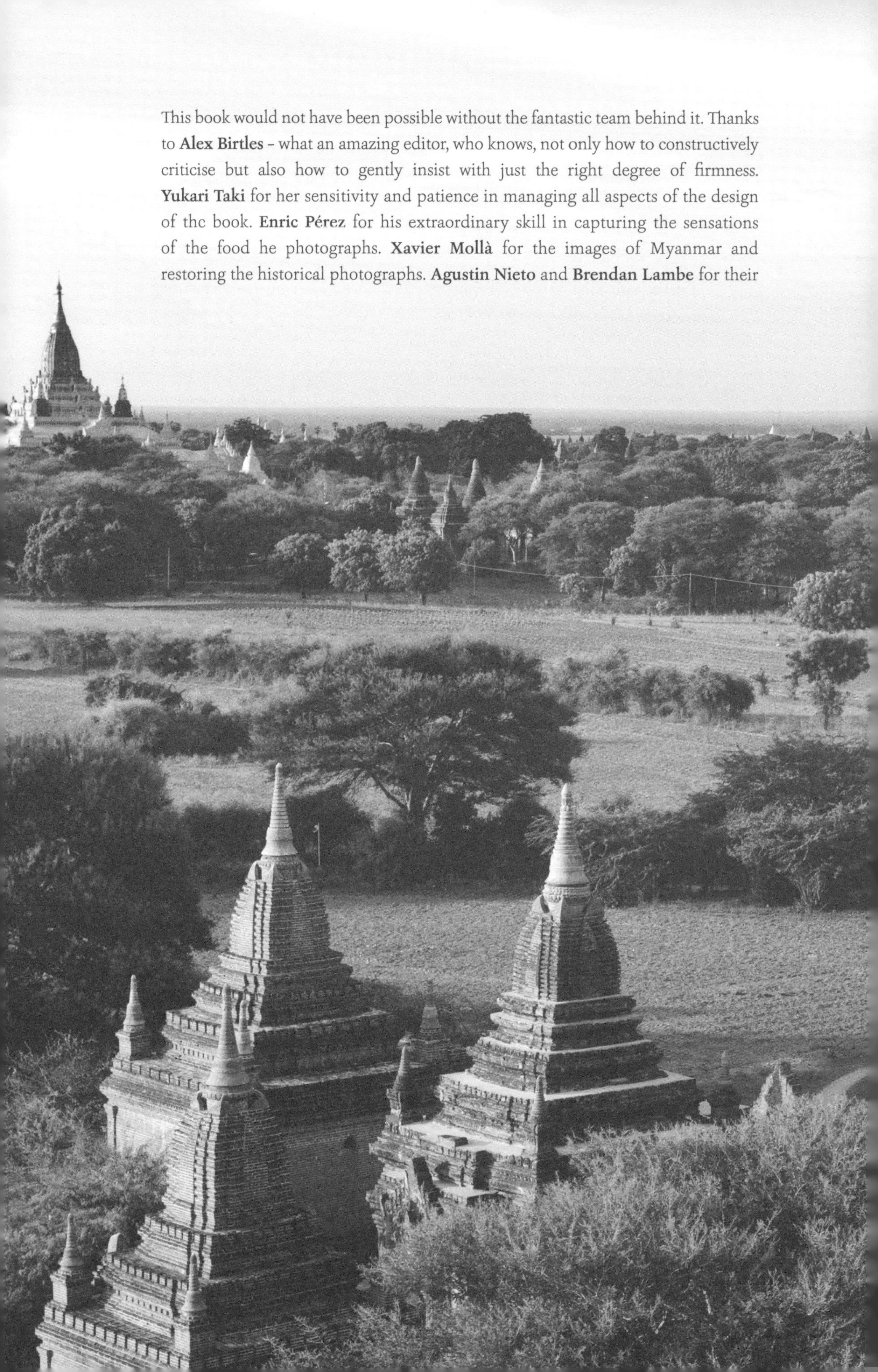

This book would not have been possible without the fantastic team behind it. Thanks to **Alex Birtles** - what an amazing editor, who knows, not only how to constructively criticise but also how to gently insist with just the right degree of firmness. **Yukari Taki** for her sensitivity and patience in managing all aspects of the design of thc book. **Enric Pérez** for his extraordinary skill in capturing the sensations of the food he photographs. **Xavier Mollà** for the images of Myanmar and restoring the historical photographs. **Agustin Nieto** and **Brendan Lambe** for their meticulous translation of the Spanish edition, and **Tomàs Belaire, Carmen Gonzalo, Jorge Cruz Orozco** and **Pablo,** Spanish proofreaders. **Nay Lin Htike** for reviewing the accuracy of Burmese names, words and phrases. **Emma Newcombe** for her tactful production management. **Julia Bell** for picking up the project, keeping us to time, and her sharp copyediting eye. **Guillermo Álvarez** for preparing and checking the recipes. **The staff at Ma Khin Café** for holding the fort. **Lorenzo López** for his unconditional support and enthusiasm.